Mastering Candlesticks, Step by Step

M. J. Kelley II

INTRODUCING THE HIGHLY ANTICIPATED SECOND EDITION OF "MASTERING CANDLESTICKS STEP BY STEP." THIS REVOLUTIONARY BOOK HAS UNDERGONE A TRANSFORMATIVE MAKEOVER, FEATURING A VISUALLY CAPTIVATING DESIGN WITH ALL DARK-COLORED CANDLESTICKS. BY ELIMINATING THE DISTRACTIONS OF GREEN AND RED CANDLESTICKS, READERS ARE NOW ABLE TO FULLY IMMERSE THEMSELVES IN THE INTRICATE WORLD OF CANDLESTICK PATTERNS. FURTHERMORE, THIS EDITION OFFERS COMPREHENSIVE UPDATES ON IDENTIFYING CANDLESTICK PATTERNS AND EXECUTING PROFITABLE TRADES. FOR THOSE WHO PREFER THE ORIGINAL COLOR SCHEME, THE FIRST EDITION REMAINS ACCESSIBLE FOR PURCHASE. IMMERSE YOURSELF IN THE ART OF CANDLESTICK ANALYSIS WITH THIS ESSENTIAL GUIDE.

Contents

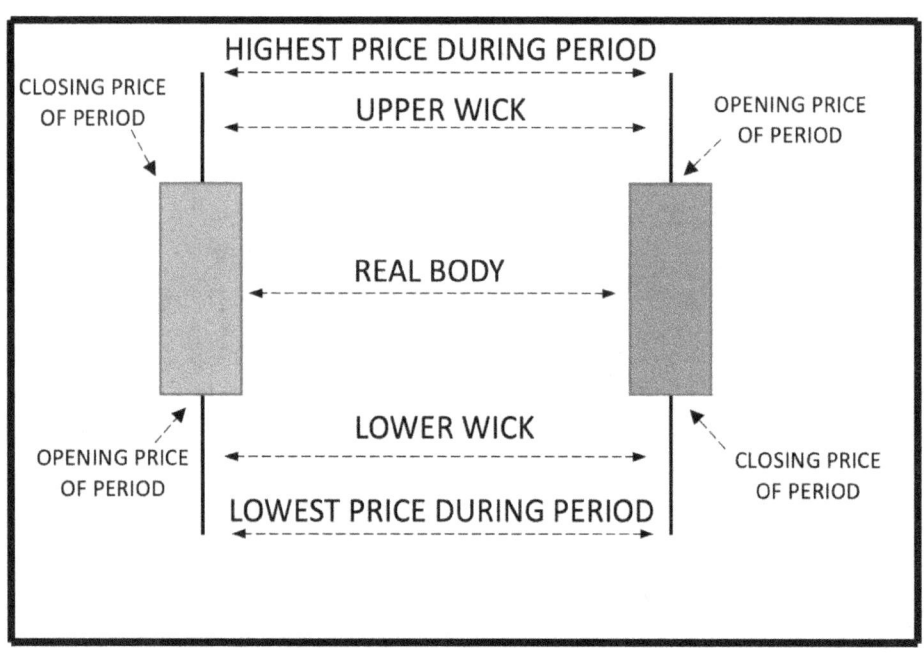

#1 - 1-2-3 Bearish Trend Change

After establishing an upward trend, look for red candlesticks that break down and close below the trendline. This will initiate a 3-wave correction. This pattern also follows a completed Elliot Wave pattern with wave 1 being bearish, wave 2 being bullish, and wave 3 being bearish. If the pattern is observed at the base of the breakout, Fibonacci numbers can be utilized.

Figure 1: 1-2-3 Bearish Trend Change

How to Trade 1-2-3 Bearish Trend Change

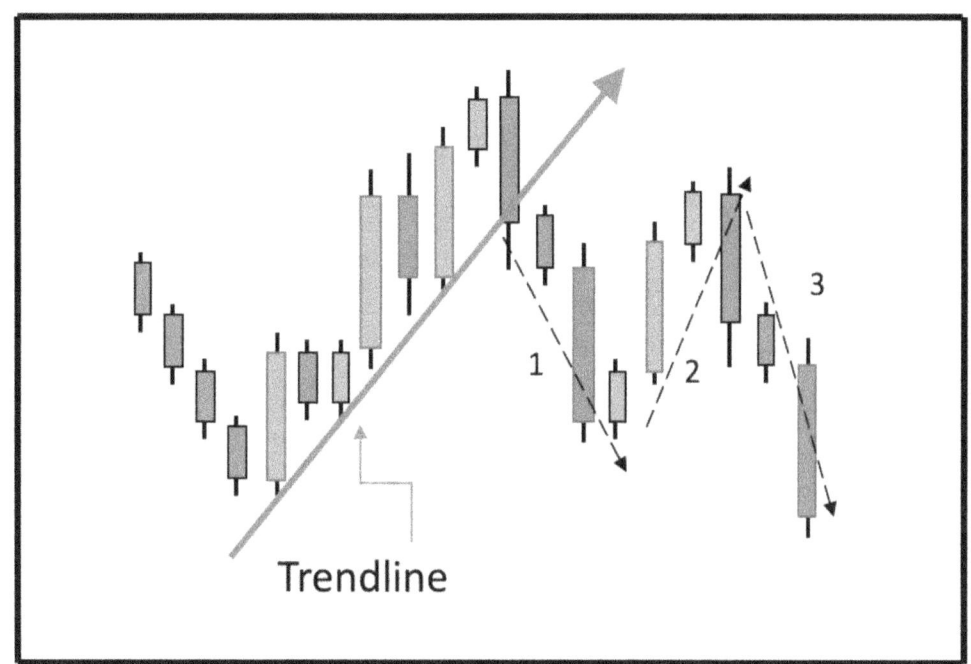

From the preceding description of this candlestick pattern, the basic idea is to follow the trendline while looking out for the short-term trend. When the candlestick breaks above the trendline and starts to fall downwards, it becomes pivot 1. Any subsequent break that goes in the upward direction after pivot 1 should be marked as pivot 2. This is crucial because pivot 2 serves as the anchor for identifying bearish momentum or trend. When the trend breaks below the anchor for some time and fails to resume the upward trend, it is a good signal to enter a short (sell) position. Another smart strategy is to use pivot 3 (which, in the figure above, is the next peak (crest) after pivot 2) as the pattern's stop-loss. In most cases, you may miss several trend reversals, which is why consistency is important. Feel free to try out different approaches to add variety   to   your   trading.

#2 - 1-2-3 Bullish Trend Change

After establishing a downward trend, look for green candlesticks that break up and close above the trendline. This pattern will initiate 3 wave corrections and follows a completed Elliot Wave pattern with wave 1 being bullish, wave 2 being bearish, and wave 3 being bullish. If the pattern is observed at the base of the breakout, there is a 70% chance of it moving 5% upward.

Figure 2: 1-2-3 Bullish Trend Change

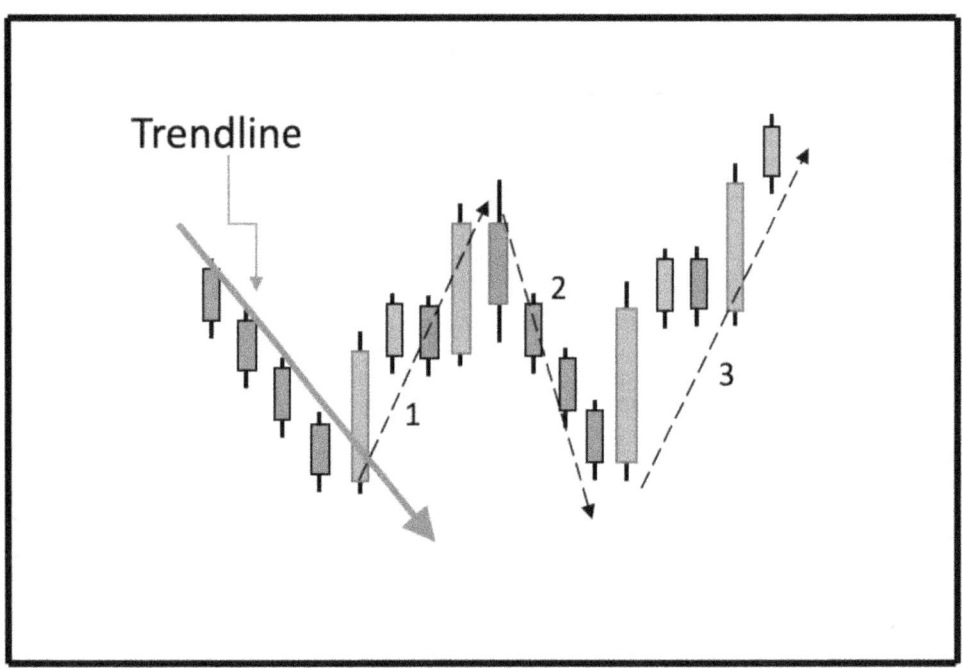

How to trade 1-2-3 Bearish Trend Change Pattern

This candlestick pattern is quite similar to the 1-2-3 Bearish Trend Change, but it is inverted. Therefore, you essentially follow the same steps as the 1-2-3 Bearish Trend Change, but in the opposite direction. Wait for the trade to retrace deeply in a downtrend and form pivot 1 (1st trough), after which it reverses to pivot 2 (peak). At this point, it is recommended to exercise patience for the formation of pivot three (2nd trough). You can then place your stop loss below pivot 1, and your confirmation support should be just above the peak at pivot 2. This provides a 100% extension of pivot 1 and 2. Once the pattern breaks above the point of confirmation support (which is pivot 2 in this case), you can confidently swing high (buy).

#3 - 3 Falling Peaks Trend Change

This pattern is easy to spot since it resembles three coffee cups heading downwards. The trend must be upward before the first cup is formed. Each peak is lower than the last one and looks similar to one another. Each valley is lower than the last one, and each peak does not have to fall on a trend line. Confirmation that you see this pattern is when the price closes below the lowest valley in the pattern.

Figure 3: 3 Falling Peaks Trend Change

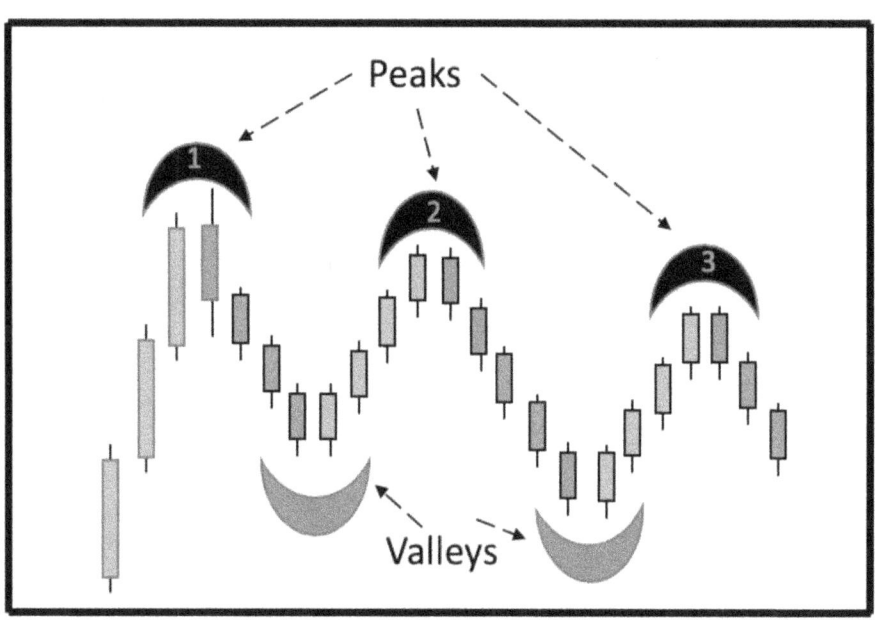

How to Trade 3 Falling Peaks

From the figure above, you can see that the three peaks are irregularly positioned, indicating a slight slant in the trend. While this may suggest a gradually decreasing momentum, it's important not to focus solely on this aspect. Many traders, in their impatience for clear evidence, enter short positions when these patterns are still in their early stages. However, such positions often close prematurely, leading to confusion. To avoid this, it's advisable to use the second crest (Valley 2) as trend support and wait for the pattern to break below this support level. It's crucial to note that breakouts below support zones offer the best opportunities for identifying short (sell) signals. Additionally, it's important to avoid trading stocks that have nearby support. Lastly, when selecting peaks, ensure that each subsequent peak is lower than its preceding peak. The initial peak you choose will determine the shape of the subsequent peaks (i.e., if your initial peak is wide, the subsequent peaks should also be wide).

#4 - 3 Rising Peaks Trend Change

This pattern is easy to spot as it resembles three coffee cups heading upwards. The trend must be downward before the first cup is formed. Each peak is higher than the last one and looks similar to the others. Each valley is higher than the previous one, and the peaks do not have to fall on a trend line. Confirmation of this pattern occurs when the price closes higher than the highest valley in the pattern.

Figure 4: 3 Rising Peak Trend Change

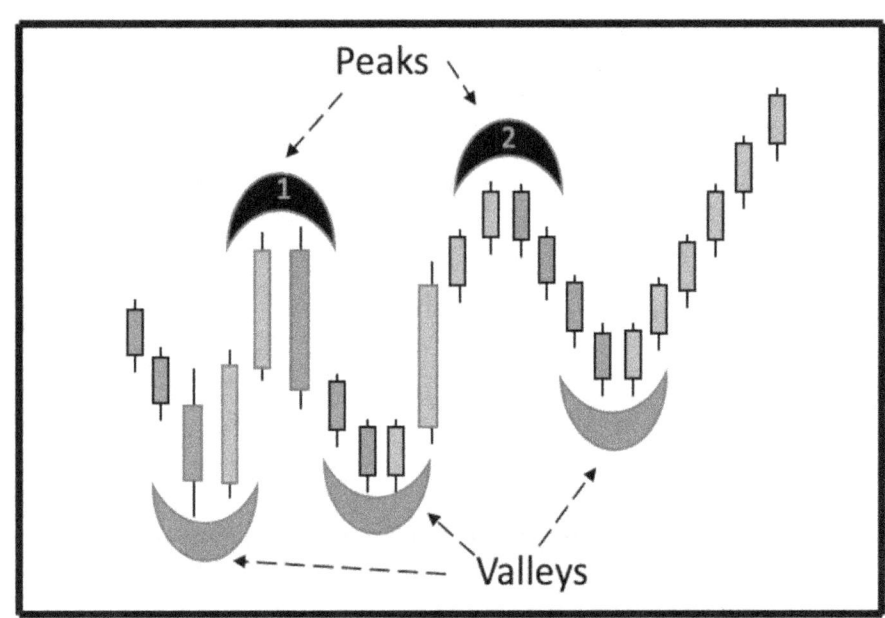

How to Trade 3 Rising Peak Trend change

When trading with the three rising peaks trend change, it is advisable to place a support line at the top of the second peak. The key is to observe patterns that break above this support line, as it indicates a potential entry for a long (buy) position. Pay attention to the trend line from the previous downward move. Tall patterns have a higher chance of performing well compared to short ones, while narrow patterns tend to outperform wider ones. It's important to note that patterns like these are often followed by pullbacks. If the valleys in the pattern are short, set your stop just below the lowest low or highest high. To maximize the potential of this pattern, it must break above the support at peak two. The profit target is determined by the difference between the confirmation price (highest high in the pattern) and the lowest low (lowest valley low).

#5 - Abandoned Baby

The first candlestick in this pattern is red, followed by a doji candlestick, and finally a green candlestick. There must be a price gap between the top of the doji and the neighboring two candlesticks for it to be considered an Abandoned Baby candlestick pattern. This pattern occurs after a downward price trend, and the breakout is upward, indicating a reversal. It's important to note that the upward price trend following the bullish Abandoned Baby pattern is usually short-lived. An upward breakout occurs when the price closes above the top of the pattern, while a downward breakout occurs when the price closes below the bottom of the three-line pattern.

Figure 5: Abandoned Baby

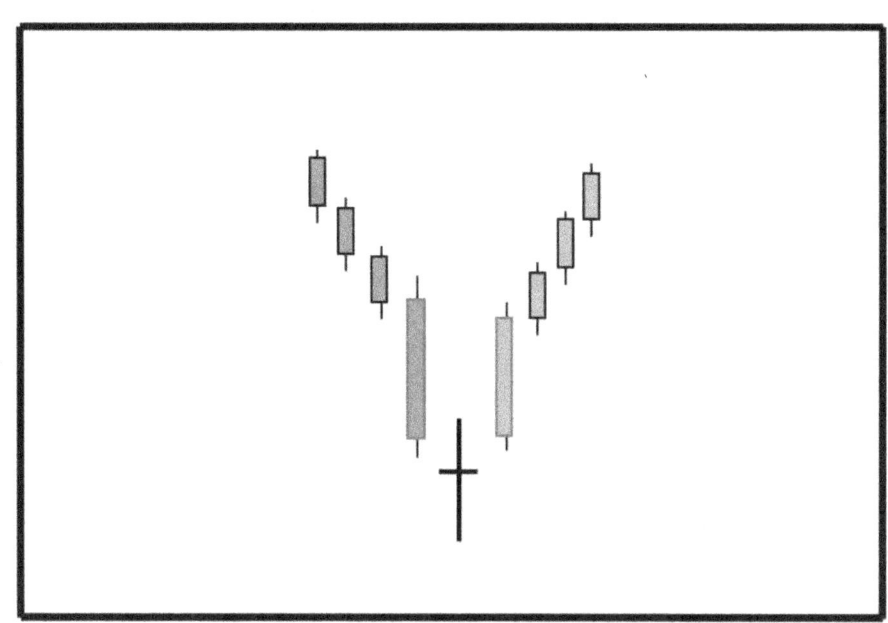

How to Trade Abandoned Baby

The Abandoned Baby pattern is often regarded as one of the most reliable trade patterns by professional traders. Its reliability stems from the fact that once this pattern is identified on a chart, it can be traded without the need for additional indicators. However, it's important to note that no pattern is foolproof. To protect your trade, it is recommended to place a stop-loss order directly below the wick of the middle candle, regardless of its size. The purpose of the stop-loss order is to minimize investment risk, and placing it tightly can result in a risk of less than 0.5%. Managing the Abandoned Baby pattern effectively can be achieved through the use of moving averages and price action rules.

#6 - Adam & Adam Double Bottom

The term "Adam" is used to describe the appearance of a narrow-pointed bottom in a pattern. In the case of Adam, it is typically formed by a single candlestick downward spike, occurring about 95% of the time. This pattern takes the shape of a "W" with the spikes at or near the same level. The two valleys in the pattern should be spaced several candlesticks apart. Approximately 65% of the time, this pattern leads to a gain of 5% or more, depending on the depth of the middle valley.

Figure 6: Adam & Adam Double Bottom

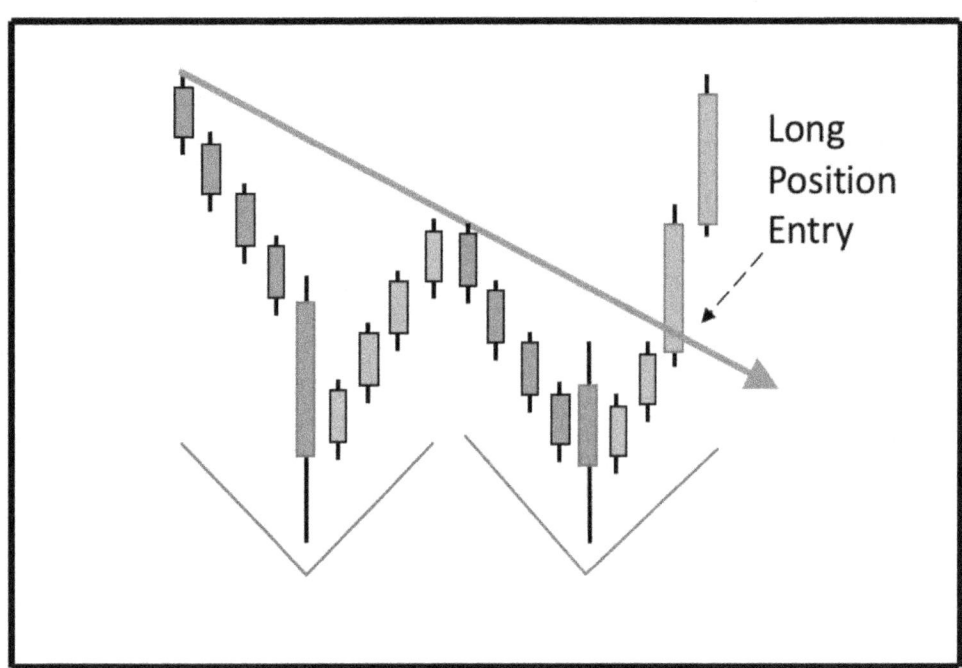

How to Trade with Adam & Adam Double Bottom

Based on the shape of this pattern, the ideal placement for support would be above the middle peak, which represents the highest high of the pattern. This is because for a true double bottom pattern, prices must close above this point to confirm a breakout. Waiting for the price to close above the support placed above the middle peak is crucial for pattern confirmation, as approximately 64% of the time, prices tend to continue lower without confirming the double bottom. To optimize your trading strategy with this pattern, consider placing a stop-loss slightly below the lower of both bottoms, but not too far below the entry price. However, it's important to note that a small rise is typically expected as prices need something to reverse, especially when the decline leading to the double bottom is minimal.

#7 - Adam & Adam Double Top

Adam is a term used to describe the appearance of a specific pattern in technical analysis. In the case of Adam, it refers to a narrow-pointed top formed by a single upward spike on a candlestick chart, which occurs around 95% of the time. The pattern resembles the letter "M" with spikes at or near the same level. The two valleys should be spaced several candlesticks apart. In approximately 55% of cases, there is a possibility of a throwback, depending on the depth of the middle valley. If the breakdown has surpassed the left side of the "M," caution should be exercised before entering a new position.

Figure 7: Adam & Adam Double Top

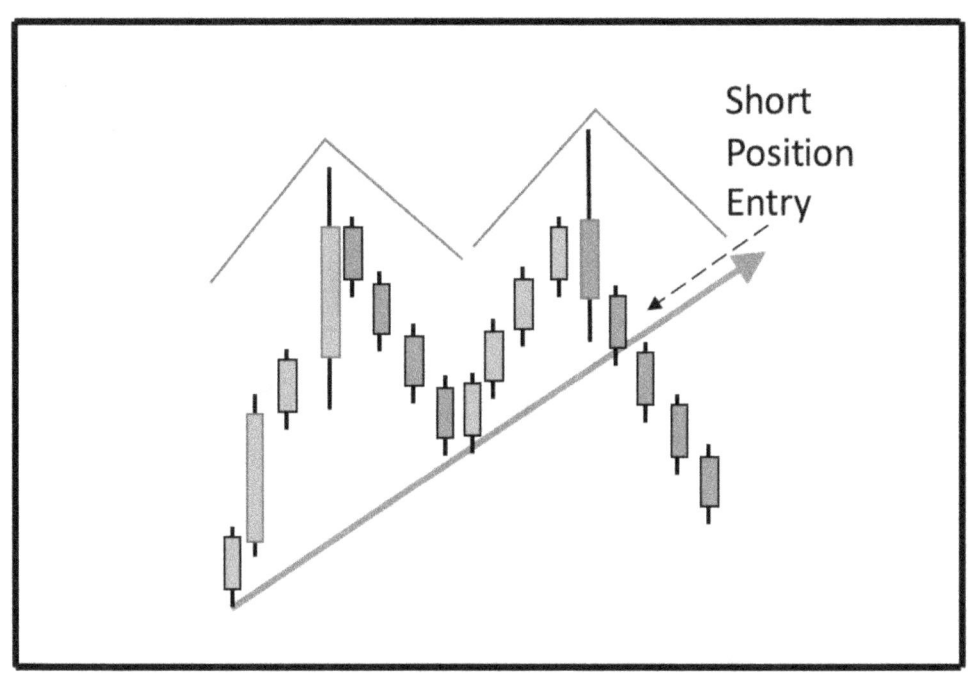

How to Trade Adam & Adam Double Top

Double top patterns, including the Adam & Adam Double Top, consist of two chart patterns. The price difference between the two peaks is typically around 3-5%, and the time frame between them ranges from two to seven weeks. To trade this chart pattern, it is recommended to set a support level just below the lower low of the trough. Wait for the prices to break below this support before entering a sell position, as there is a 65% chance that the price will not confirm the double top and will continue to rise. This pattern shares similarities with the Adam & Adam Double Bottom pattern, but in reverse. So, if you understand how to trade the double bottom pattern, you can apply a similar strategy in reverse for the double top pattern.

#8 - Adam & Eve Double Bottom

The term "Adam" is used to describe the appearance of the bottom of a chart. In this case, it refers to a narrow, pointed bottom, often accompanied by a single candlestick downward spike. On the other hand, "Eve" bottoms have a more rounded and wider appearance. The Adam and Eve Double Bottom pattern typically exhibits a higher rise both before and after a throwback. This pattern has a higher likelihood of breaking upward and sustaining an upward trend for a longer period of time, resulting in potentially higher returns.

Figure 8: Adam & Eve Double Bottom

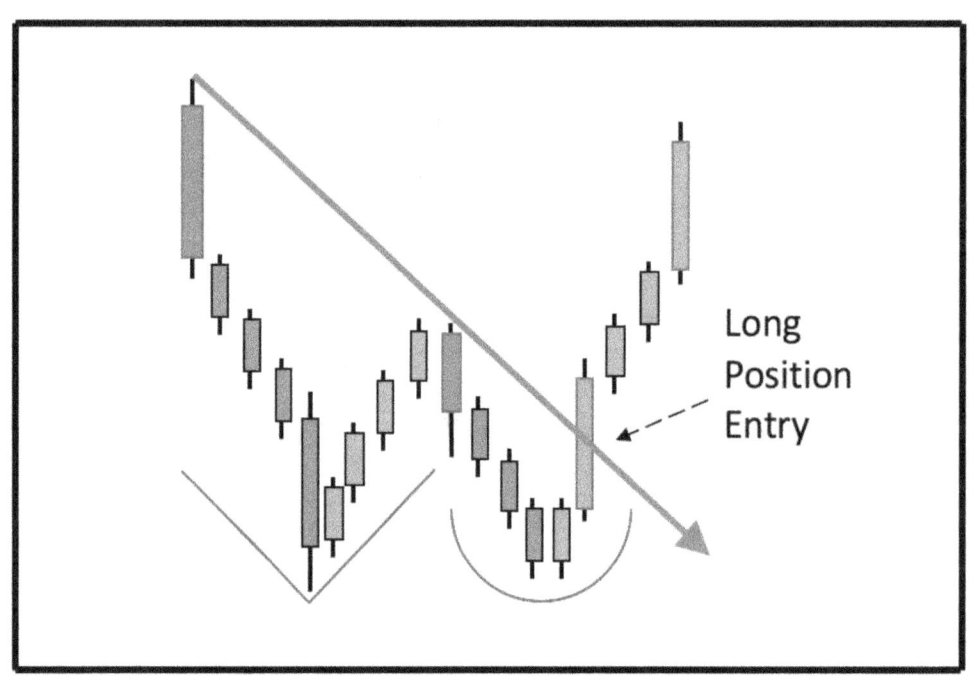

How to with Trade Adam & Eve Double Bottom

The identification of the Adam and Eve Double Bottom pattern is relatively straightforward. The key difference lies in the width of the bottoms. The Adam's bottom remains narrow, while the Eve's bottom widens out, creating a noticeable difference in width throughout their entire height. Both bottoms should experience a rise of at least 10%, although some variation is allowed. It is crucial to note that there should be an average time separation of approximately two months between the two bottoms. To confirm the pattern, the price must close above the peak formed between the two valleys, which becomes the support point for a buy confirmation. Waiting for this confirmation is important because prices can sometimes continue to decline without confirming the double bottom pattern.

#9 - Adam & Eve Double Top

The Adam and Eve Double Top pattern is characterized by two distinct peaks in the price chart, with the first peak referred to as the Adam top. This initial peak is typically narrow in width. After the Adam top, there is a valley that measures around 10% before the formation of the second peak, known as the Eve top. The Eve top is usually wider than the Adam top. The time frame between the two peaks is typically within a range of two to seven candlesticks. Overall, this pattern suggests a potential reversal in the upward trend of the price.

Figure 9: Adam & Eve Double Top

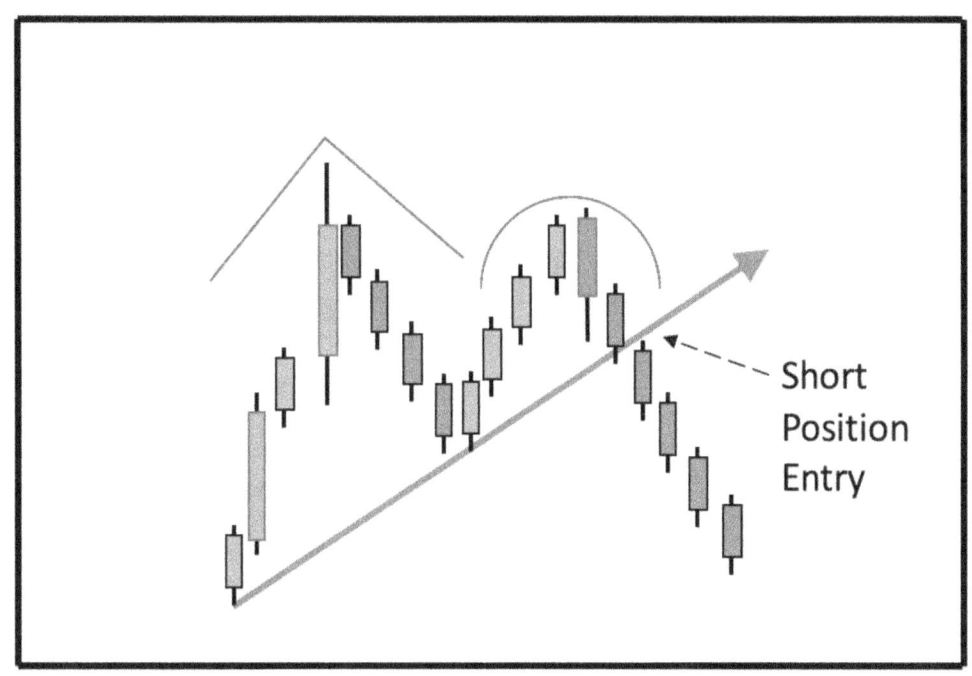

How to Trade with Adam & Eve Double Top

To increase the likelihood of accurate confirmation in trading the Adam and Eve Double Top pattern, it is advisable to exercise patience and wait for the price to close below the middle valley. Once the price has closed below the middle trough, it is expected to continue downwards, presenting an opportune time to enter a short (sell) trade. To achieve a more precise confirmation, you can establish a support line at the bottom of the lowest candle in the middle valley, as illustrated in the figure above. It is common to observe a minor decline, particularly when the preceding rise before the double top is relatively small, as the price requires a reversal catalyst. To manage investment risk effectively, it is recommended to place a stop loss just above the second peak (Eve), which can serve as a significant resistance level.

#10 - Advance Block

Although this pattern may initially appear to be a bearish signal and exhibit signs of weakness, it is actually a bullish continuation pattern. In this pattern, the upper wicks become longer as the body diminishes, and prices continue to rise. This pattern is characterized by a series of three candles and is commonly observed in both uptrends and downtrends. The opening prices of these candles typically fall within the range of the previous candle's real body. This pattern tends to perform best during temporary uptrends within a broader downtrend and is often used as a confirmation of other signals.

Figure 10: Advance Block

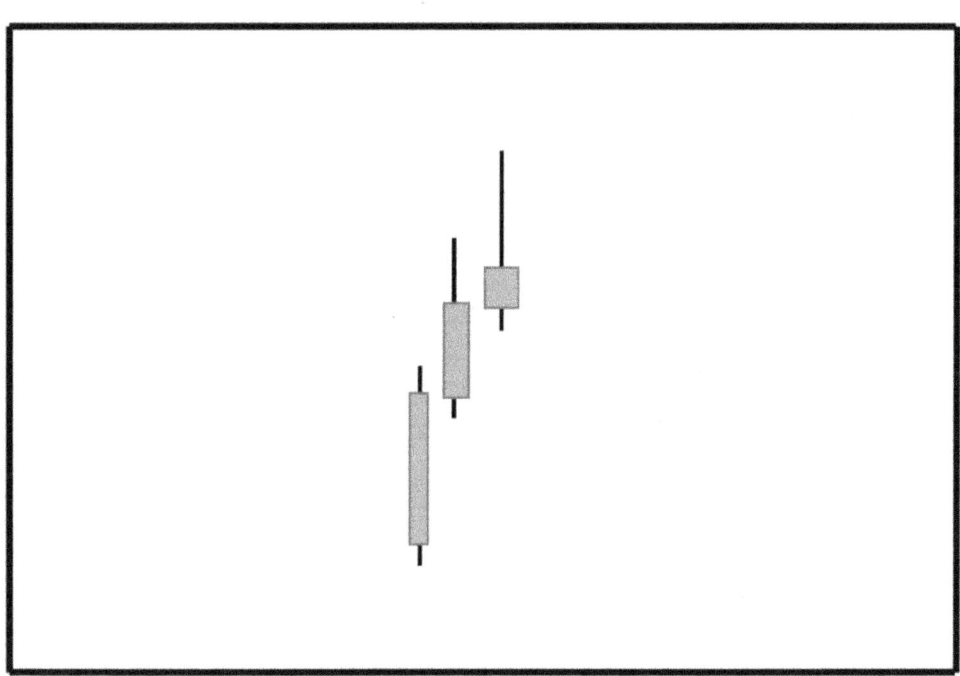

How to Trade with Advance Block

When trading this pattern, it is important to consider that the confirmation level is typically located just above the body of the first candle, serving as a reference point. To ensure safety, a stop loss should be set slightly above the highest point of the last candle's tip. Once the stop loss is in place, it is recommended to exercise patience and wait for the price to cross below the confirmation level before entering a trade position. It is advisable to use the advance block pattern as a confirmation tool rather than relying solely on it for buy or sell signals. Additionally, it is worth noting that tall real bodies have a tendency to increase the likelihood of a reversal.

#11 - Ascending and Broadening Wedge

This pattern is frequently observed in cryptocurrency markets and can be somewhat challenging to interpret. It has an equal probability of being bullish or bearish, with each outcome occurring approximately 50% of the time. In a bull market, the breakout tends to be predominantly downward, accounting for around 90% of cases. Conversely, in a bear market, the breakout is typically bullish around 60% of the time. The price trend leading to this pattern can be either upward or downward, and both trendlines display an upward slant, with the upper slope being steeper than the lower slope.

Figure 11: Ascending and Broadening Wedge

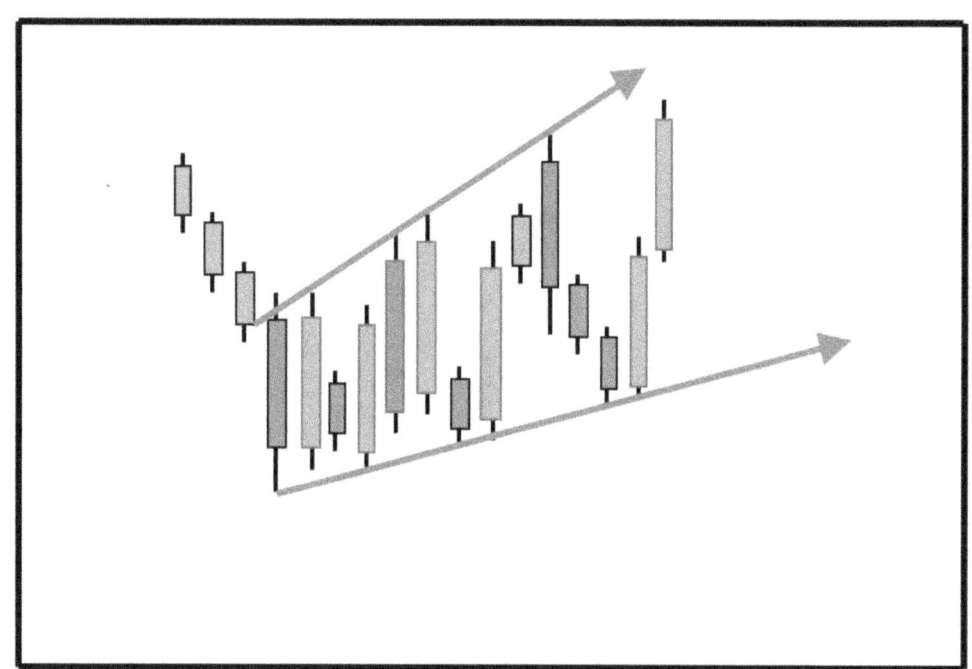

How to Trade with Ascending and Broadening Wedge

Based on the bottom line trends in the upward direction, it is advisable to consider going long at the bottom of this pattern. Typically, when the price bounces off the bottom trendline and starts to rise after the third touch, it presents an optimal opportunity for a buy trade. The third touch is a signal for a buying opportunity, and in around 60% of cases, a partial rise tends to be successful, while a partial decline works in the remaining 65% of instances. This pattern is often associated with aggressive traders due to its tendency to exhibit a downward breakout.

#12 - Ascending and Inverted Scallop

This pattern is often referred to as a "pirate's hook" due to its distinctive shape. When this pattern is identified, it has one of the highest completion rates, reaching an impressive 97%. To calculate the percentage target, measure from the tip of the hook to the top of the hook when entering a position. These patterns are typically observed in an upward trend or during a bullish reversal in a downtrend. Confirmation of the pattern occurs when the price closes just above the highest high within the pattern.

Figure 12: Ascending and Inverted Scallop

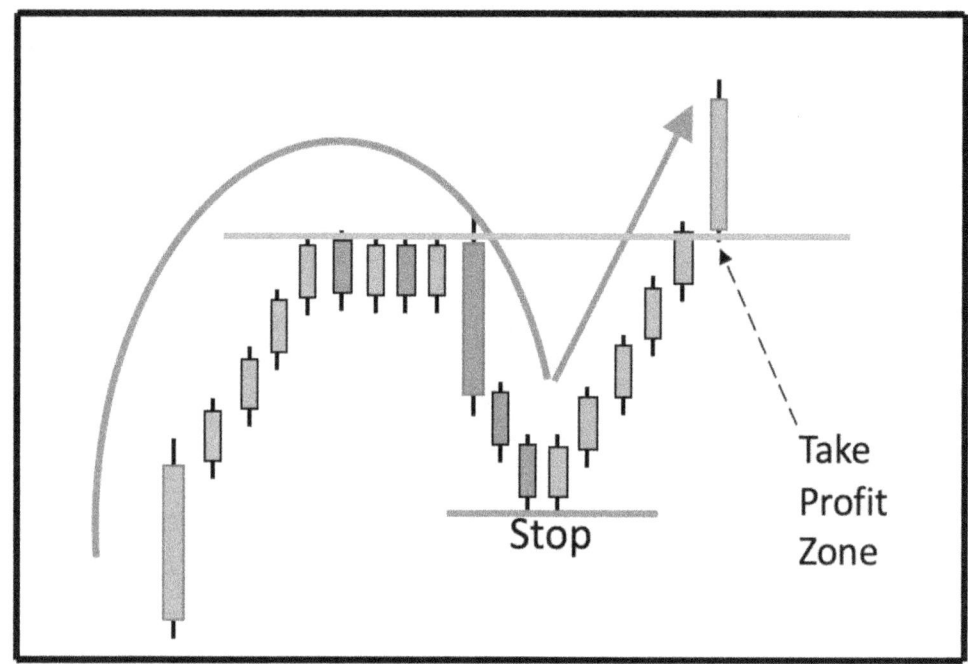

How to Trade with Ascending and Inverted Scallop

When trading this pattern, it is recommended to place a support line just above the highest peak and set a stop at the right scallop. Once these levels are established, it is crucial to monitor the price movement. If the prices close below the scallop edge, it signals a potential entry point for a long trade. Conversely, if the prices close above the highest point of the peak, it indicates a buying opportunity. It is important to avoid prices that drop below the starting point. In some cases, prices may form distinct new right valleys after the scallop, and if the price drops below this valley, it is advisable to sell. However, if the prices rise again to form a new scallop, it can be used as the new stop location. Notably, heavy breakouts have shown better performance in the Ascending and Inverted Scallop pattern.

#13 - Ascending Triangle

This pattern is often associated with weak performance, especially in cryptocurrency markets where it is commonly observed. Many traders find it challenging to profit from this pattern. The crucial factors to consider are the starting point of the triangle and the entry points of the candlesticks into the triangle. Around 40% of the time, this pattern experiences a breakout that is opposite to the entry point. When an uptrend enters the triangle, there is a 60% chance that it will result in an upward breakout at the end of the triangle.

Figure 13: Ascending Triangle

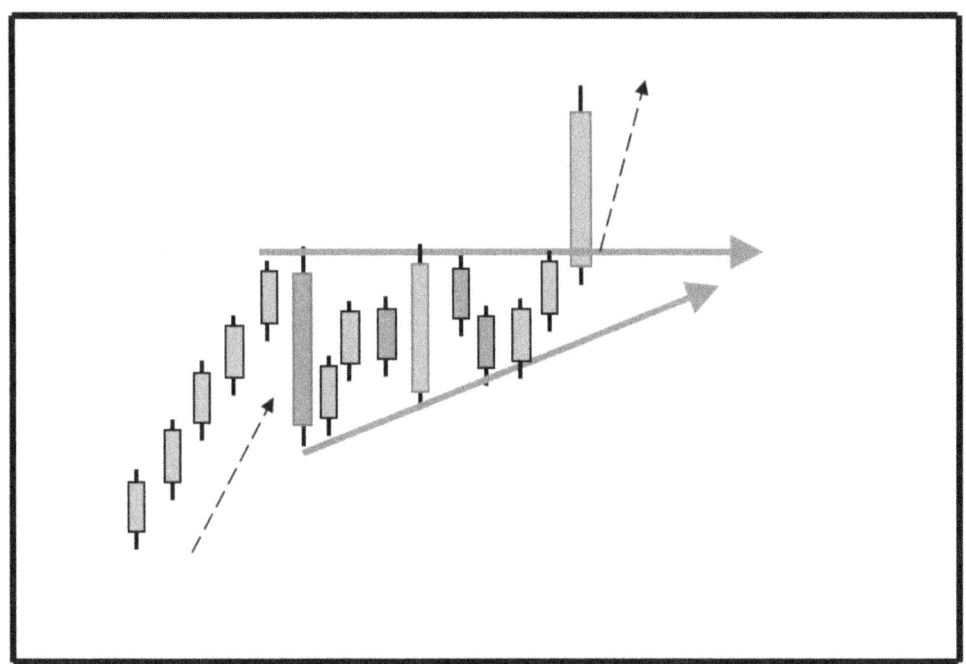

How to Trade with Ascending Triangle

When trading this pattern, it is important to ensure that the trendlines of the triangle are formed by connecting at least two swing highs and lows. If the price breaks above the top of the pattern, it is a signal to enter a buy trade. Conversely, if the price breaks below the lower trendline, it indicates an opportunity to enter a short trade. To manage risk, it is recommended to place a stop loss just outside the pattern. It is worth noting that any breakout, regardless of its direction, should be taken into consideration. This pattern can last from a few weeks to several months, with an average duration of one to three months. It is important to consider an ascending triangle invalid if a more recent reaction low is lower or equal to the previous reaction   low.

#14 - Bearish Bat

This pattern, known as the Bearish Bat, is frequently observed in cryptocurrency markets but is rare in the stock market. It resembles a large "W" chart pattern, with uneven bottoms and points referred to as the "Adam" or "Eve" points, identified using Fibonacci ratios. Interestingly, the breakout direction is upward approximately 80% of the time. However, there is a high likelihood of a significant pullback occurring in around 95% of cases, with the resulting gains being less than 3%. It is important to note that relying solely on Fibonacci ratios for predicting the pullback can be misleading.

Figure 14: Bearish Bat

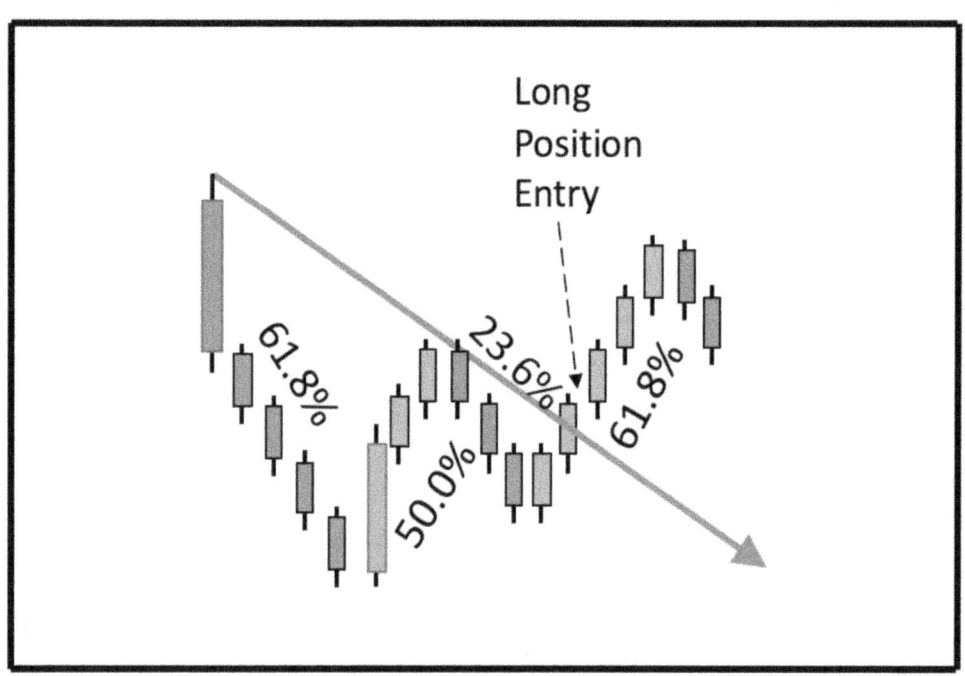

How to Trade with Bearish Bat

When trading the Bearish Bat pattern, it is important to watch out for strong moves in either direction (up or down), as the direction of the move depends on the structure of the bat. These patterns often resemble butterflies. To set profit targets, look for Fibonacci lines between the first valley and the last breaking point (last candle in the pattern). You can enter pending trades by setting profit targets within this range. For example, you can set a pending buy stop order to be triggered when the price reaches 23%. However, the main profit targets should be set at 38%, 50%, and 100%. It is crucial not to be tempted to increase the position size unless the trend extends towards the higher profit targets. Additionally, place your stop loss at the initial point, which is the beginning of the candle in the pattern.

#15 - Bearish Engulfing

This pattern signals lower prices ahead. It consists of a large green candlestick followed by another large red candlestick, both surrounding smaller candlesticks (two in the case of the figure below). This pattern can occur anywhere on the chart, but it is more noteworthy when it happens after a price advance, indicating a potential pullback to the upside with a larger downtrend. In this pattern, prices are on an uptrend, even if it is short-term. When a fast spike occurs and an engulfing pattern forms, there will be less supply of stock to slow down a potential reversal.

Figure 15: Bearish Engulfing

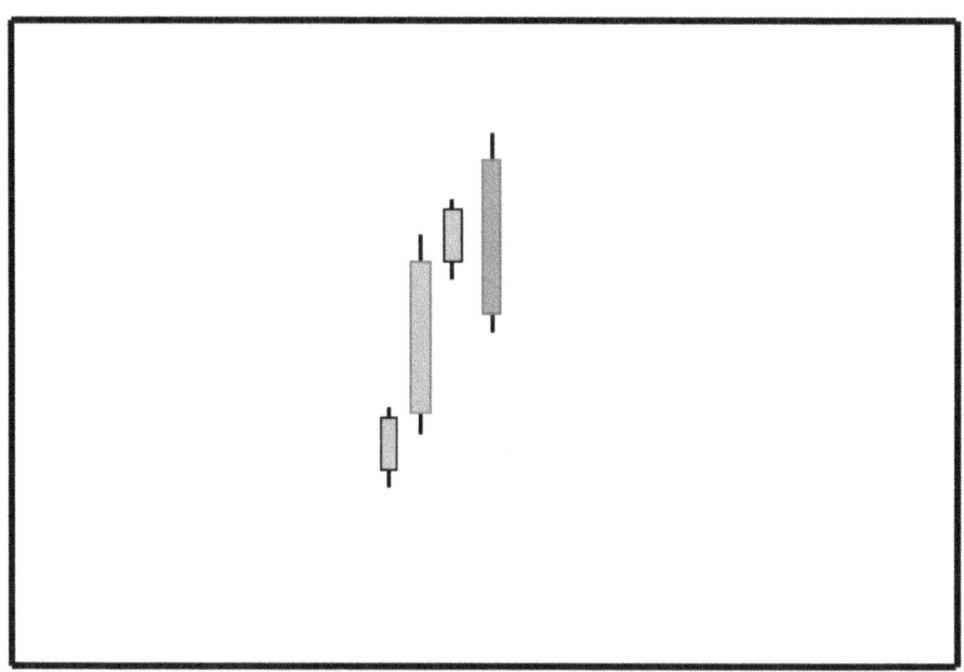

How to Trade Bearish Engulfing

When it comes to this pattern, the first candle signifies that buyers control the market, resulting in a higher close during this period. The second candle indicates a buildup of selling pressure, which is confirmed by the fourth candle closing below the low of the third candle. Traders often mistake this pattern as a sign of market weakness and are tempted to go short. However, it is important to note that the ideal scenario is to look for bearish engulfing patterns that reverse at the highs. There are two possible ways to trade with this pattern. First, you can sell a candle after the occurrence of the bearish engulfing pattern to confirm the bearish reversal. Alternatively, you can wait for an increase in volume accompanying the large downward price movement, as this is a strong indication to sell.

#16 - Bearish Gartley

This is a great pattern in that it strictly uses Fibonacci ratios. Without a computer, it is impossible to locate this pattern. The pattern resembles a Bat or a Double Bottom pattern, which is why Fibonacci is key to this pattern. This pattern has to align with specific Fibonacci levels, as it is a member of the harmonic family.

Figure 16: Bearish Gartley

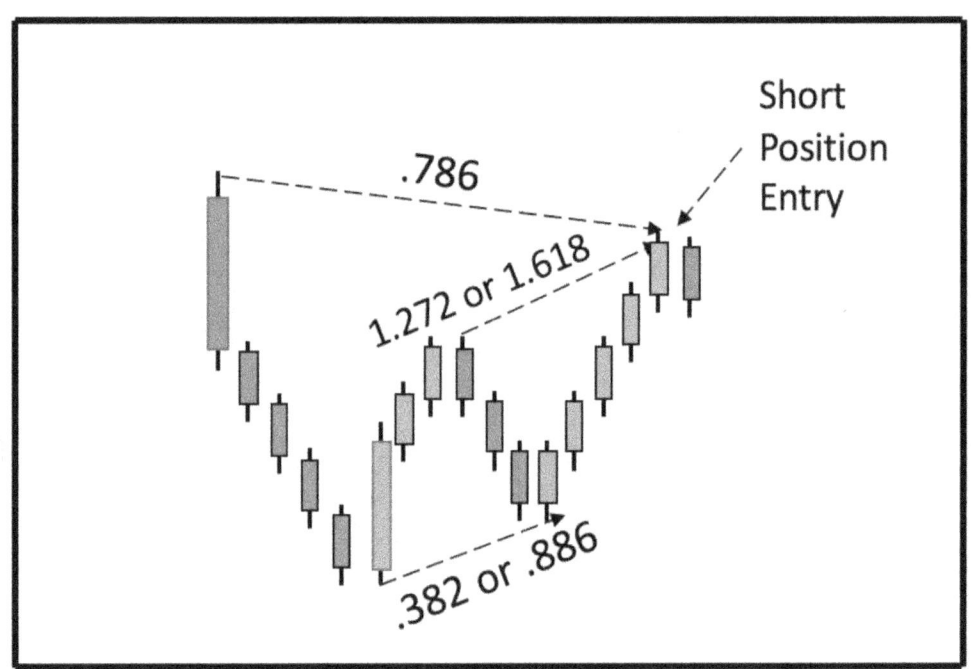

How to Trade Bearish Gartley

The Bearish Gartley pattern requires you to identify the pattern and confirm its validity. To do this, you must first outline the four price swings and ensure that each corresponds to their respective Fibonacci levels. With this information, you can easily estimate the general size of the pattern and establish clear parameters. This will help you determine whether the pattern is bearish or bullish. If the pattern is bearish, you should open a short (sell) trade.

#17 - Bearish Harami

This pattern consists of an initial green or white candlestick followed by a second red or black body. In the case of an uptrend, a green candle appears at the end of the trend. The open of candle two is always lower than the close of candle one, and the close of candle two is higher than the open of candle one (as shown in the figure below). The openings and closes of the second candle must be contained within the body of the first candle. This signifies an impending reversal, which is typically more significant with longer candlesticks.

Figure 17: Bearish Harami

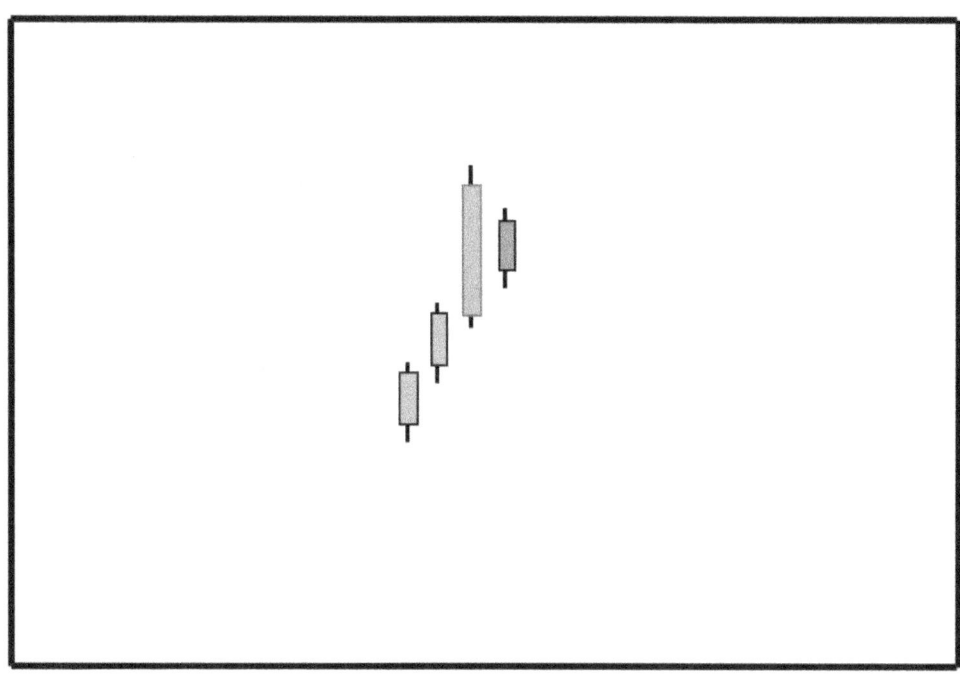

How to Trade Bearish Harami

Given the condition that the second body must be contained within the first, you can place your support directly below the wick of the small bearish candle. If you still have doubts about the trend, you can place your support below the wick of the bullish candle. If the price closes below the support, it indicates a sell signal. Combining this pattern with a trendline break can create a potential sell signal. Remember that the key to maximizing the potential of this pattern is to place a stop-limit order slightly below the low of the Bearish Harami candle. This method is commonly used by traders who don't have time to monitor the market. Another way to trade this pattern is by placing a market order at the breakout point.

#18 - Bearish Wolfe Wave

This pattern resembles a rising wedge pattern with a twist. The distinguishing feature of this pattern is that the candlesticks do not reach the end of the wedge. Wave 5 often breaks the resistance line, but this breakout is followed by a rapid drop. In cryptocurrency trading, the optimal re-entry point would be at the support line connecting points 1 and 4, where a breakdown occurs and the price drops by more than 10%.

Figure 18: Bearish Wolfe Wave

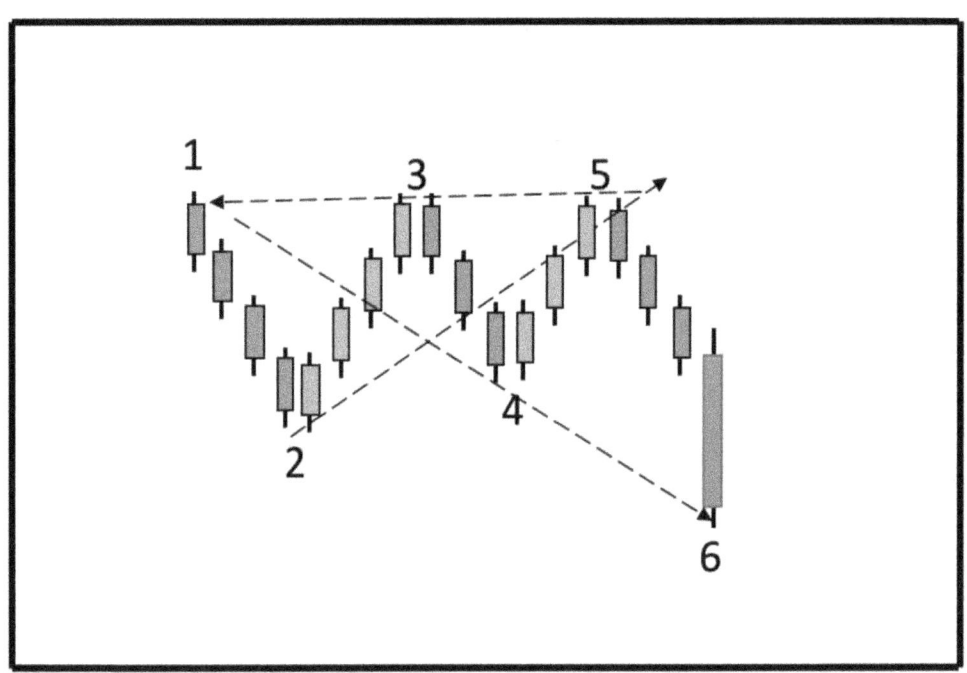

How to Trade Bearish Wolfe Wave

Considering the figure above and following the flow from left to right, let's number the points as 1, 2, 3, 4, 5, and 6. The optimal entry point for a sell trade is at Point 5, which is where the trend breaks into a downtrend. This point is often referred to as the "sweet spot." Your take profit level can be set at the point where the trendline from Point 1 intersects with Point 6, also known as the Estimated Price at Arrival. At this point, the downward trend begins to lose momentum. Trading the Wolfe Wave pattern requires sufficient trading experience, as these setup charts can be challenging to identify. To recognize this pattern, look for three points aligned along a trendline and then examine Points 2 and 4 to confirm if they match the characteristics of a bearish pattern.

#19 - Belt Hold

Belt hold lines are single candlestick patterns characterized by a gap up on the open of the bar. Bullish belt hold patterns occur when there is a significant gap down in a downtrend, and these candlesticks are typically green or white. Conversely, bearish belt hold patterns form with a gap away from existing uptrends, and they are usually red or black. The real body of the pattern has no shadow at the open end. These candlestick patterns are also referred to as white and black opening Marubozu.

Figure 19: Belt Hold

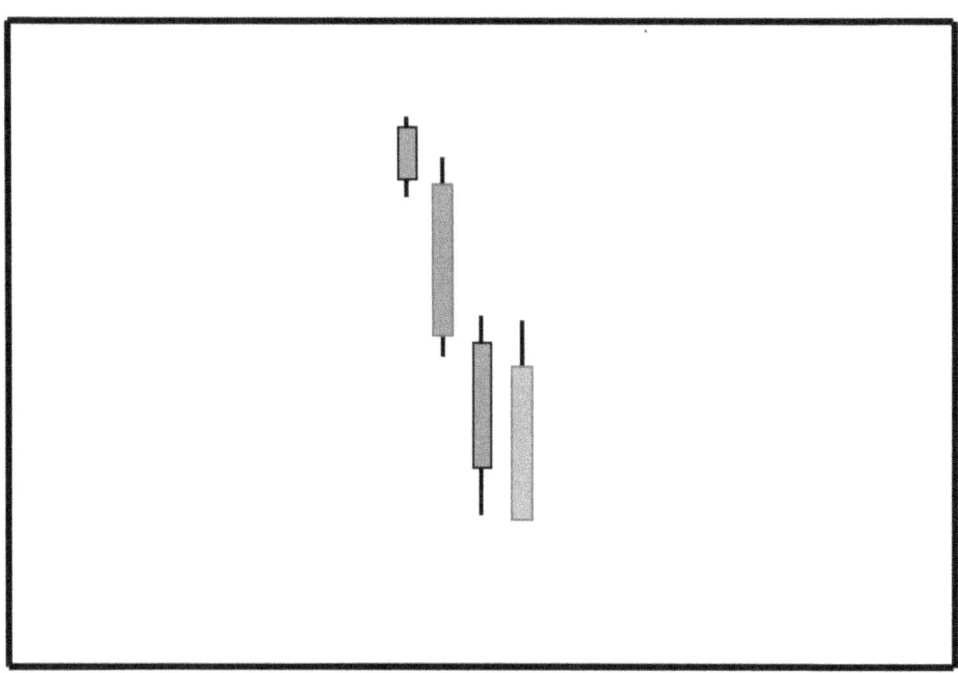

How to Trade with Belt Hold

Before trading this pattern, it's important to understand that the signal validity of the Belt Hold pattern increases when used in conjunction with other technical indicators. However, implementing Belt Hold pattern principles is relatively straightforward. The key is to identify candlesticks with a single wick sticking out from them. When you spot such a candlestick, open a position in the direction of the candle. If the candle is green and facing up (bullish), there is a high likelihood that prices will move upward. The same principle applies to red candles (bearish), but in the opposite direction. In this pattern, place your stop loss just below the low of the entry candle to protect your trades.

#20 - Breakout Through Major Moving Averages

When attempting to identify the Belt Hold pattern, it is important to pay attention to breakouts, as they often indicate important technical levels. Another key indicator is a significant moving average that triggers the breakout. The pattern stands out due to the irregular candles that appear at a different level. In this pattern, large volumes typically accompany significant price movements. Furthermore, a prolonged trend often follows after the breakout of this pattern.

Figure 20: Breakout Through Major Moving Averages

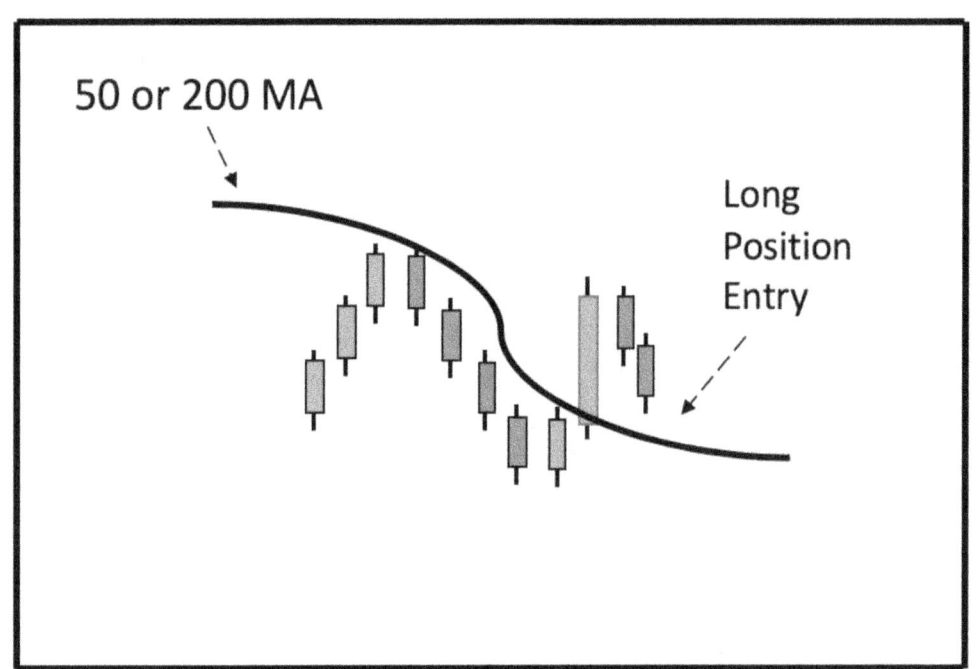

How to Trade with Breakout Through Major Moving Averages

When using the Belt Hold pattern in your trades, it is crucial to consider the price resistance and support levels. One advantage of this breakout pattern is its applicability to any trading chart. The support and resistance levels play a significant role in trading this pattern, as the confirmation of its validity relies on how many times the price touches these areas. A longer-lasting support or resistance level tends to yield better results after the price breakout. For a bullish trade entry, it is best to wait for prices to close above the resistance level. Conversely, for a bearish position, enter when prices prepare to close below a support level. Additionally, pay attention to the recent behavior of the stock, as recent price actions can confirm price targets, particularly in price trading patterns.

#21 – Bullish Bat

The Bullish Bat pattern is frequently observed in cryptocurrency trading but is relatively rare in the stock market. It resembles a large "M" chart pattern, although the tops are not evenly formed. The points referred to as "Adam" or "Eve" are identified using Fibonacci ratios. Notably, the breakout direction is downward around 70% of the time, with a pullback of approximately 90% and resulting in gains of less than 7%. It is important to note that the throwback can be misleading when using Fibonacci analysis.

Figure 21: Bullish Bat

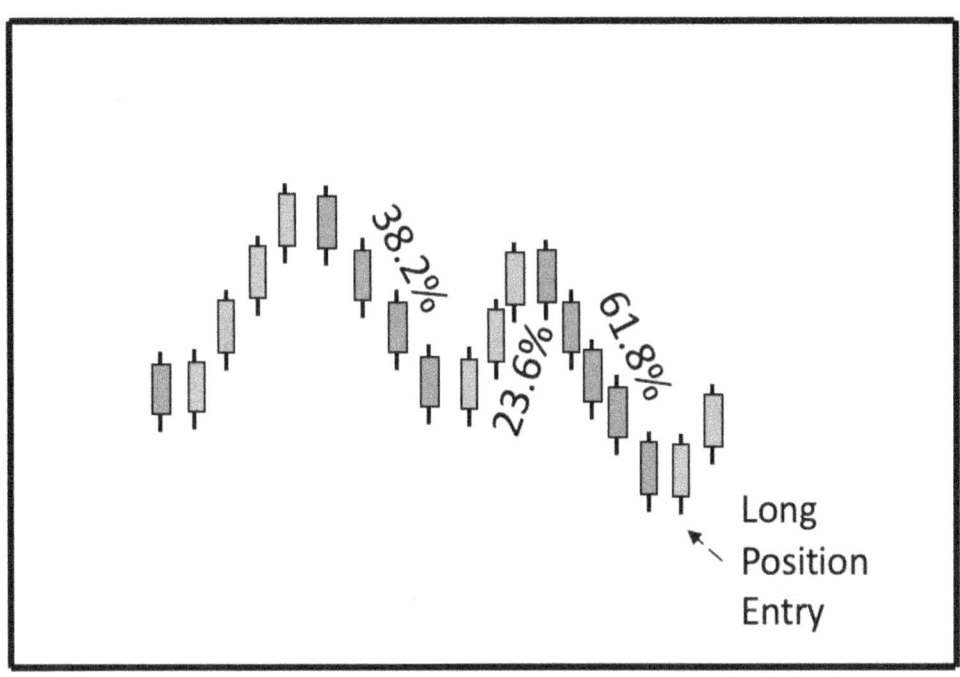

How to Trade with Bullish Bat

When trading the Bullish Bat pattern or any bat pattern, it is crucial to ensure that the Fibonacci levels align correctly. Since this pattern follows a harmonic approach, any misalignment can make the pattern unreliable. In the Bullish Bat pattern, the Fibonacci lines between Point A (peak 1) and Point D are used as profit targets. Assuming the figure above is labeled X, A, B, C, D, you can set your profit target levels at 38%, 50%, and 100% by selecting Point A and Point D using a Fibonacci retracement tool. For optimal trading, set your trade entry levels for pending orders at the lower profit targets. To manage potential reversals that often occur at Point D in bat patterns, it is advisable to place a pending buy stop order at the 23% target level. If the reversal does not occur, you can set the order to expire. To limit losses in bat patterns, only increase the position size if the breakouts fail. Remember to set your stop loss at Point X and not lower to protect your trades.

#22 – Bullish Engulfing

Bullish Engulfing patterns typically occur at the end of a downtrend. These patterns focus on the body of candle 2, which completely engulfs the body of candle 1 (without considering the wicks). The confirmation comes from the fact that the real body of Candle 2 is the opposite color of Candle 1, which matches the color of the previous trend. The body of candle 2 (represented by the green candle in the figure) is crucial as it serves as the actual reversal signal. When there is a rapid downward move, it indicates a smaller amount of stock available to impede a reversal, leading to the engulfing pattern. Conversely, when there is a swift upward move, stock prices may overextend, increasing the potential for taking profit.

Figure 22: Bullish Engulfing

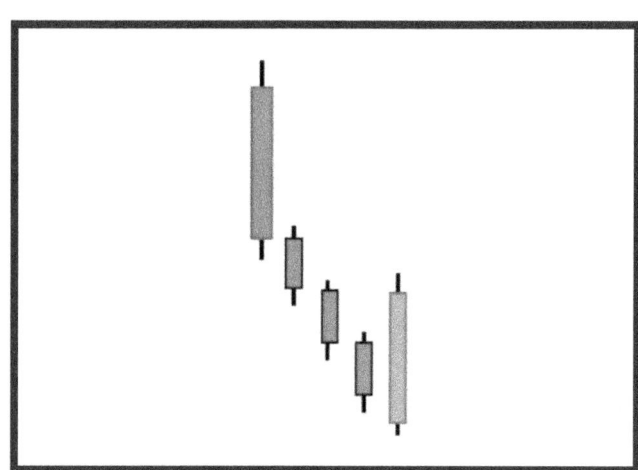

How to Trade Bullish Engulfing

The Bullish Engulfing pattern is a relatively common chart pattern, but it presents an opportunity for traders to capitalize on it. There are several ways to trade this pattern, such as waiting for a pullback to support or buying immediately when the candle closes. Many traders prefer buying at the close of candle 2 because there is often a morning gap down followed by a rally in prices. This is seen as a reversal of market sentiment, especially when accompanied by a significant increase in volume. Some traders may choose to confirm the price trend by waiting for the pattern to form before entering a buy position. While the Bullish Engulfing pattern shares similarities with the Bearish Engulfing pattern and can sometimes be indistinguishable, noting the dominance of either a red/black candle or a green/white candle helps avoid confusion between the two.

#23 – Bullish Gartley

A Bullish Gartley pattern is a popular harmonic trading formation that can provide traders with potential buying opportunities in the financial markets. This pattern is composed of specific Fibonacci retracement and extension levels, forming a distinct shape on a price chart. To spot a Bullish Gartley pattern, traders should look for a sequence of price swings that follow the pattern's specific ratios. The key levels to watch for are the 0.618 retracement of the XA leg, a 0.382 retracement of the AB leg, and a 0.786 retracement of the XC leg. Additionally, the CD leg should ideally complete at a 1.27 or 1.618 Fibonacci extension of the AB leg. By identifying these specific price relationships, traders can potentially identify Bullish Gartley patterns and take advantage of potential market reversals.

Figure 23: Bullish Gartley

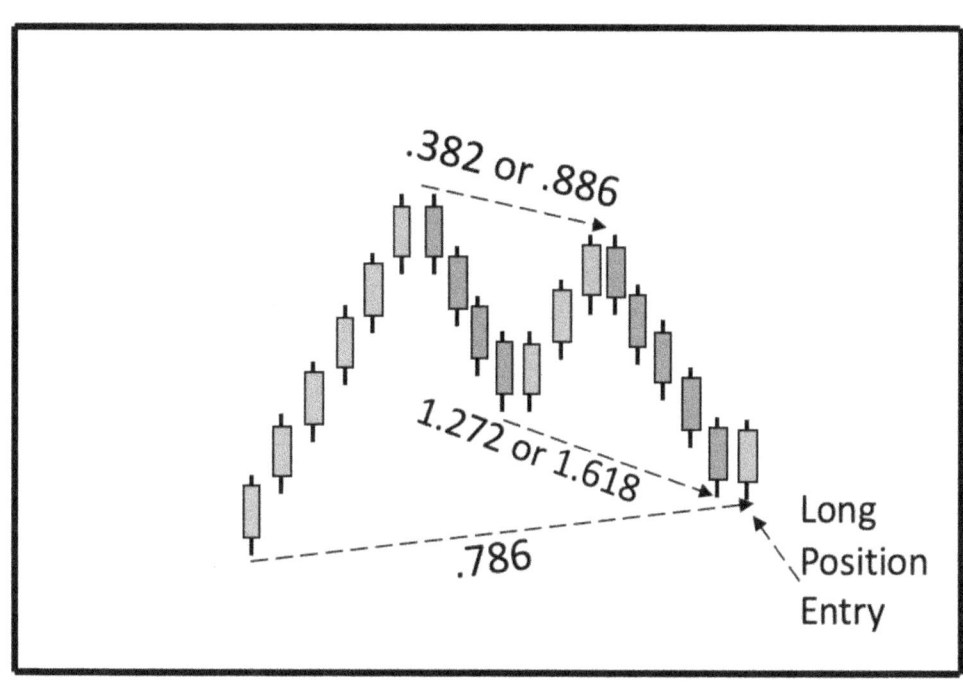

How to Trade Bullish Gartley

One characteristic feature of this chart is its X, A, B, C, D pattern, where X signifies high or low precedence. The XA line is the longest of the pattern. After the swing up from X to A, it reverses down from A to B but not as far down as from XA. The 61.8% retracement of XA marks the end of B, which is very important. Point C is at a 38.2% to 88.6% retracement of points AB. Finally, point D is at a 78.6% retracement of XA. These points are important because they help you understand when and where to enter a buy position, place a stop loss, or take profit. In this case, Point D is a potential reversal zone, making it a good spot to buy.

#24 - Bullish Harami

The Bullish Harami pattern is the reverse version of the Bearish Harami. Unlike the Bearish Harami pattern, this pattern relies heavily on the initial candle to indicate the continuity of a downward trend, signifying a bearish market. The real body of the first candle is red, while the second candle is green, but the first candle is bigger. In this pattern, the downtrend is evident for a substantial period, creating a long red candlestick at the end of the trend. The opening of candle 2 is higher than the close of candle 1 but closes lower than candle 1. Further confirmation of reversal is required for an uptrend indication, and the longer the red and green candles, the more forceful the reversal becomes.

Figure 24: Bullish Harami

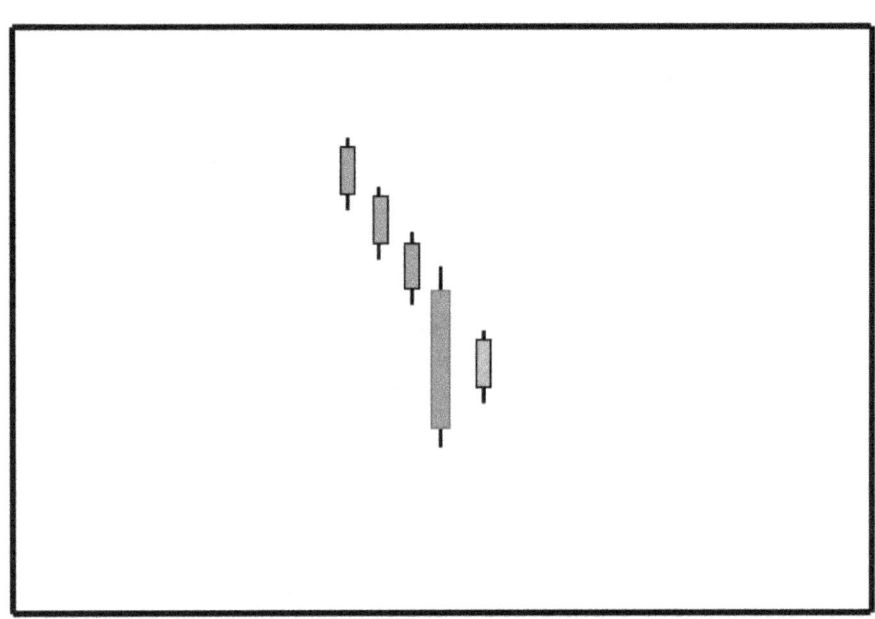

How to Trade Bullish Harami

When trading the Bullish Harami pattern, it's important to watch for a rise in prices, particularly those that close above the downward resistance trendline after the pattern occurs. When combined with a trendline break, this pattern can potentially signal a buy opportunity. There are four ways to trade this pattern effectively. The first is to rely solely on price action without any indicators. The second involves combining the pattern with a fast EMA and Fibonacci levels, using the moving average to determine entry points and Fibonacci levels for exit points. The third approach is to trade the pattern with a fast oscillator, and the fourth involves using Bollinger Bands. Keep in mind that while these strategies are effective for trading the Bullish Harami pattern, it is advisable to use additional trading tools to confirm the signal, as the pattern is considered a secondary candle pattern.

#25 – Cat's Ears

The Cat's Ear pattern is not as common as other chart patterns, but when identifying this pattern, the following six phases are commonly observed about 85% of the time. Phase 1 involves a price decline, typically accompanied by a severe sell-off of around 30%. This is followed by a horizontal pause in Phase 2. Next, there is a sudden upward movement and a subsequent sharp decline, creating the shape of the cat's left ear in Phase 3. The pattern then ranges for a while, resembling Phase 2, and eventually rises and falls to form Phase 5, which is usually smaller than Phase 3 about 95% of the time.

Figure 25: Cat's Ears

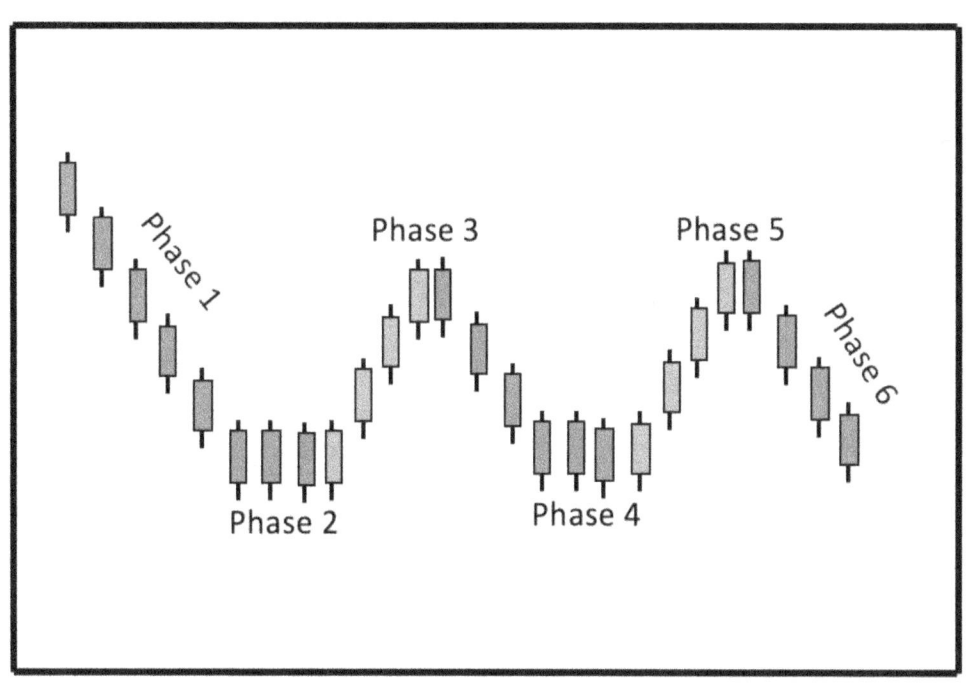

How to Trade Cat's Ears

When trading the Cat's Ear pattern, it is advisable to create a support line at the cat's scalp in Phase 4 and monitor the price movement in relation to this line. It is important to be cautious when the price breaks below this support line. While Phase 5 suggests a bearish turn, this indication is only valid if prices close below the pattern's support line. If the prices drop below Phase 4, it serves as a signal to sell. The Cat's Ear pattern typically spans from ten candles to two months (60 days), so a 14-period Relative Strength Index (RSI) can be applied. Throughout the pattern, the RSI should remain below 65. If the RSI rises above 65 during this pattern formation, it suggests that the Cat's Ear pattern may be less bearish.

#26 – Combination of Bullish Signals at Bottom

This particular chart pattern is an extended downtrend with numerous bullish signals like the Doji, Hammers, Bullish Haramis, and Bullish Engulfing signals. They usually indicate that prices are starting to turn bullish. Also known as bullish reversal patterns, they serve as an indication that buyers have overcome the previous selling pressure. However, there is still no confirmation whether there will be higher price bids from new buyers. Unless there is confirmation, these patterns remain neutral and are merely an indication of a potential support level.

Figure 26: Combination of Bullish Signals at Bottom

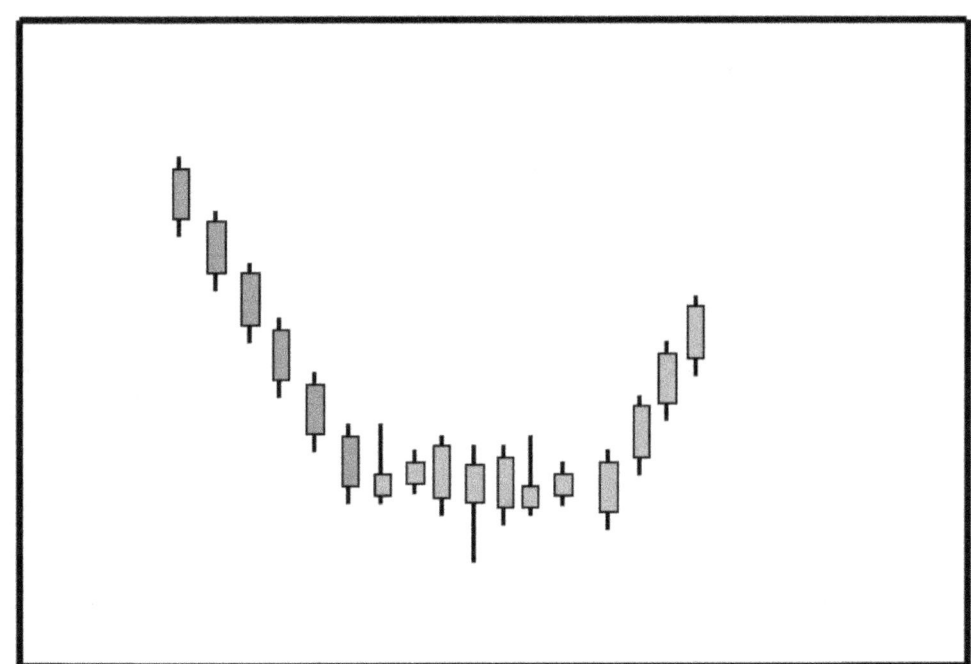

How to Trade Combination of Bullish Signals at Bottom

For this pattern to be considered a potential bullish reversal, there must be an existing downtrend to reverse (as seen in the figure above). If a Bullish Engulfing with new highs is the only visible pattern, it is hardly considered a bullish reversal pattern but rather an indication of continued buying pressure. First, look for the existence of a downtrend using moving averages, trend lines, or crest/trough analysis. Look for trades below a security's 20-day EMA and consider that each crest and trough is always lower than the previous, and the security must be trading below its trendline. The combination of bullish signals at the bottom indicates an impending uptrend, which presents a great opportunity to enter a buy position once confirmed.

#27 – Combination of Sell Signals at Top

This pattern is similar to the combination of bullish reversal patterns, but unlike its counterpart, it consists of an extended uptrend followed by numerous bearish reversal patterns like the Bearish Abandoned Baby, Bearish Engulfing, Bearish Harami, and Shooting Star signals. These patterns typically indicate an impending downtrend, suggesting that the market sentiment is likely to turn bearish soon. However, these patterns are not considered definitive without further bearish confirmation, which can be challenging to identify without the use of other technical analysis tools. Additionally, these patterns must form within an uptrend and are also known as bearish reversal patterns.

Figure 27: Combination of Sell Signals at Top

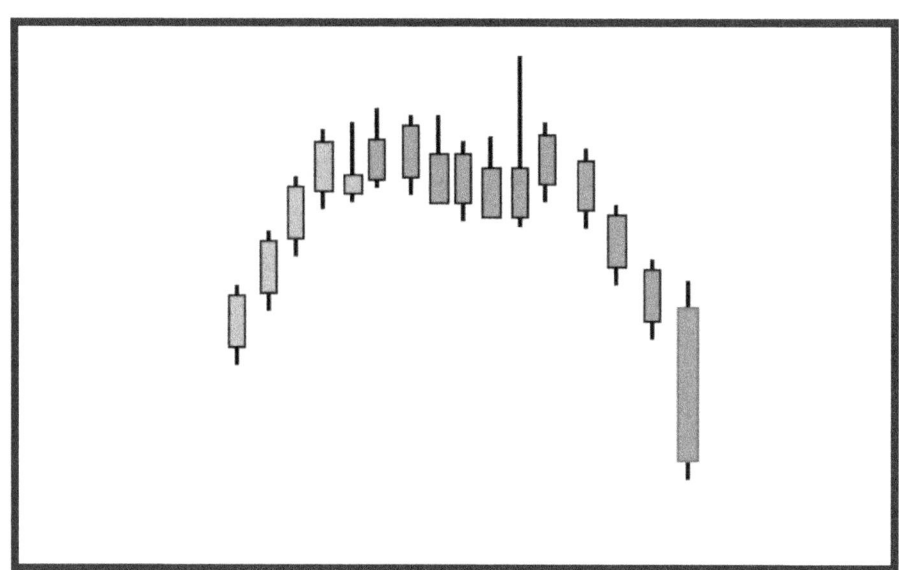

How to Trade Combination of Sell Signals at Top

There has to be an existing uptrend before this pattern can be considered a bearish reversal, even if the uptrend is not major, but it must have lasted for a short period (at least a few days). Otherwise, it is simply a confirmation of existing selling pressure, making it a continuation pattern instead. Similar to its counterpart, the security must trade above its 20-day EMA, with higher reaction troughs and peaks, and the commodity must trade above an existing trendline. The way you choose to trade this pattern depends on your personal preferences, trading style, and time horizon. To make the most of these patterns, it is advisable to incorporate other technical analysis tools. Some useful analysis tools to consider include MACD, PPO, Stochastics, RSI, and StochRSI, as they can help identify negative divergences that indicate weakening momentum.

#28 – Concealing Baby Swallow

This is a bullish reversal pattern that occurs at the end of downtrends and consists of four red candlesticks. These candlesticks usually indicate the weakening of an existing downtrend. It is a four-candle signal with two red Marubozus on the first two candles, representing the downtrend, and an inverted hammer on the third candle, indicating a potential trend reversal. On the third candle, the candlestick gaps down at the open and trades up, demonstrating buying strength. On the fourth candle, the candlestick opens higher than the third candle's close and engulfs the entire candle, closing just below the third candle's close. This particular pattern is quite rare and not widely discussed.

Figure 28: Concealing Baby Swallow

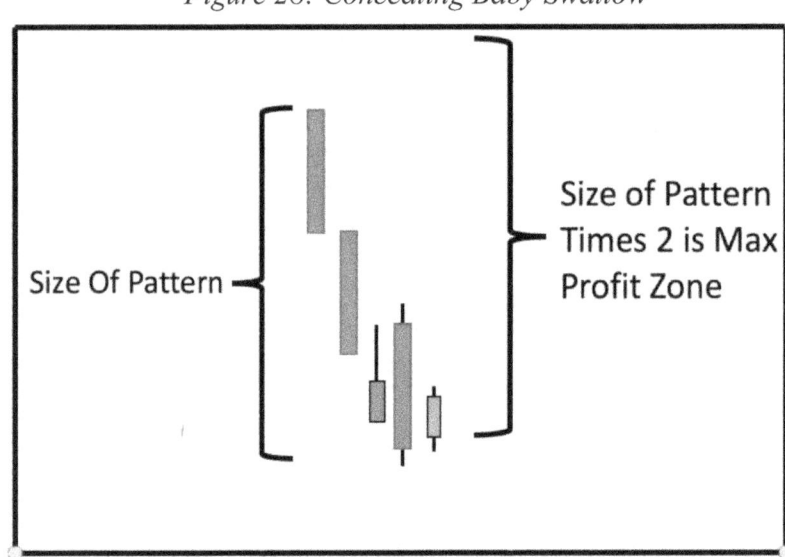

How to Trade Concealing Baby Swallow

Although this pattern occurs right after the formation of the fourth candle, it is still not sufficient to enter a trade position. Before entering any trades, make sure to identify a close above the upper body of the engulfing candle (i.e., the fourth candlestick). However, keep in mind that the candle after the fourth does not necessarily have to close above it; it may take some time for the pattern to develop a breakout. In most cases, the confirmation of this pattern comes with the fifth candle, presenting a good opportunity for the trader to take a long position. As always, it is important to place a stop-loss order for risk assessment, and in this case, the stop-loss should be placed just below the lowest level (i.e., below the lower wick of the fourth candle). On the other hand, the profit target should be equal to the size of the pattern, which can be measured by calculating the distance between the first Marubozu and the lower wick of the engulfing candle. Apply this measurement upwards from the lower point of the engulfing candle to the upper body. If the price action breaks above the upper body, then the trade is confirmed.

#29 – Cup and Handle

This pattern bears resemblance to a large coffee cup with a handle. In cryptocurrency, the left side of the cup is usually taller than the right side, occurring about 85% of the time. Additionally, throwbacks can be observed approximately 60% of the time. On average, the rise beyond the handle formation can range from 20-40%, depending on the timeframe being observed. It's worth noting that the handle does not necessarily have to experience a drop in price; it can also appear horizontal. The cup and handle pattern tends to perform best when the handle forms a bullish flag. Typically, there is low trading volume on the right-hand side of the pattern, which can span anywhere from as little as seven candles to as long as 65 candles. Depending on the timeframe.

Figure 29: Cup and Handle

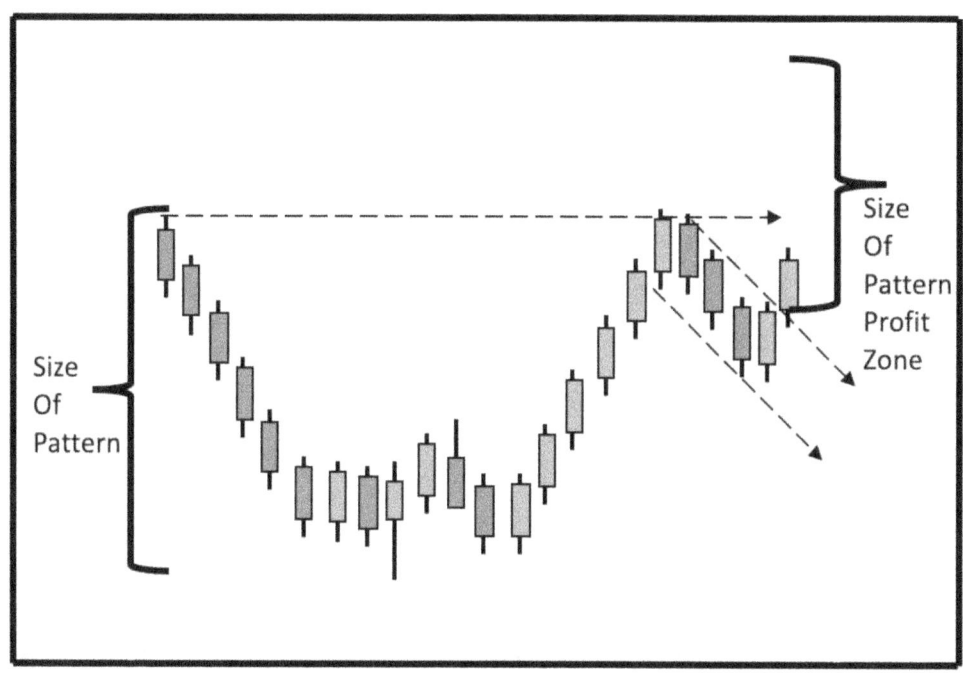

How to Trade Cup and Handle

This pattern is typically considered a bullish continuation pattern that helps identify buying opportunities. When trading this chart pattern, pay attention to the shape of the bottom. Stronger signals tend to come from patterns that have a U-like shape, while patterns with sharp V bottoms should be avoided. While U-like shapes generate stronger trade signals, it's advisable to avoid cups that are excessively deep or have deep handles. As always, placing a stop-loss order is important, and for this pattern, it should be set slightly above the upper trendline of the handle. The key with this pattern is to wait for the formation of the handle because the pattern remains incomplete until the price breaks out of the handle. However, once the price does break out of the handle, expect a rise in price.

#30 - Cup and Handle Inverted

This pattern, also known as the inverted cup and handle, resembles a large coffee cup with its handle turned upside-down. In cryptocurrency, the left side of the cup is typically taller than the right side, occurring about 70% of the time. Pullbacks are observed approximately 80% of the time, so traders should exercise caution. On average, there is a 40% drop beyond the handle formation, depending on the timeframe being observed. Handles can sometimes appear horizontal and do not necessarily have to experience a climb in price. Unlike its counterpart, the inverted cup and handle pattern performs best when the handle forms a bearish flag. The handle should not rise above the top of the cup but should retrace 30-60% of the cup's height.

Figure 30: Cup and Handle Inverted

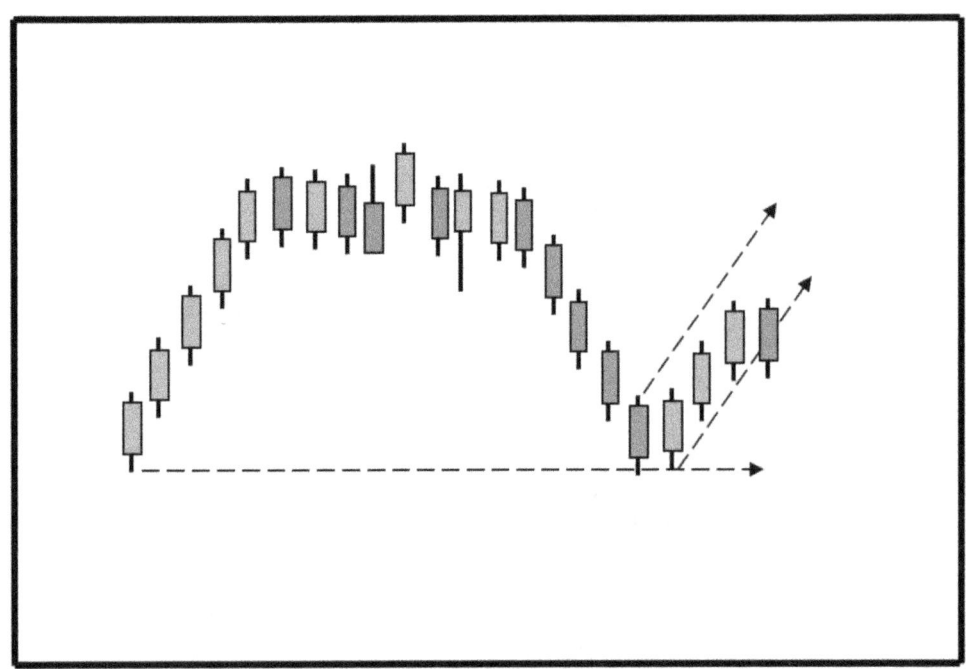

How to Trade Cup and Handle Inverted

This pattern typically takes a few months to form, but it is easily identifiable on daily chart timeframes. Due to its formation time, traders often look for other patterns that may develop within the inverted cup and handle. It's important to note that this is a bearish pattern, so it is crucial to determine the trade direction before entering. Having a good understanding of candlesticks, support and resistance levels, and volume is essential for successful trading. Paying close attention to volume is particularly important as it plays a vital role in confirming breakouts and completing the pattern. This pattern is used to identify selling opportunities and can confirm the absence of buying pressure during the assessed timeframe.

#31 – Cradle Pattern

This pattern is formed by a series of Doji candles at the bottom. Its name is derived from its cradle-like appearance, making it easily recognizable as a reversal pattern. It is a symmetrical bottom pattern characterized by a large bearish candle at the bottom of a downtrend, indicating significant selling pressure. The subsequent trading days show candles such as Doji, Harami, Hammer, Spinning Top, or Inverted Hammer, signifying an indecisive period. If a bullish engulfing signal occurs, approximately equal in magnitude to the preceding bearish candle at the end of the downtrend, it indicates that the indecisive period has ended and the bulls have taken control of the market.

Figure 31: Cradle Pattern

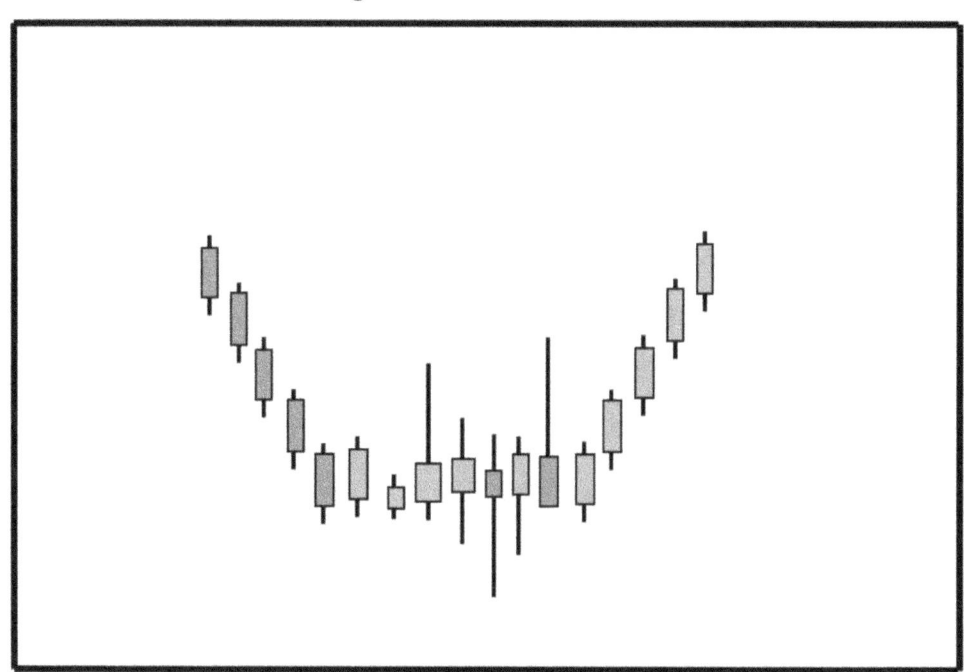

How to Trade Cradle Pattern

Not much can be said about this pattern, except that you should be on the lookout for the next long green (white) candlestick, as they are known to indicate strength in the rising prices. If the candle following this is also green (white) and closes above the previous candle's close, then you can be confident that the upward trend will continue, suggesting a favorable time to enter a buy position.

#32 - Dark Cloud Cover

This is a three-candlestick pattern consisting of a green candlestick as the first, followed by a red candlestick, and another red candlestick as the third. It is formed when a bearish candle opens above the close of a preceding bullish candle, with a confirmation candle in the process of forming. This pattern confirms a trend reversal. The red candle closes at least halfway below the green candle. On the second candle, the price may gap up but eventually fills the gap and closes near the opening of the bullish candlestick from the first candle.

Figure 32: Dark Cloud Cover

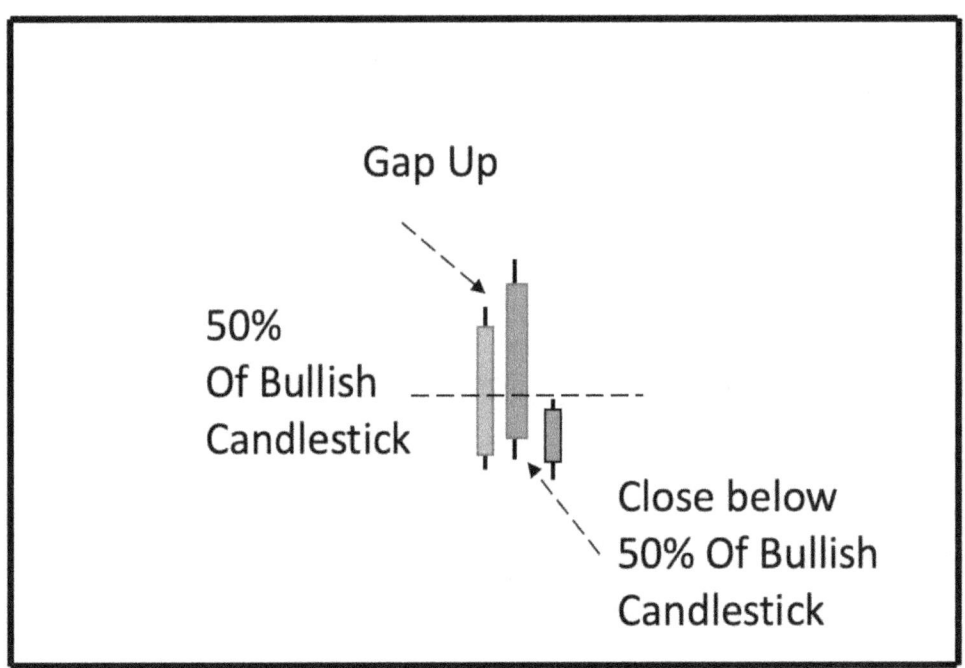

How to Trade Dark Cloud Cover

A strong reversal is identified when the lower red candle closes below the green candle. This indicates that demand is unable to match the supply. It is important for traders, especially beginners, to avoid the temptation of selling immediately upon observing the first and second candles of the Dark Cloud Cover pattern, as this is incorrect. The key is to wait for additional confirmation signals to occur. Some signals to watch for include existing uptrends, a gap on the following candle, and breaks in the upward trendline or other technical indicators. This is because, even as a bearish pattern, it retains a portion of the gains from the first candle.

#33 - Deliberation

This pattern occurs during an uptrend and signals a potential bearish reversal. It is similar to the Three White Soldiers pattern and is formed by two long, green bodies followed by a small green body. The third candle sometimes gaps up or opens at or near the close of the previous candle. Both the first and second candlesticks are relatively equal in size. Also known as a Stalled Pattern, this formation indicates market indecisiveness.

Figure 33: Deliberation

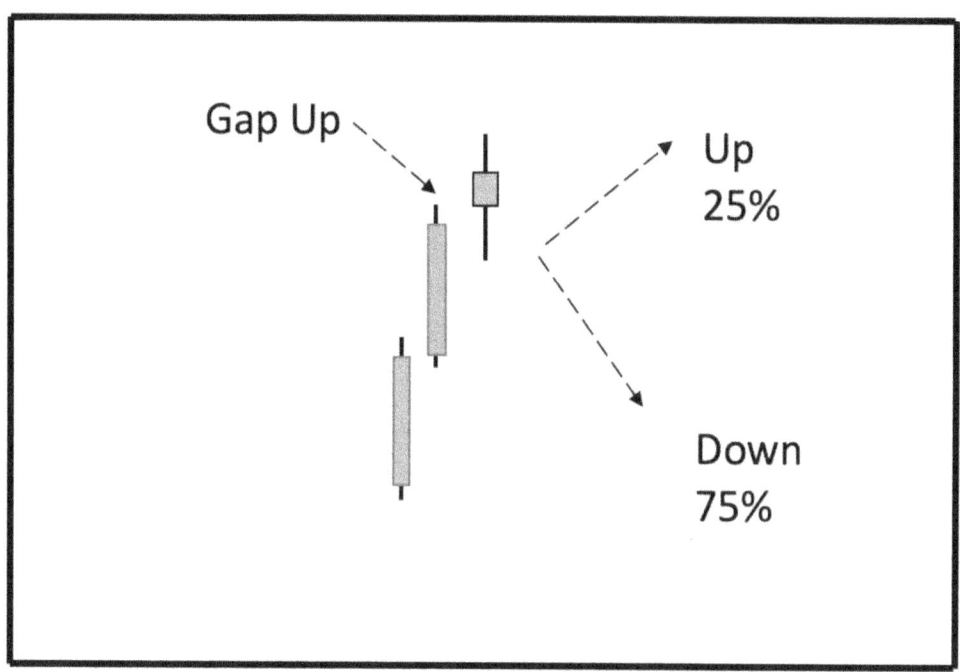

How to Trade Deliberation Pattern

The pattern may not actually indicate an impending bearish reversal, but if it falls below the midpoint of the second candle's real body, then a bearish reversal is likely to occur. Traders view this as an opportunity to limit their losses. While reversals can also happen within daily trades, traders generally prefer to observe the market for reversals over longer periods of time, often weeks. This is because such reversals occur rapidly and are influenced by events that quickly impact investor confidence. To identify a bearish trend, look for a series of lower lows and lower highs. When a market turns bearish, it is likely to reverse into an uptrend, especially if the lows and highs start moving higher.

#34 - Descending Broadening Wedge

Wedge patterns are extremely common in cryptocurrency and are definitely worth exploring. Approximately 70% of the time, the breakout occurs at the point where the wedge begins, regardless of whether it is a bullish or bearish condition. Throwbacks and pullbacks also occur about 65% of the time. In this pattern, both the upper and lower trendlines should slope, but the lower trendline should be steeper than the upper one. Similar to the Ascending Broadening Wedge, wider and taller patterns tend to work better than narrow and short ones.

Figure 34: Descending Broadening Wedge

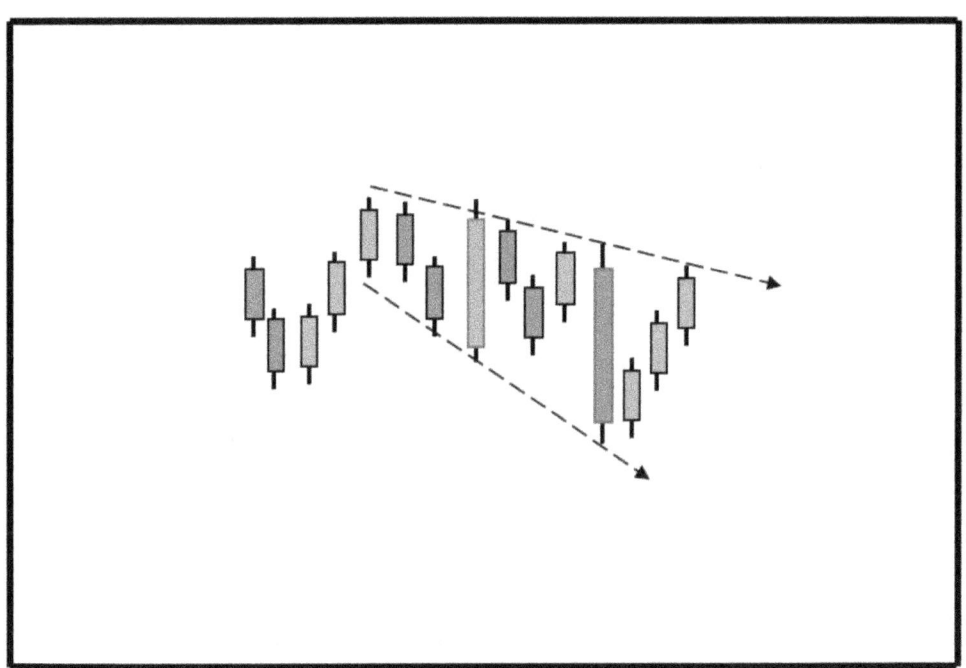

How to Trade Descending Broadening Wedge

In this pattern formation, you should look out for two touches on each trendline. These patterns typically result in upward breakouts. The advantage of this pattern is that it can be traded both from top to bottom and from bottom to top. The goal is to buy once the price starts to rise after touching the bottom trendline for the third time. Pay attention to the preceding pattern for a long-term rise, especially in the case of upward breakouts. In this pattern, the breakout direction is upwards around 72% of the time. Place your stop loss below the lower trendline. For buy signals, keep an eye out for breakouts that occur when the price breaks the upper trendline and closes above   it.

#35 - Descending Scallop

Descending Scallops are common but tricky to trade in cryptocurrency. It is best to avoid this pattern unless you are comfortable with a high-risk strategy. This pattern has a 50/50 ratio of bullish to bearish performance. Descending Scallops are characterized by backward J-shaped charts and often appear in downtrends, although they can also be seen in retracements of uptrends. When it comes to pullbacks, smaller pullbacks tend to create better patterns.

Figure 35: Descending Scallop

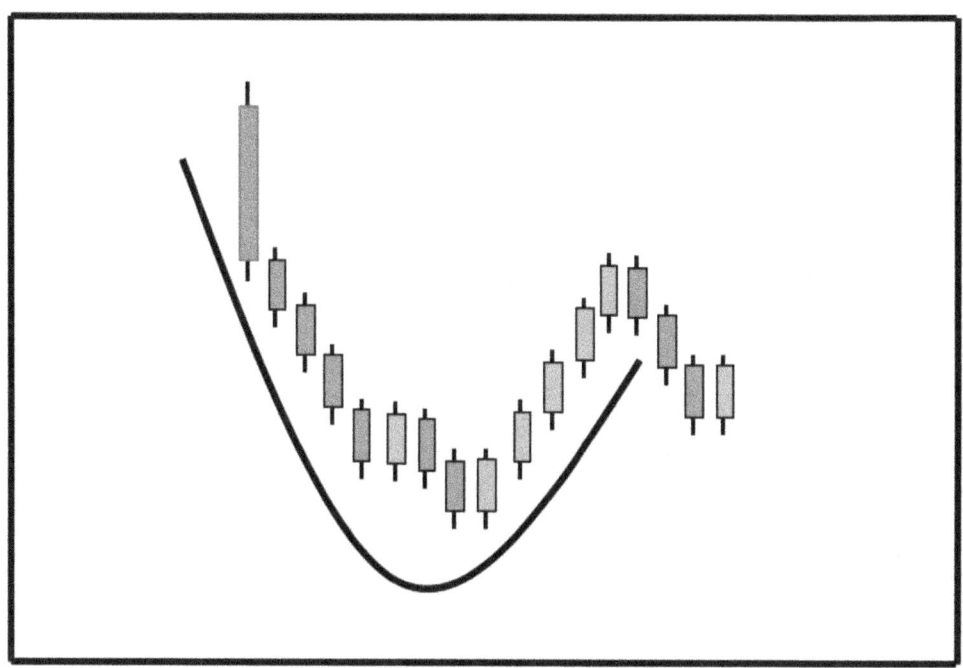

How to Trade Descending Scallop

When trading this pattern, it is recommended to place a support line just below the lowest trough and a stop at the right scallop. Once set, monitor the price movement, and if the prices close above the edge of the scallop, enter a short trade. Conversely, if the prices close below the lowest point of the valley, sell. Avoid prices that rise above the starting point. In some cases, prices may form distinct new right peaks after the scallop, and if the price rises above this peak, consider buying. In the case of the Ascending and Inverted Scallop pattern, heavy breakouts have shown better performance.

#36 - Descending Triangle

This is another common pattern found in all markets. It is easy to spot and trade. The key to this pattern is that the support and resistance lines should have two or more touches. The breakout typically occurs in the direction in which the triangle started, with a success rate of around 85% or higher. Throwbacks and pullbacks happen about 50% of the time, so there's no need to worry. This pattern is considered a universal pattern and can be seen as both a reversal and a continuation pattern simultaneously. On average, this pattern lasts from one to three months. However, if the high of a recent reaction surpasses that of a previous one, the pattern becomes invalid.

Figure 36: Descending Triangle

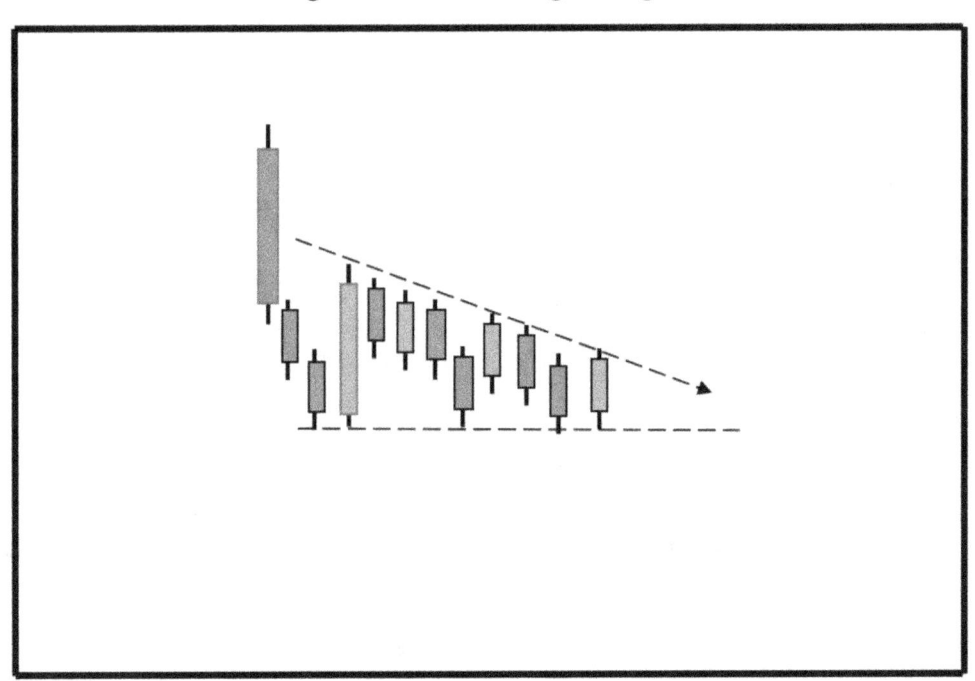

How to Trade Descending Triangle

There is typically a contraction in volume as the descending triangle pattern develops, but it expands once the downside breakout occurs, serving as confirmation. The tendency for the descending triangle pattern to be bullish before the breakout is definite. Once the pattern breaks below the lower support, there is a high probability that the downtrend momentum will strengthen. Many traders enter a short position after the breakdown. To determine the price target for this pattern, subtract the vertical height between the trendlines at the time of the breakdown from the entry price. Risk reduction is important, so don't forget to apply a stop-loss order, which can be placed at the upper trendline resistance.

#37 - Descending and Inverted Scallop

This pattern can become a bit tricky when trying to determine whether the Scallop is Ascending or Descending. It is important to clearly identify if it is inverted. There are two main ways to determine the nature of the pattern. Firstly, check if the Scallop pattern stops at the left side of the scallop or starts at the front of the Scallop. Secondly, after the handle is formed, observe whether the price continues its downward trend. Caution is advised as this pattern can be easily misinterpreted as a Head and Shoulders pattern or an Inverted Cup and Handle pattern.

Figure 37: Descending and Inverted Scallop

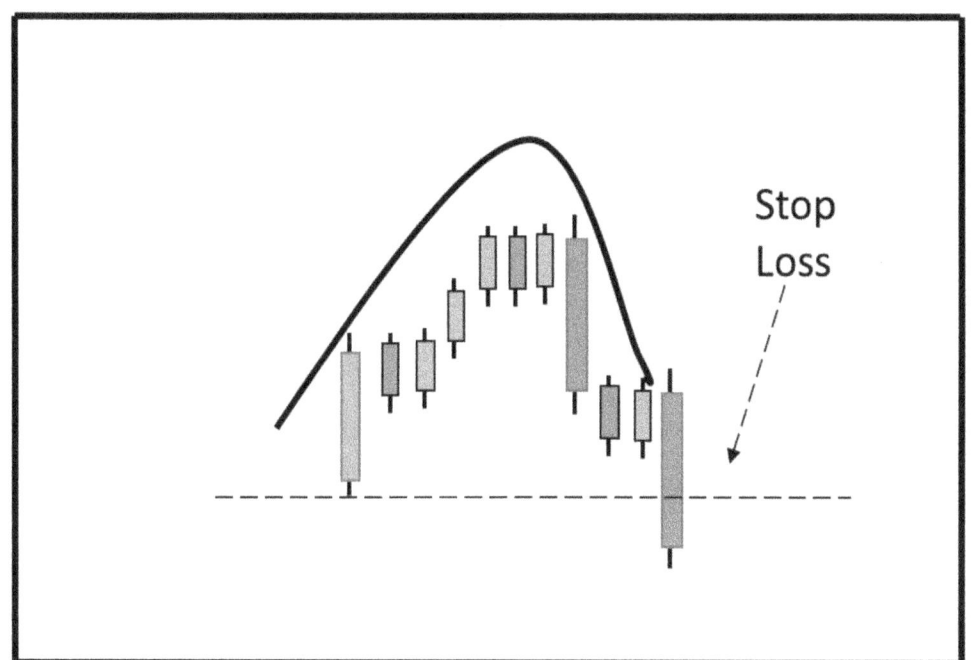

How to Trade Descending and Inverted Scallop

Before entering a trade with this pattern, it's important to note that tall patterns tend to perform better than short ones, and scallops with a decreasing volume trend are more successful in bearish markets. A buy signal can be identified when the price closes below the lowest low but does not surpass the high. This presents a great opportunity to initiate a short position. However, if the price rises above the start of the pattern, it is advisable to close your short position. If the price goes any higher than that, it's recommended to exit the trade. Confirmation of this pattern occurs when the price closes below the low of the pattern formation.

#38 - Diamond Bottom

This pattern is often overlooked and considered one of the most challenging to spot. However, if correctly identified, it has the potential to generate profitable trades. It can be easily confused with a double bottom pattern, creating an illusion of something that isn't there. Throwbacks occur approximately 50% of the time, while pullbacks happen around 75% of the time in a bullish trend and about 42% of the time in a bearish market. The pattern represents a struggle between buyers and sellers, eventually leading to a breakout as one party emerges as the victor due to the pressure of buying and selling.

Figure 38: Diamond Bottom

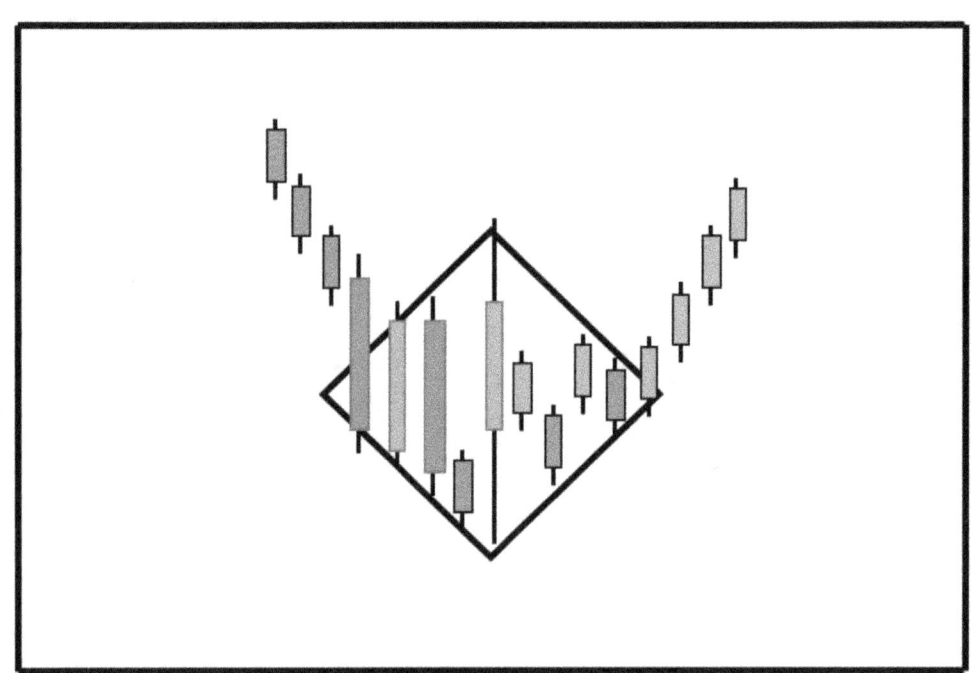

How to trade Diamond Bottom

Given the complexity of this pattern and its tendency to break out in any direction, it is crucial to exercise patience and wait for the breakout to occur. It is common for prices to retrace back to their base after shooting upwards, resulting in a quick decline. Diamond patterns have highly unpredictable breakout directions, emphasizing the importance of patience when trading this pattern. While a premature breakout is possible, it is exceedingly rare. In this pattern, the highest high of the highest candle within the diamond serves as the support level.

#39 - Diving Board

This pattern offers exciting trading opportunities, akin to taking candy from a baby. However, it still requires discipline and patience. Timing is crucial! It's worth noting that trading this pattern alone has yielded an average return of just over 50%. This chart pattern can be easily identified using the weekly chart. Pay attention to prices with flat bottoms, as this is a key characteristic. For optimal performance, look for regions of horizontal congestion and anticipate a subsequent price plunge, which is likely to reach the bottom of the diving board.

Figure 39: Diving Board

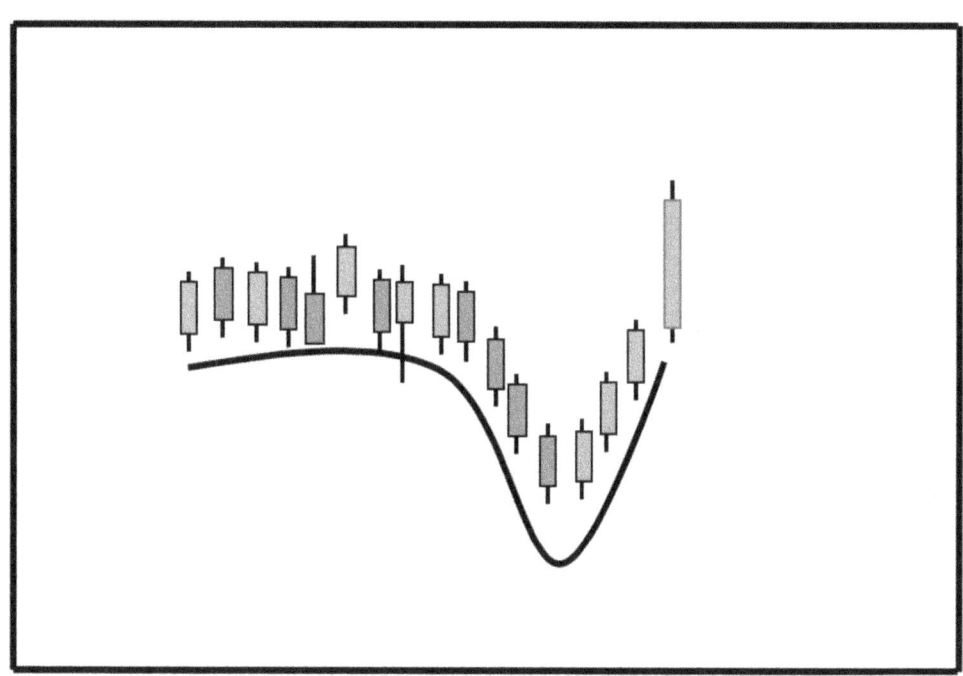

How to Trade Diving Board

Before trading this chart pattern, it's important to note that longer diving boards tend to yield better performance, and prices often return to the bottom of the diving board around 88% of the time. To determine when the plunge has ended, you can use a downward sloping trendline, which increases the likelihood of entering an early trade. A buy signal for this pattern is confirmed when the price closes above the chart pattern. As long as the upward trend continues, you can confidently maintain your trade position. Now you can see why I described it as an exciting pattern to trade.

#40 - Doji Dragonfly

This pattern is formed when the coin opens and closes at approximately the same price as its high, although not exactly. The Doji Dragonfly pattern serves as a potential signal for an upward or downward price reversal. The long lower shadow indicates aggressive selling during the candle's period. However, since the open and close prices are close to each other, it suggests that buying pressure pushed the price back up despite the selling pressure. Although not very common, when this pattern occurs, traders can expect a definite change in the trend direction. This is particularly true when the pattern emerges after a significant price rise or decline.

Figure 40: Doji Dragonfly

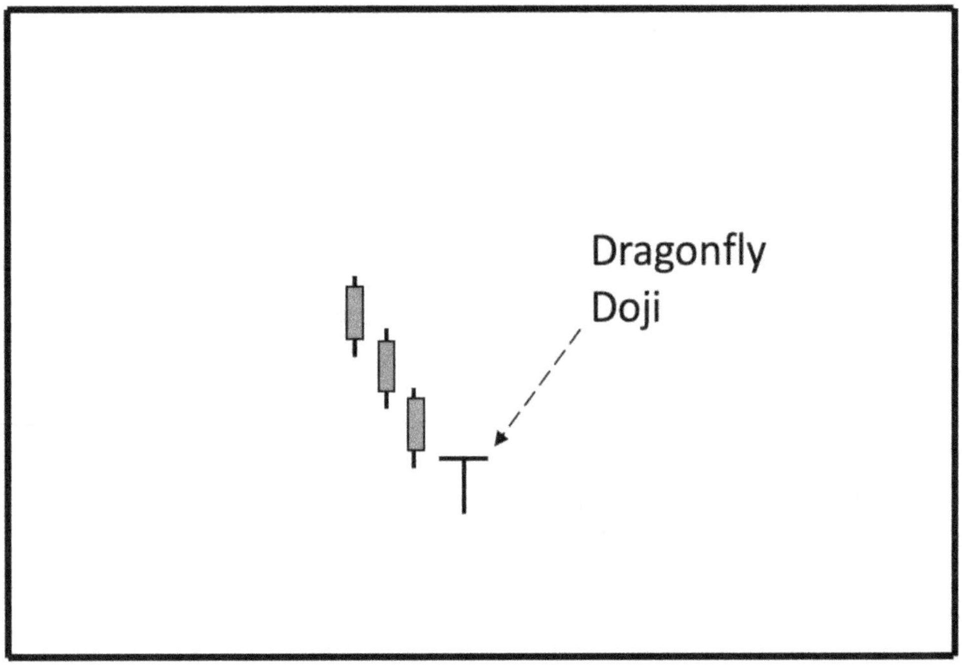

How to Trade Doji Dragonfly

To make this pattern tradable, it must be valid, which requires the candle following the Doji Dragonfly to drop and close below the close of the Doji Dragonfly candle. If the confirmation candle shows a rise in price, it confirms the price reversal signal, indicating a likely continuation of the upward trend. Most traders prefer to enter trades shortly after the completion of the confirmation candle, as this is considered the optimal timing. For a bullish reversal, a stop-loss order can be placed below the low of the Doji Dragonfly, while for a bearish reversal, the stop loss can be placed above the high of the Doji Dragonfly. To enhance the effectiveness of this pattern, it can be combined with other technical indicators.

#41 - Doji Gravestone

This pattern can be seen as a reverse version of the Doji Dragonfly, as they share similar characteristics. It typically occurs at the top of uptrends. Like the Doji Dragonfly, the open, close, and low prices are approximately the same. This pattern suggests that the market initially shows bullish pressure, pushing prices higher, but eventually, the bears gain control and suppress the upward momentum. The interpretation of this pattern can be controversial because while it can indicate a market reversal, it can also be a sign of market continuation, especially in a bearish market trend.

Figure 41: Doji Gravestone

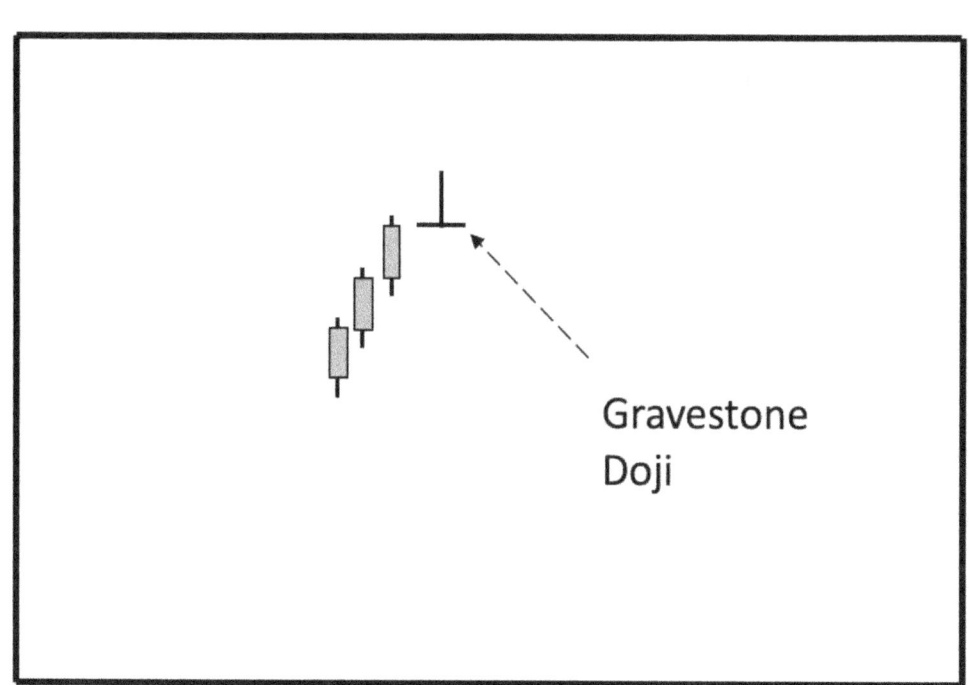

Gravestone Doji

How to Trade Doji Gravestone

This pattern indicates the potential for a bearish reversal, providing traders with an opportunity to take a bearish trade position or secure profits. However, it is crucial to accurately identify the pattern before entering or exiting a trade. To do so, it is recommended to use this pattern in conjunction with other technical analysis tools. Pay close attention to the context in which the Doji Gravestone appears. If it appears in an uptrend (which is most likely), it suggests the end of that uptrend in most cases, prompting traders to prepare for a trend reversal. Conversely, in a downtrend, it indicates a continuation of the downtrend, leading many traders to hold their positions until the market indicates otherwise.

#42 - Doji Long Legged

This candlestick pattern is commonly known as a Doji, and it represents market indecision. It can be observed at both the bottom and top of trends, serving as a signal for potential price trend reversals. However, it can also indicate market continuation. The Doji has a small body with long upper and lower shadows or wicks. It tends to appear after significant price advances or declines, regardless of the timeframe. However, its significance is more pronounced on longer timeframes such as days, weeks, and months.

Figure 42: Doji Long Legged

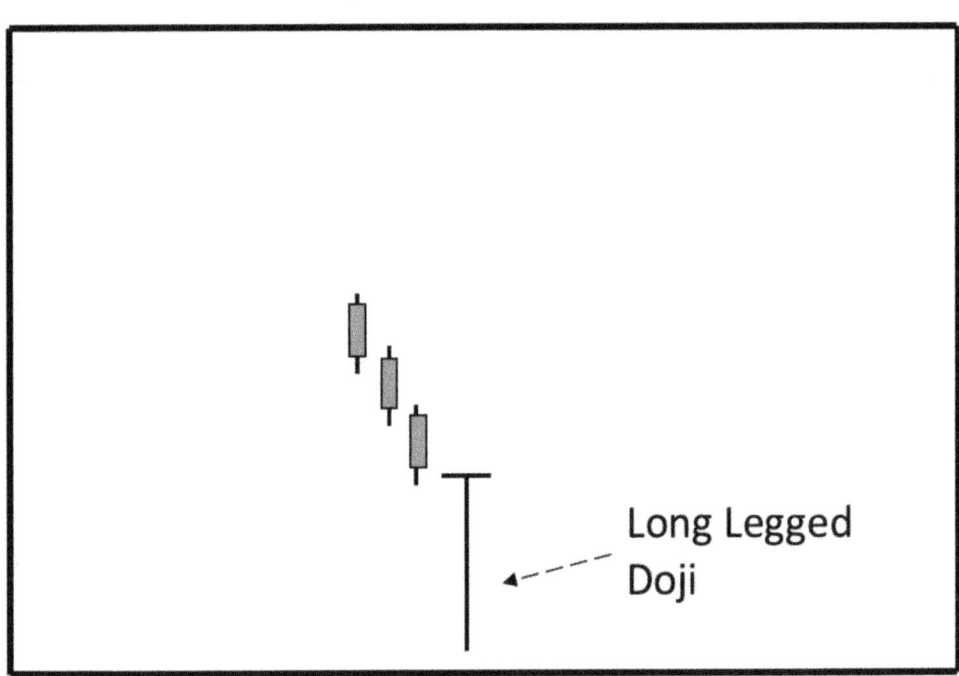

How to Trade Doji Long Legged

When trading this pattern, it is important to focus not just on the individual candle itself, but also on the trends that occur before and after its formation. Since there is no significant price movement at the close of the Doji Long Legged candle, it is crucial to wait for confirmation of the chart pattern through subsequent price movements. In many cases, especially when the pattern appears in clusters, it could either indicate a continuation of the existing trend or a reversal. Therefore, it is advisable to exercise patience and wait for price movements above the high (wick or shadow top) or below the low (wick or shadow bottom) of the Doji Long Legged candle pattern before entering any trade position. Movements above the high suggest a long opportunity, while movements below the low indicate a short opportunity. To mitigate risk, consider placing stop-loss orders above or below the wick, depending on your chosen position.

#43 - Doji Neutral

The Doji Neutral, also known simply as the Doji, is a candlestick pattern characterized by a closing price that is nearly identical to its opening price. This pattern is often mistaken for the Spinning Top candlestick pattern. The Doji Neutral takes the shape of a plus sign and, depending on market sentiment, can indicate either a trend reversal or continuation. As a result, it is commonly viewed as a signal of indecision in the market. This candle pattern can also be found in conjunction with other patterns. Analysts utilize the Doji to filter out market noise and identify trades with the highest probability of success. Dating back to the 17th century, the Doji is considered one of the oldest chart patterns, if not the oldest.

Figure 43: Doji Neutral Example

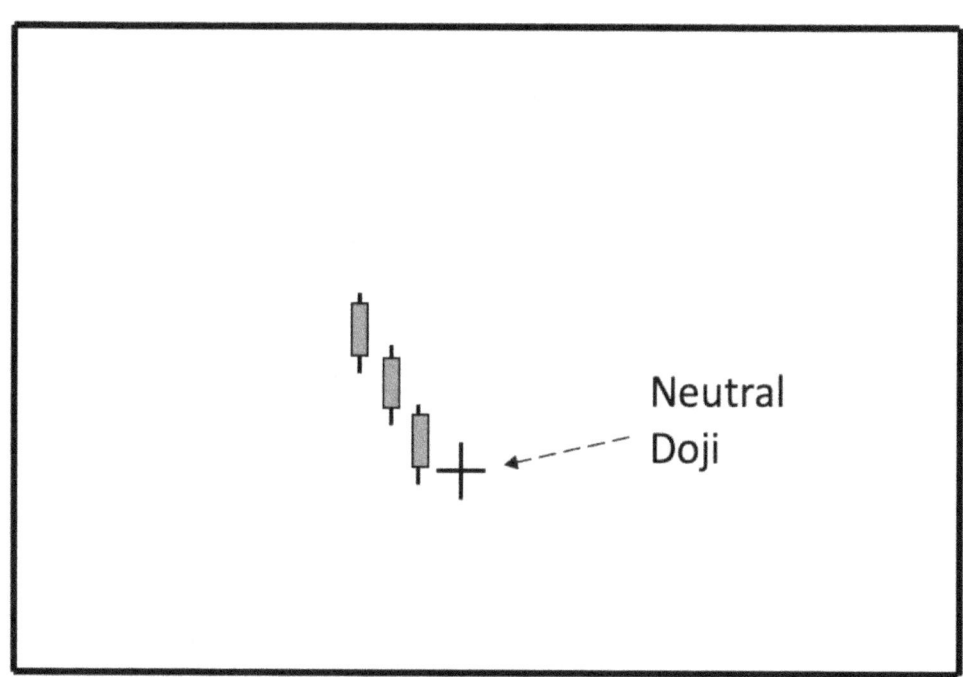

How to Trade the Doji Neutral

The Doji Neutral pattern is primarily used to determine potential market direction based on its position and the prevailing trend. Regardless of where the pattern appears, it is crucial to focus on the preceding and succeeding candlesticks. For example, if bullish candlesticks precede the Doji, it suggests that the market sentiment is likely to turn bearish. Conversely, if bearish candlesticks precede the Doji, it indicates that the market sentiment is about to become bullish. Keep an eye out for such opportunities, but always confirm the trends before entering any positions. If the pattern occurs at the peak of a bullish trend, exercise patience and wait for a bearish candlestick to form afterward before considering exiting your position or entering a new one.

#44 - Doji End Flat Trading Range Bottom

Identifying the Doji End Flat Trading Range Bottom pattern can be challenging, but not impossible. This pattern occurs when prices stabilize after a prolonged downtrend. There is no clear bullish signal, and bearish candlesticks outnumber bullish ones. At the end of the flat trading range, a Doji candlestick appears, serving as a signal for a potential strong price movement in either direction. If there is a gap up from the last Doji formation, it suggests the possibility of an emerging uptrend.

Figure 44: Doji End of Flat Trading Range Bottom

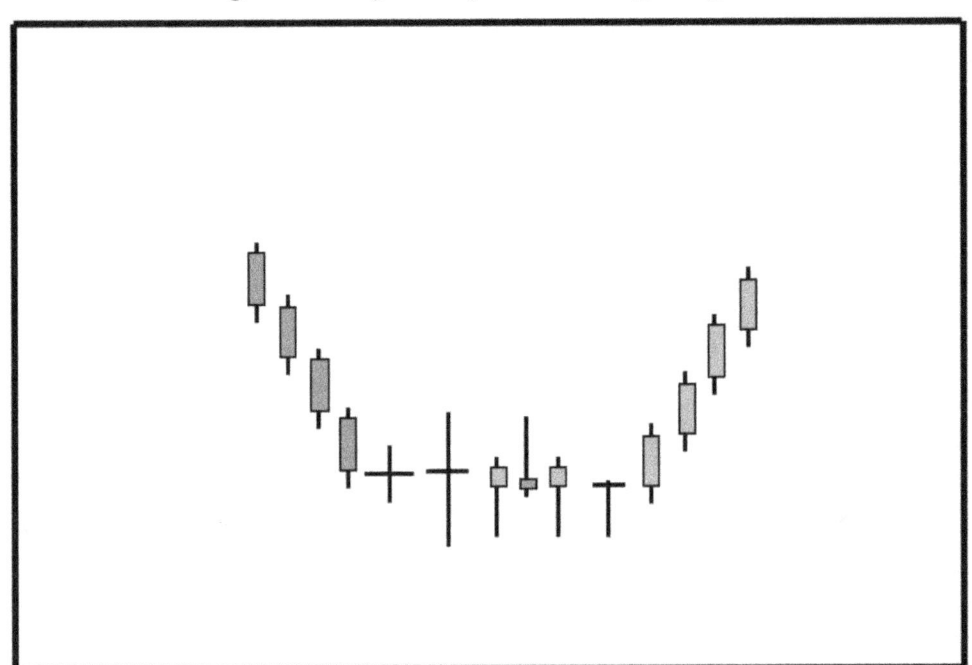

How to Trade the Doji End Flat Trading Range Bottom

Trading this pattern requires first identifying it. Now that you know its appearance and formation, it's important to note that the pattern can signal both a potential trend continuation and a potential trend reversal. Until either is confirmed, there is a level of uncertainty. To confirm the trend direction from this pattern, place a support line at the top wick of the last candle before the flat range. If the price breaks out of the support line, it suggests a high likelihood of an uptrend. At that point, you can choose to enter a long position or wait for a second confirming candle before making a decision.

#45 - Doji End of Flat Trading Range Top

This chart pattern is similar to the Doji End of Flat Trading Range Bottom, but it is the exact opposite. Following an extended uptrend, prices consolidate and trade within a narrow range for a short period. At the end of this trading range, a Doji candlestick appears, indicating a potential price movement in either direction. If the market is overbought, there is a higher probability of a subsequent downtrend. Confirmation of a downtrend occurs if there is a gap down from the last Doji formation. This confirms the likelihood of a downtrend in the following price action.

Figure 45: Doji End of Flat Trading Range Top

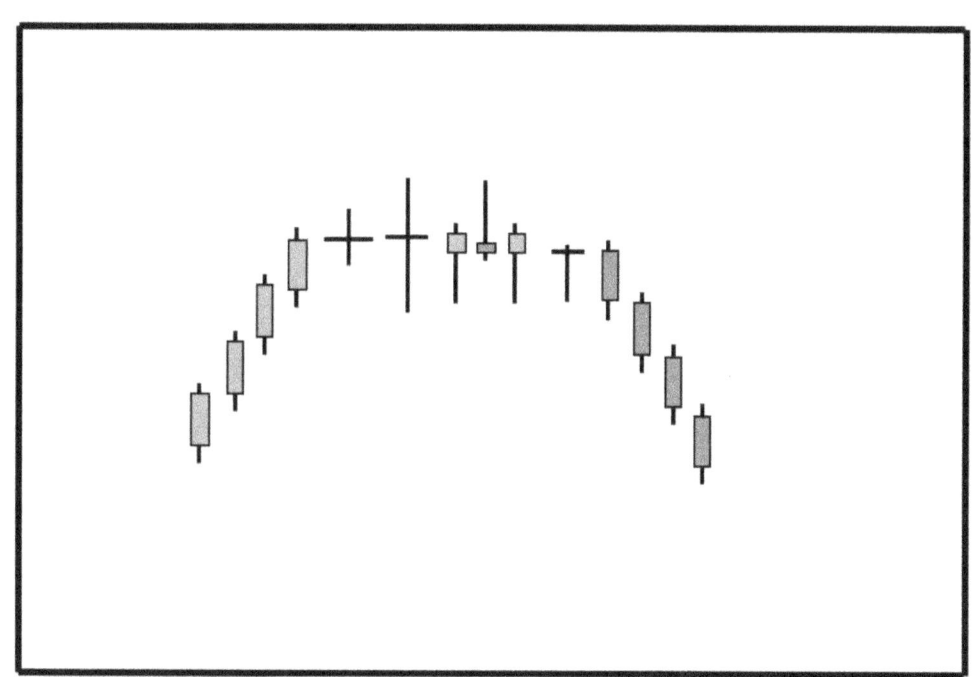

How to Trade Doji End of Flat Trading Range Top

Although this pattern indicates the potential end of an uptrend, it can also signal a continuation of the same trend. Therefore, it is crucial to confirm the trend before entering a trade position. Relying solely on the appearance of the Doji increases the likelihood of being incorrect. To confirm the trend, place a support line below the third candle prior to the trading range and observe if the price breaks below the support level. If it does, it confirms the presence of a downtrend. At that point, you can consider entering a short position or wait for a second confirming candle. The key takeaway is that patience and astuteness are essential for maximizing the potential of this pattern.

#46 - Doji Series at Bottom

This pattern is formed by the occurrence of several Doji candlesticks after a prolonged downtrend, indicating a period of significant indecision in the market. When the market is oversold, the presence of a single Doji serves as the initial signal that the market sentiment is changing or likely to change. However, the presence of multiple Doji candlesticks suggests a strong reversal from the current trend is imminent. Additionally, a long bullish candle or a gap up away from the Doji signifies the end of the indecision, indicating the beginning of an uptrend.

Figure 46: Doji Series at Bottom

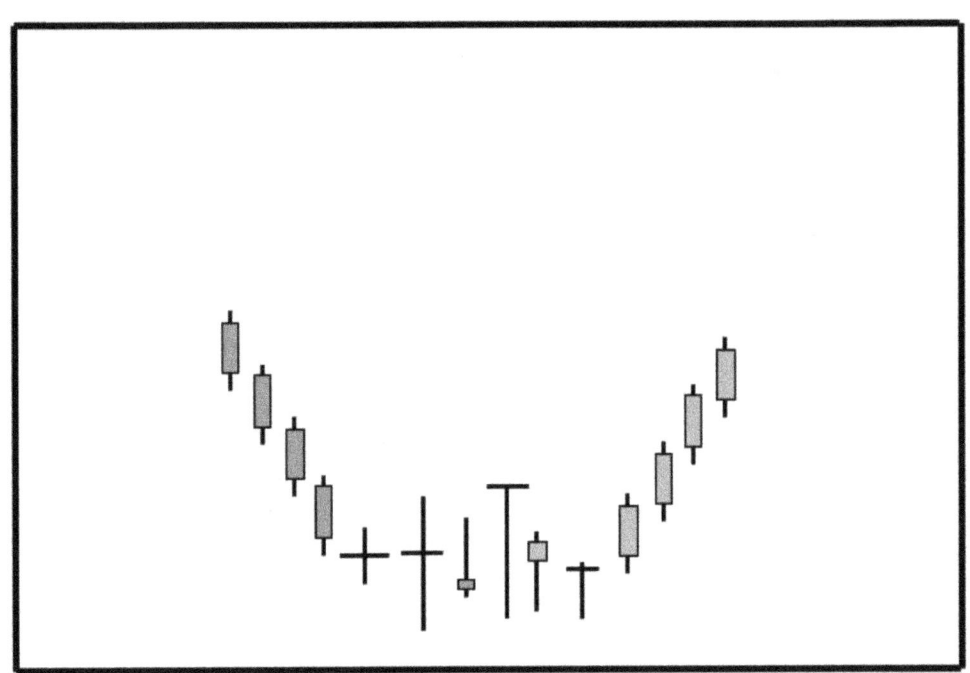

How To Trade Doji Series at Bottom

When trading this candlestick pattern, it is crucial to closely observe the series of Doji candles that form a brief range, particularly the first two that initiate the uptrend. If these candles are green (or white), it suggests an upcoming uptrend. Some traders prefer to wait for the second candle after the gap before making a buying decision. This cautious approach is considered a smart move and reduces the likelihood of incurring losses.

#47 - Doji Series at Top

Unlike its counterpart, the Doji Series at Top occurs following a prolonged uptrend, characterized by a series of Doji candles at the top of the trend. Confirmation of an impending strong reversal occurs when the first Doji is followed by another Doji, forming a brief range of Doji candles within a short timeframe. This series of Doji candles signals market indecision. The trend subsequently reverses, often accompanied by a gap down or a strong bearish signal, typically represented by a red or black candlestick.

Figure 47: Doji Series at Top

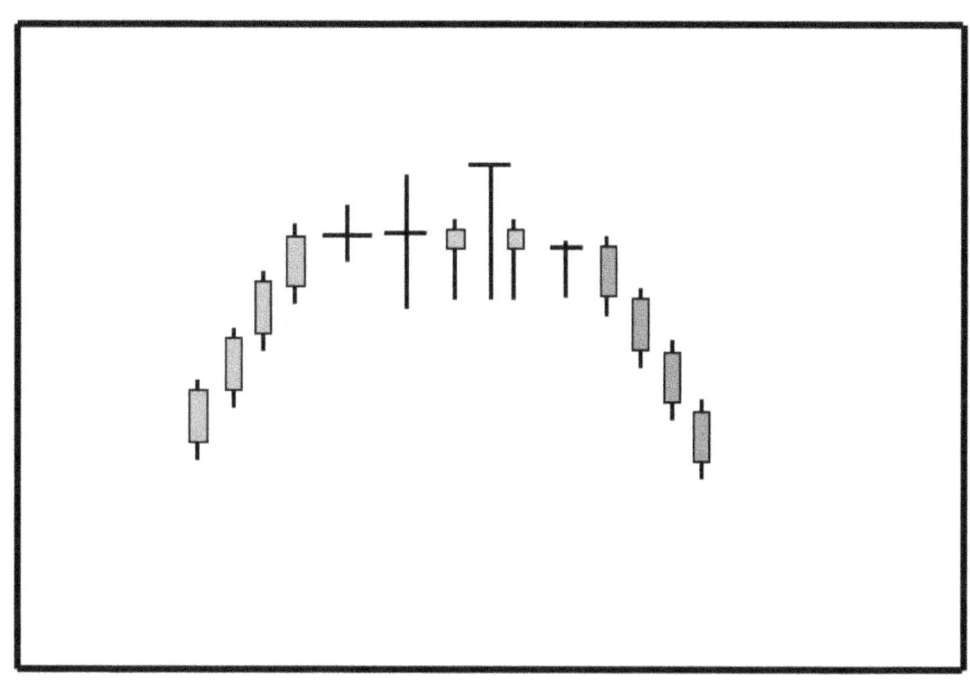

How to Trade Doji Series at Top

The key to trading this pattern, like any other pattern, is to wait for confirmation of the trend. The Doji Series at Top pattern is confirmed when a bearish candle gaps below the last Doji in the series (in this case, the Doji gravestone). At this point, you have two options. The first is to take this as a signal and trade at the close of the initial bearish candle after the gap. Alternatively, you can choose to wait for a second candle before entering your sell position. Both approaches have their merits, and it depends on your trading strategy and risk tolerance.

#48 - Double Bearish Engulfing

This pattern serves as a signal that sellers are beginning to take control of the market through a Bearish Engulfing Signal. During an extended uptrend, there may be a final attempt to push the trend higher, but the subsequent downtrend starts with limited force. However, even with the presence of the first bearish engulfing pattern, the pattern itself is not fully confirmed. It is the appearance of a second bearish engulfing signal that provides stronger evidence of the bears taking over the market, indicating that traders should anticipate a downtrend from that point onwards.

Figure 48: Double Bearish Engulfing

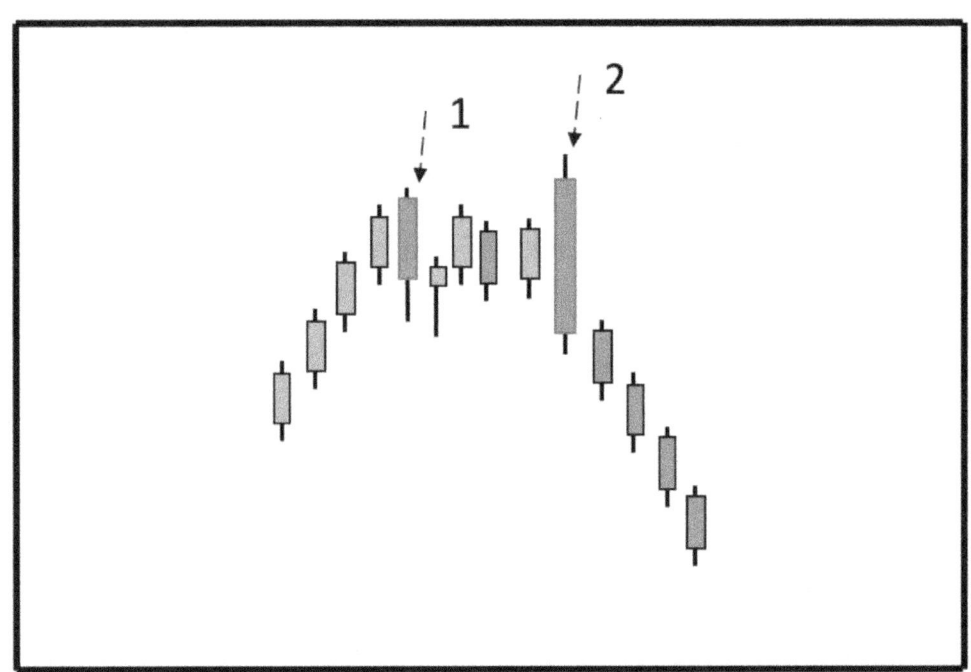

How to Trade Double Bearish Engulfing

When it comes to this pattern, the first Bearish Engulfing is a sign that buyers still control the market, but sentiments are changing. By the second Bearish Engulfing candle, there is an increase in selling pressure, which finally manifests in the bearish candles that follow. Traders are mostly tempted to go short during the second Bearish Engulfing; however, it is wiser to wait for a second bearish candle to confirm the pattern. With patience, you could wait to observe if an increase in volume accompanies the large downward price movement, as this has been known to be a strong indication to sell, allowing you to get the best from this pattern.

#49 - Double Bottom

The Double Bottom Pattern is the opposite of the Double Top Pattern, and it occurs when a bearish trend is about to come to an end, making it an indication of a likely reversal. The pattern consists of three parts: the first price rejection level (also the first low), the neckline (also the area of resistance), and finally, the second price rejection level (or second low). The Double Bottom begins with a downtrend that gets interrupted at a certain point and then ranges, creating a chart with two bottoms. After this, the range breaks, and a new bullish trend begins.

Figure 49: Double Bottom Pattern

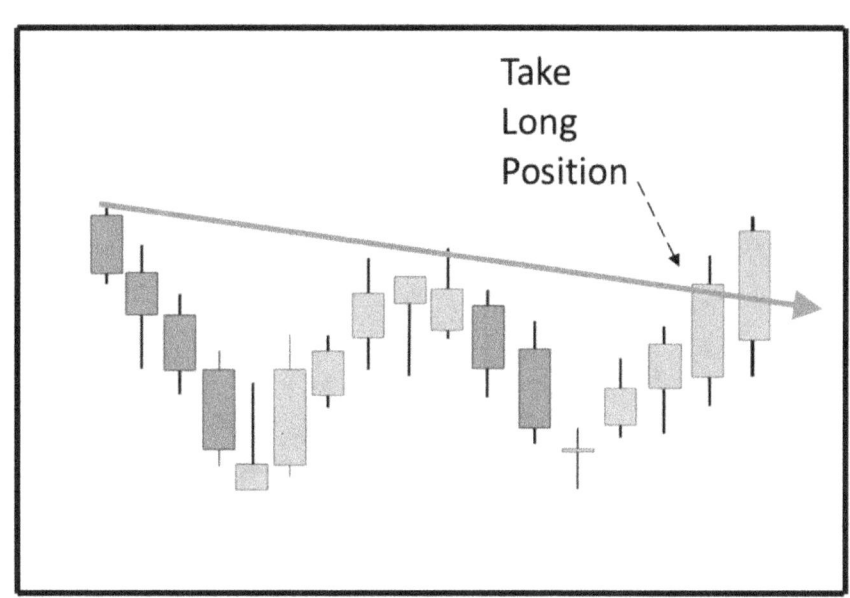

How to Trade the Double Bottom Pattern

This pattern is one of the most common chart patterns. Like the Double Top, it also describes the retesting of temporary extremes. However, executing a real-time trade with this pattern is not easy. Despite its common occurrence, identifying it can be challenging. Even if the pattern seems recognizable, it is still important to wait for confirmation to ensure its validity. To confirm the pattern, draw a neckline (a support line on the peak between both bottoms) and wait. If the price breaks above this support, the pattern is confirmed. The double bottom is also useful for predicting the potential price movement. However, traders should avoid trying to anticipate the trade and instead apply stops to manage risks. Patience and careful observation of the market are key to successfully trading the Double Bottom Pattern.

#50 - Double Bullish Engulfing Signal

This candlestick pattern is similar to the Bullish Engulfing Signal, but it is even more bullish. It occurs when a downtrend is reversed with a Bullish Engulfing Signal and is further confirmed by witnessing a second Bullish Engulfing Signal within the next few days. The second Bullish Engulfing Signal indicates that bulls have taken control at the end.

Figure 50: Double Bullish Engulfing Signal

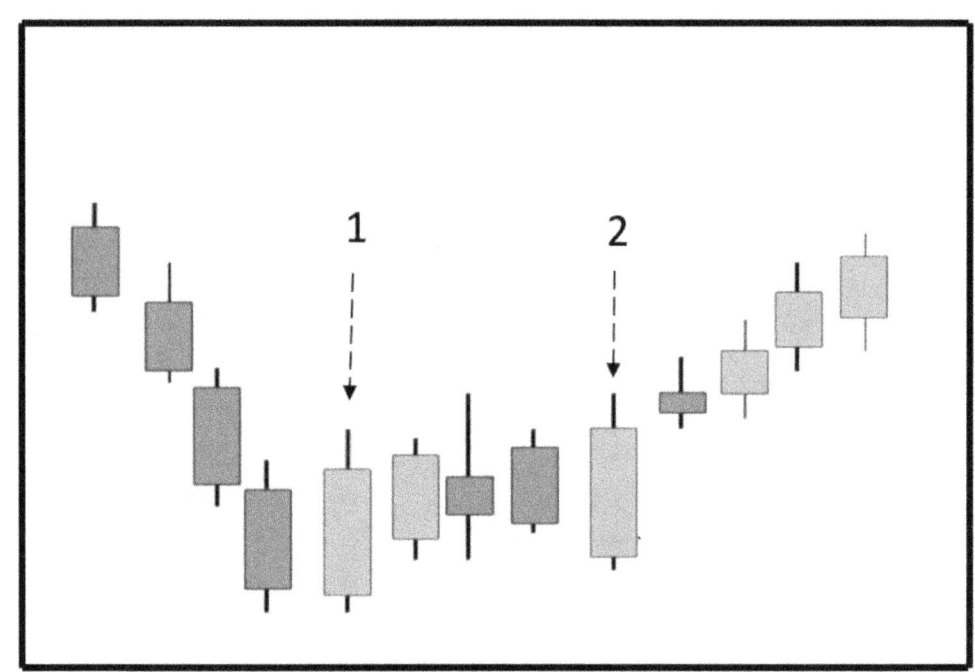

How to Trade Double Bullish Engulfing Signal

This pattern bears a remarkable resemblance to its bearish counterpart. However, in the case of this pattern, the first Bullish Engulfing is a sign that sellers still control the market, but sentiments are changing. By the second Bullish Engulfing candle, there is an increase in buying pressure, which is eventually reflected in the bullish candles that follow. Traders are often tempted to go short during the second Bullish Engulfing; however, it is wiser to wait for a second bullish candle to confirm the pattern. With patience, you can observe if an increase in volume accompanies the large upward price movement, as this is a strong indication to buy and allows you to maximize the potential of this   pattern.

#51 - Double Top

The Double Top chart pattern occurs during an ongoing bullish trend when the price is interrupted and starts ranging, forming two prominent peaks on the chart. Once the second peak is formed, the price drops, indicating the beginning of a new bearish trend. These two peaks suggest an impending bearish trend. It is worth noting that while many believe the peaks to be of equal height, the second peak is usually slightly lower than the first. Misinterpreting this pattern can lead to significant losses as it is not only easy to identify but also carries substantial risk unless properly understood and traded.

Figure 51: Double Top

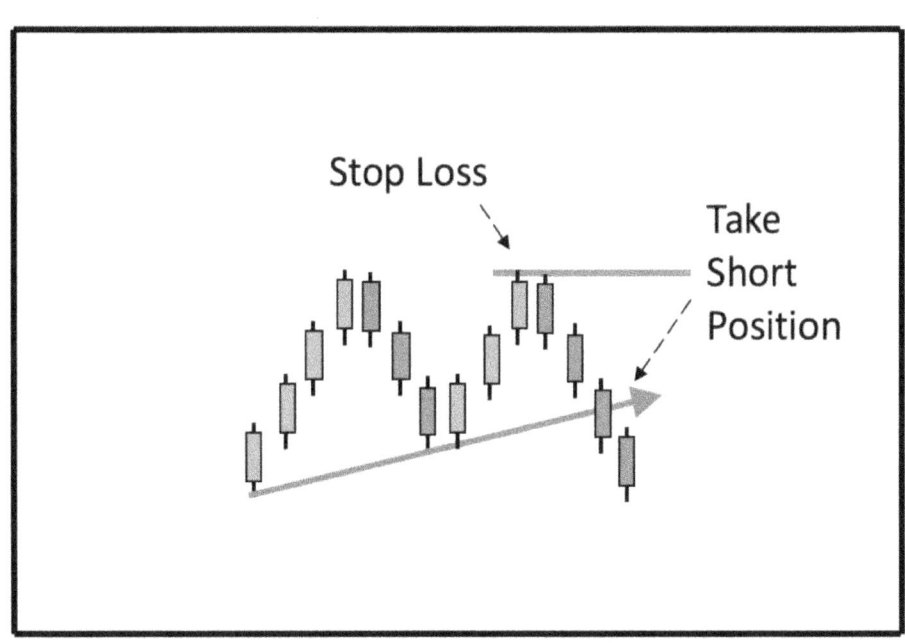

How to Trade Double Tops

Being easy to spot doesn't mean this pattern isn't tricky. It requires a great deal of patience from traders. The first step is to draw a neckline just below the valley between both peaks, aligning it with the close of the lowest candle. This neckline serves as a confirmation support, and if the price breaks below it, it indicates a bearish market. Some traders may be tempted to buy weaknesses and sell strengths, which is risky. To manage this risk, you can use other technical tools in conjunction with this pattern. For instance, the Bollinger Bands with four standard deviation parameters can be helpful. Draw a line from the first peak to the Bollinger Band and place a stop where they intersect.

#52 - Downside Tasuki Gap

This pattern is known for signaling the continuation of a downtrend. It is formed by two consecutive red candlesticks, with the second bar opening below the close of the previous bar. The third candle is a green candle with an opening price within the range of the first body and a closing price just below the close of the first line, but it doesn't close the gap. To confirm this pattern, it needs to appear within a downtrend, with the first two candles being red and the third candle being green.

Figure 52: Downside Tasuki Gap

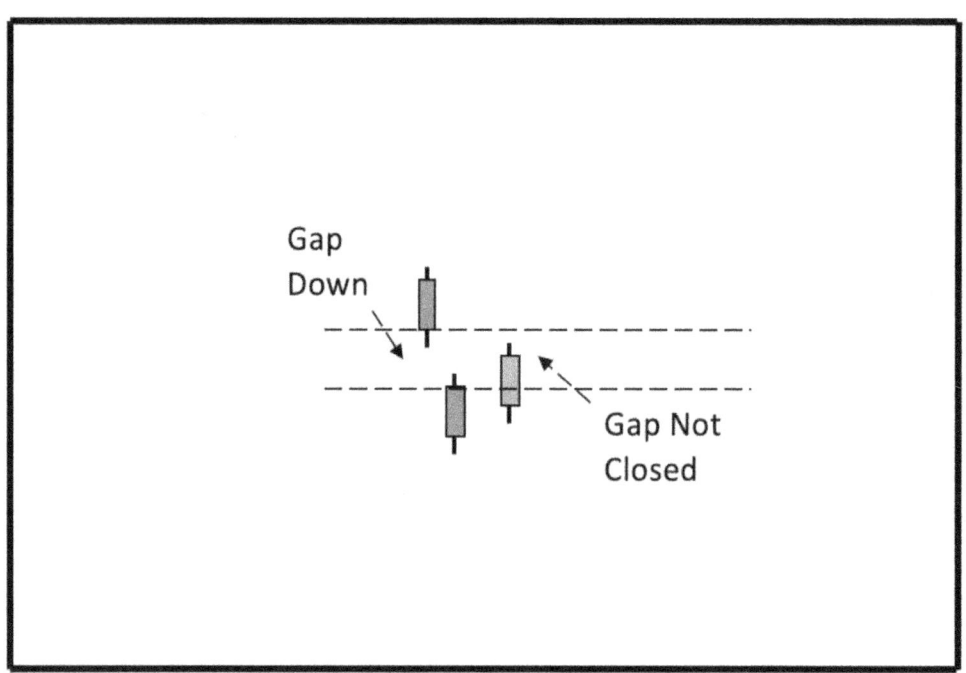

How to Trade Downside Tasuki Gap

You can gauge the strength of the downtrend by observing the gap down, which also indicates the level of control the bears have in the market. Despite the bulls' attempt to regain control, as evidenced by the single green candle, they fail to close the gap. This failure to reclaim the market confirms the continuation of the downtrend. To effectively trade this pattern, it is crucial to exercise patience and observe the candles that follow the third green or white candle in the Downside Tasuki Gap. Confirmation is essential to avoid any misinterpretation of the pattern.

#53 - Dumpling Top

This pattern consists of a series of candles with small bodies that form a convex shape, clearly indicating a loss of interest from buyers. It serves as a clear indication that buying momentum is diminishing and the market is poised for an imminent downtrend. The presence of a gap down between two candles, accompanied by selling pressure, signifies the strength of the bearish sentiment. Subsequently, the volatility in pricing significantly decreases. Skilled traders recognize this gap down as a signal of growing bearish activity.

Figure 53: Dumpling Top

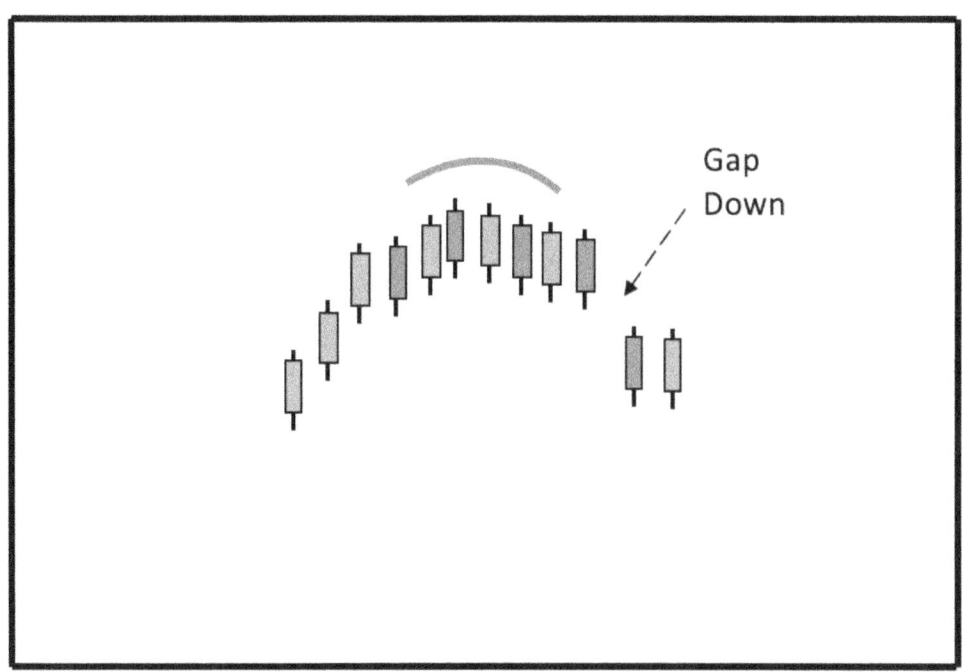

How to Trade Dumpling Top

This pattern presents a challenging trading opportunity. The convex shape and small bodies in each candle indicate investor interest in sustaining the uptrend. However, the optimal time to trade is at the close of the candle following the gap, or alternatively, waiting for a second candle after the gap for a more cautious approach. Occasionally, a green or white candle may appear (as shown in the image above), but it is crucial to grasp the chart pattern and exercise patience. To mitigate risks, consider placing a stop loss order above the highest candle in the curve.

#54 - Eve Eve Double Bottom

"Eve" is a term used to describe the point at the bottom of a chart pattern. In the case of Eve, it forms a rounded and pointed bottom. This pattern typically occurs in a series of two to three candlesticks, accounting for about 95% of the time. The pattern resembles a "W" shape, with the bottoms positioned at or near the same Satoshi. The two valleys should be separated by several candlesticks, indicating a throwback change of 55% or more, depending on the depth of the middle valley. Ideally, a target of 4% is suitable for this pattern.

Figure 54: Eve Eve Double Bottom

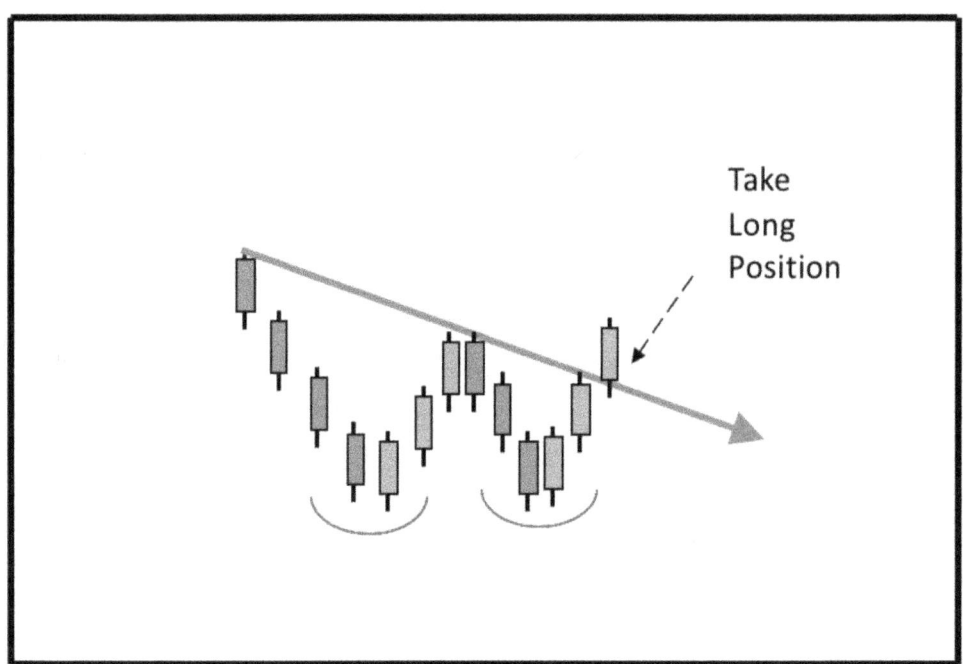

How to Trade Eve Eve Double Bottom

Trading this pattern is similar to trading the Adam & Eve Double Bottom pattern. To begin, draw a support line on top of the highest candle in the crest between the left and right troughs. Patiently observe for any breakout above this support line. Once the price breaks above the line, it serves as a signal to trade long. Patience is crucial here, as depicted in the figure above, as impatience may lead to missed profitable opportunities. It is important to remain calm and composed to fully take advantage of the potential for profit.

#55 - Eve Eve Double Top

"Eve" is a term used to describe the point at the top of a chart pattern. In the case of Eve, it forms a rounded and pointed top. This pattern typically occurs in a series of two to three candlesticks, accounting for about 95% of the time. The pattern resembles an "M" shape, with the tops positioned at or near the same Satoshi. The two valleys should be separated by several candlesticks, indicating a pullback change of 55% or more, depending on the depth of the middle valley. It is important to exercise caution if the breakdown passes the left side of the "M" before taking a new position.

Figure 55: Eve Eve Double Top

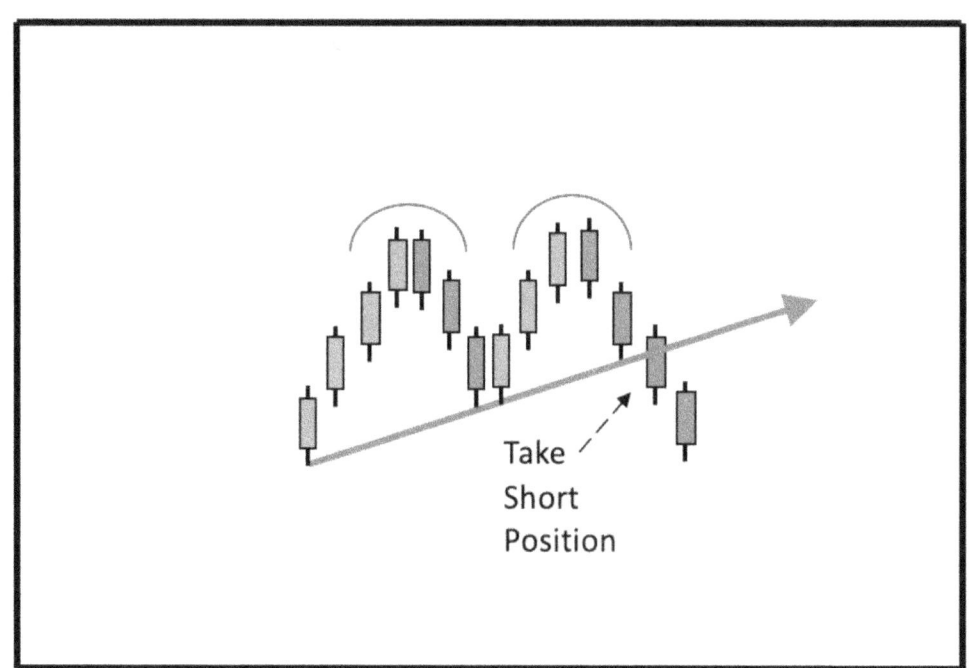

How to Trade Eve Eve Double Top

Trading this pattern is similar to trading the Adam & Eve Double Top pattern. Start by drawing a support line below the lowest candle in the trough between the left and right peaks. Patiently observe for any breakout below this support line. Once the price breaks below the line, it serves as a signal to trade short. Remember, patience is crucial here, as depicted in the figure above. If you are not patient, you may lose your nerve and miss out on a great opportunity for profit. Stay composed and vigilant to capitalize on potential gains.

#56 - Evening Star

In this pattern, an uptrend is apparent. The real body of the first candle continues the current trend while the second is an indecision indicator. It is a three-day pattern where Candle 1 shows that the price is very bullish, Candle 2 suggests that the prices may not go much higher and the candlestick is much smaller, and Candle 3 shows that the bears have stepped in by closing at least halfway down the green candle. The longer the candlesticks, the more forceful the reversal. If Candle 2 indicates more indecision, there is a better probability that a reversal will occur. A gap between Candle 1 and Candle 2 adds to the chances of a reversal taking place.

Figure 56: Evening Star

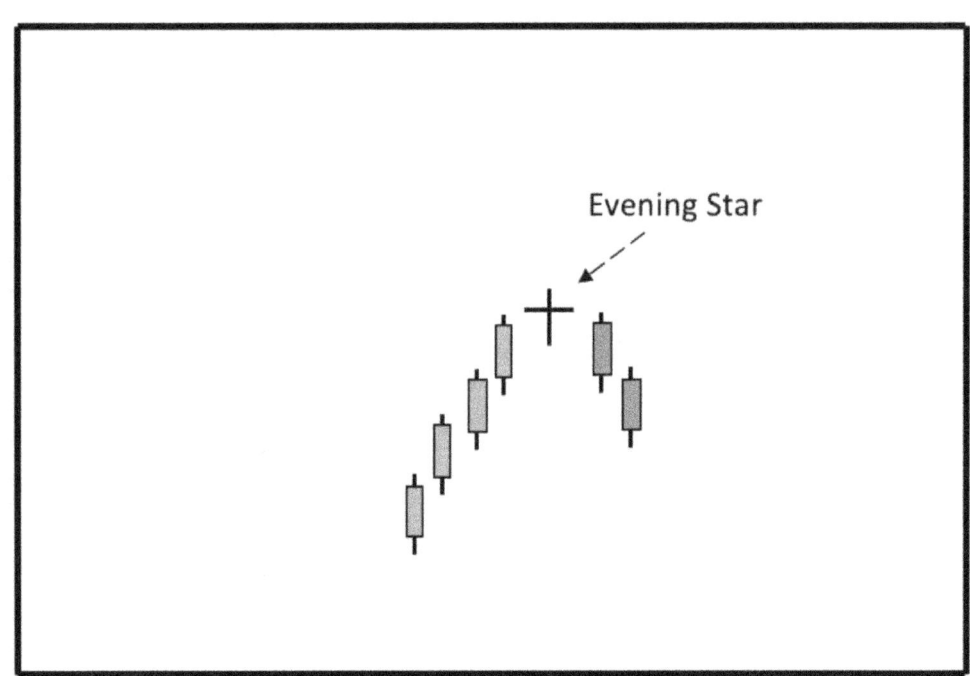

How to Trade Evening Star

When attempting to trade this pattern, it is important for you to have knowledge of a commodity's open, close, high, and low over whatever time period you choose to analyze. The length of each candle is worth noting because they represent the highs and lows of a price within a specific timeframe. The first candlestick is bullish and indicates a significant upward move, while the second is a shorter candlestick, indicating price indecision. This suggests that the momentum behind the bullish candlestick is waning, and the final candlestick, a bearish one, opens lower than the previous one. This clear sign indicates an impending trend reversal and the start of a new trend. You have two options: either enter a trade once the reversal begins or wait for a second candle to form before entering your position.

#57 - Faked Ya Bearish

The traditional name of this pattern presents a false impression. The name seems to suggest that it will move downward in a "bearish" direction; however, in reality, it does not behave that way. So, why is this pattern called "Fake Ya"? The pattern is a 4-candlestick pattern that can appear in three different intervals. If spotted, it can provide insights into entering a position too early or too late. The only candlestick they all have in common is the second one.

Figure 57: Faked Ya Bearish

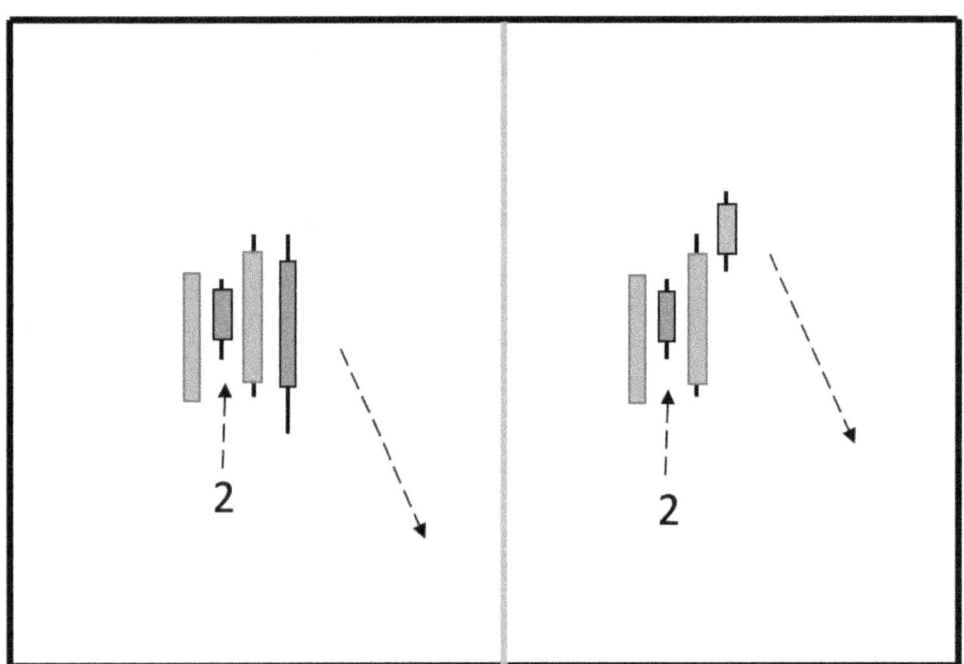

How to Trade Faked Ya Bearish

Trading this pattern is not as tricky as it may initially seem. It is a versatile pattern that can be traded in various market conditions, including trending, range-bound, and even against the trend from key levels. It provides traders with a high-probability entry point. To effectively trade this pattern, you can choose to enter a trade as the price breaks below the low of either (1) the mother bar or (2) the inside bar, which in the case of the figure above (right), corresponds to the first and second bars, respectively.

#58 - Faked Ya Bullish

The traditional name of this pattern presents a false impression. The name seems to indicate that it will move upward in a "bullish" direction, but in reality, it behaves differently. So, why is this pattern called "Faked Ya"? The pattern is a four-candlestick pattern that can appear in four different intervals. If spotted, it can provide insights into entering a position earlier than most. The only candle they all have in common is candlestick number two.

Figure 58: Faked Ya Bullish

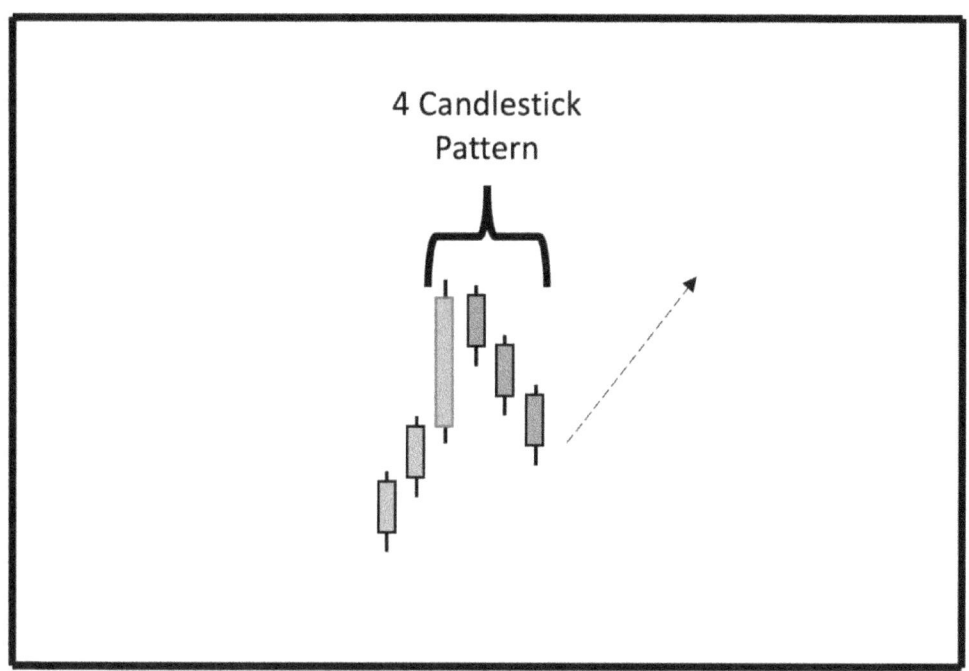

How to Trade Faked Ya Bullish Pattern

Trading this pattern is not so different from its counterpart, the Faked Ya Bearish Pattern. It is also a pattern that can be traded in any market condition, whether trending, range-bound, or even against the trend from key levels. It provides traders with a high-probability entry point. To properly trade this pattern, you can choose to enter a trade as the price breaks above the high of either (1) the mother bar or (2) the inside bar, which in the case of the above figure, corresponds to the first and second bar respectively.

#59 - Flag Pattern

This is a fairly common pattern that can be identified early on and indicates an opportunity to enter a position early. However, caution is advised. Patience is key! The breakout point typically occurs in a bullish or bearish direction about 80% of the time when the pattern forms.

Figure 59: Flag Pattern

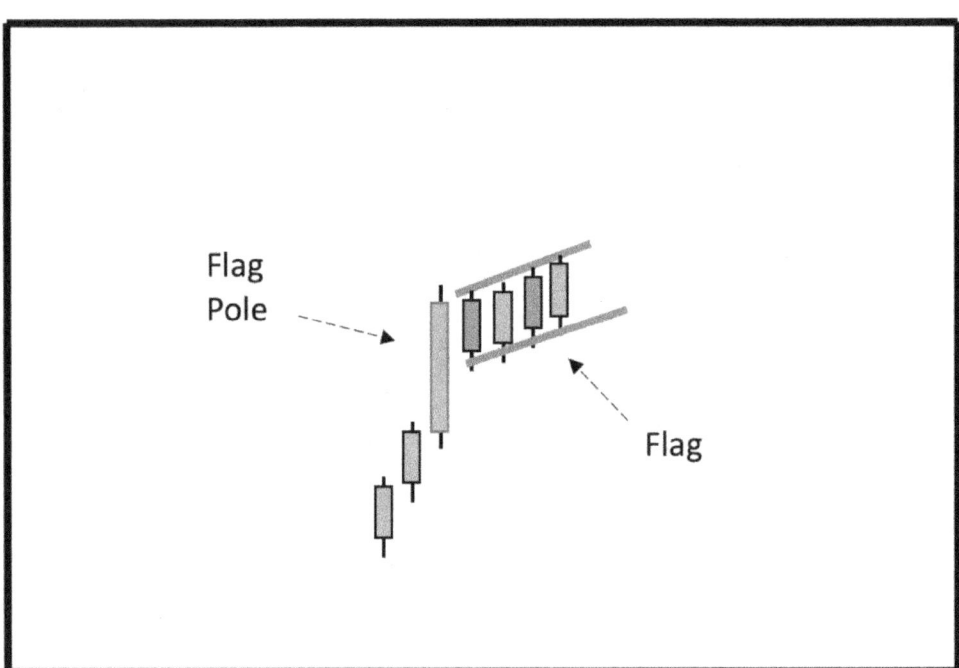

How to Trade Flag Pattern

The Flag Pattern is a relatively simple pattern to trade. Based on the direction of the trend, you create a trendline above and below the current trend and patiently wait for the price to break above or below the trendline of the flag. While there are two types of flag patterns - bullish (as shown in the figure above) and bearish - the same principle applies to both. Therefore, as a trader observing any flag pattern (whether bullish or bearish), you should look to enter sell positions with breakouts.

#60 - Frying Pan Bottom

Small trading bodies indicate a downtrend. This pattern, known as the Inverted Cup and Handle, is the opposite of the Dumpling Top and forms a convex shape. It provides a clear indication of buying power as the price gradually rises. The upward movement of the convex formation occurs after a week or two of bottoming. While the curve formation is significant, the focus should be on the gap that follows the curve. This gap confirms the pattern and also confirms the direction of the trend.

Figure 60: Frying Pan Bottom

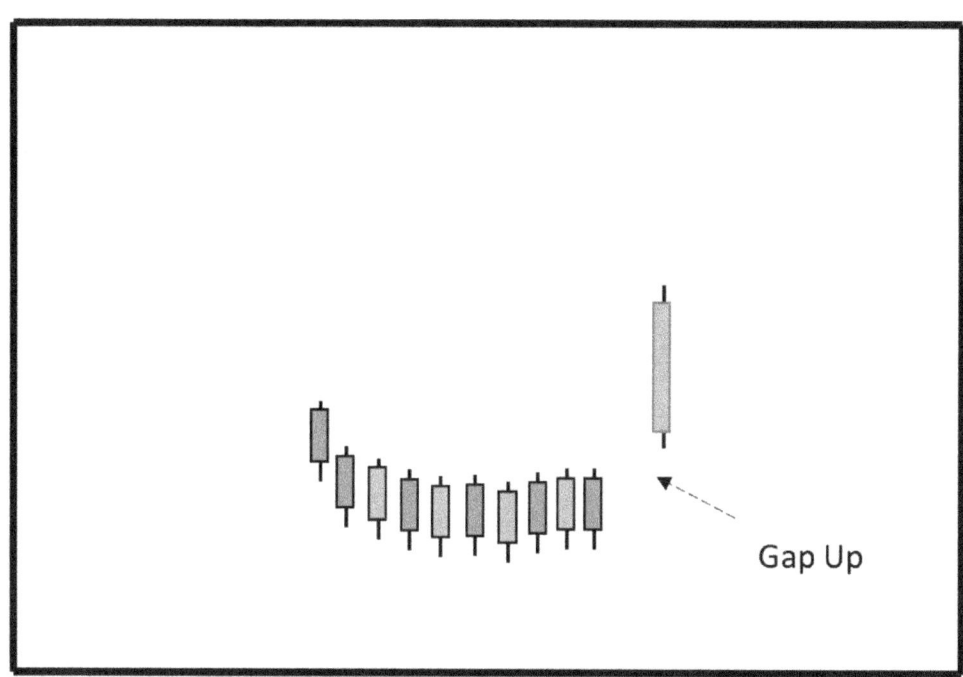

How to Trade Frying Pan Bottom

As a bullish reversal pattern that signals the exhaustion of sellers, the Inverted Cup and Handle pattern is traded similarly to the Dumpling Top pattern. Like the Dumpling Top, the key focus area is the gap formed at the end of the curve. However, if the gap is filled by the last candlestick, the pattern becomes invalid. Being a rare pattern, trading it requires a great deal of patience, so exercising patience is highly recommended. To enter a trade, wait for the candle after the gap to close and place a stop loss order below the lowest candle in the curve.

#61 - Gaps

Gaps are the primary patterns to identify and locate. They can occur in an upward or downward direction. Gaps are crucial as they assist traders in determining the next move in a pattern. This makes them suitable for both beginners and experienced professionals. On stock charts, there are specific regions where prices experience a significant upward or downward movement, with little or no trading activity in between; these regions are known as gaps. Gaps happen when the opening price of a day is higher than its previous close.

Figure 61: Gaps

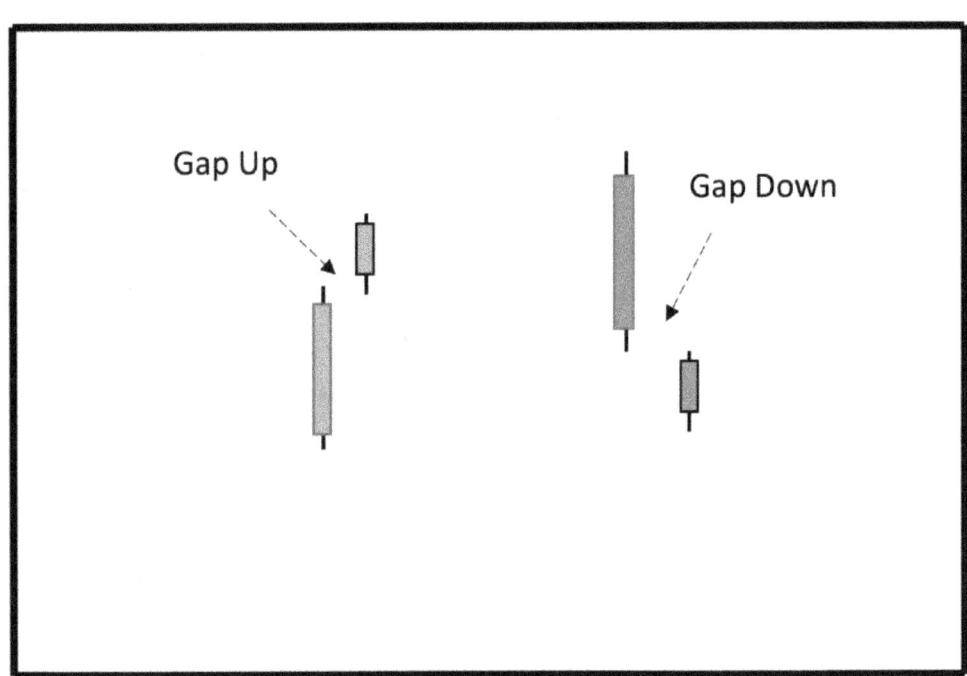

How to Trade Gaps Pattern

There are two types of traders who focus on Gap patterns. The first group buys when the essential factors align with the Gap the day after it occurs. The second group tries to fade the Gaps by taking positions in the opposite direction once a high or low point has been established. Regardless of the approach, it is crucial to have strict entry and exit rules to minimize risks and generate trade signals. When entering a trade position, it is important to calculate and set a trailing stop of 8% for exiting a long position and 4% for exiting a short position. Trailing stops determine the exit point after a price rise or fall.

#62 - Gap down After Bearish Harami

This pattern features a Bearish Harami at the top of an extended uptrend. To confirm a downtrend, sell trades must persist into the following day. A gap down indicates highly negative investor sentiment, signaling the imminent start of a strong downtrend.

Figure 62: Gap Down After Bearish Harami

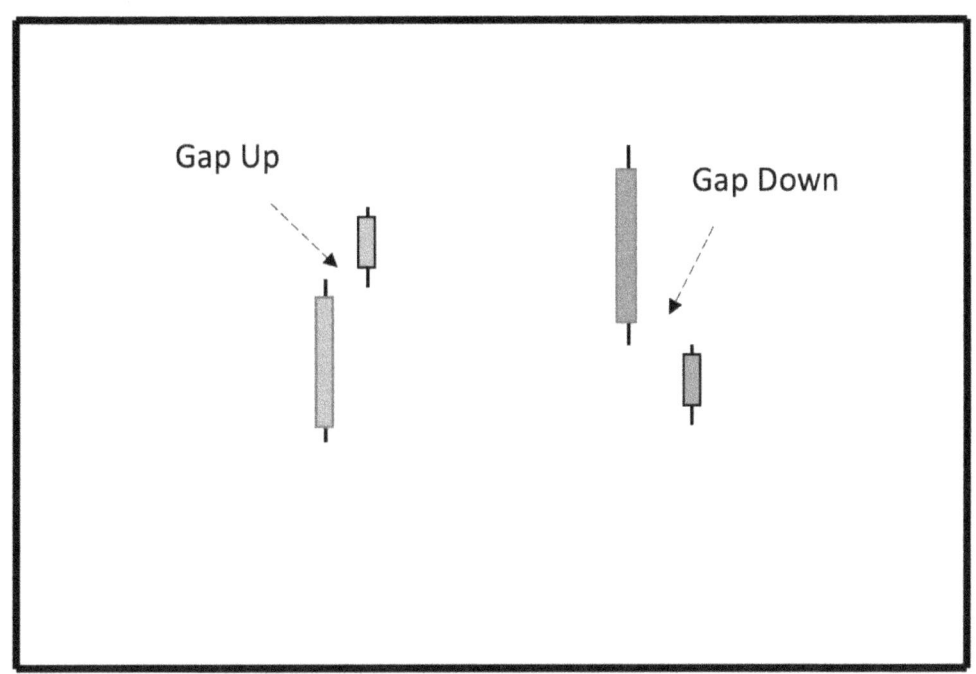

How to Trade Gap Down After Bearish Harami

Trading this pattern is relatively straightforward. It is important to closely observe the inside bar and the gap. While many traders consider the appearance of a bearish gap as sufficient reason to enter a short trade, it is advisable to wait for the opening of a second bearish candle after the gap, or even better, its close. This caution is necessary because although trader sentiment may be weakening, the market remains unpredictable. In the case of the figure mentioned above, you can place a support line below the opening of the third candle before the Harami, while setting a stop loss order above the wick of the inside bar.

#63 - Gap down After a Doji at the Top

A Doji candlestick at the top indicates indecision following an extended uptrend. A bearish candlestick on the day after the Doji serves as a signal to sell. A gap down from the Doji is a reliable indicator of a strong downward trend. The Doji at the top is a clear sign that the price is in an overbought condition, suggesting that investors are likely to liquidate their positions at the first signs of a weak opening.

Figure 63: Gap Down After Doji at the Top

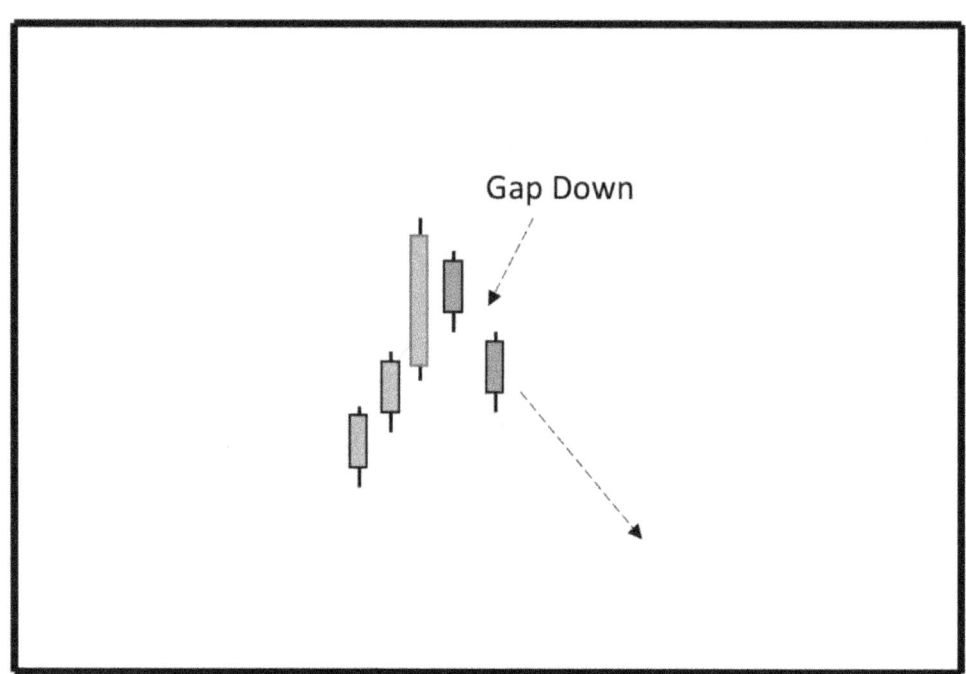

How to Trade Gap Down After Doji at the Top

In the Gap Down After Doji at the Top pattern, the presence of a gap indicates that sellers have entered the market, signaling a downward trend. As a candlestick investor, taking advantage of this gap down can lead to profitable trades. Individually, gaps are reliable indicators of trend direction, while Doji candles are well-known reversal signals. When combined, these two elements create a formidable pattern. While some investors may wait for a second confirming candle, seizing the opportunity without hesitation can result in significant profits instead of leaving   them   for   others.

#64 - Gap Down After Hanging Man Signal

In this pattern, an extended uptrend is observed, but the bulls start to feel nervous during the sell-off. When the price opens at the top of the current trend on the following day, it forms a Hanging Man Signal. As confirmation, additional selling can be seen on the next day. A gap down in price from the Hanging Man Signal further amplifies the nervousness of the bulls, leading them to start selling. This weakening sentiment serves as an indication that a downtrend is likely to be confirmed.

Figure 64: Gap Down After Hanging Man Signal

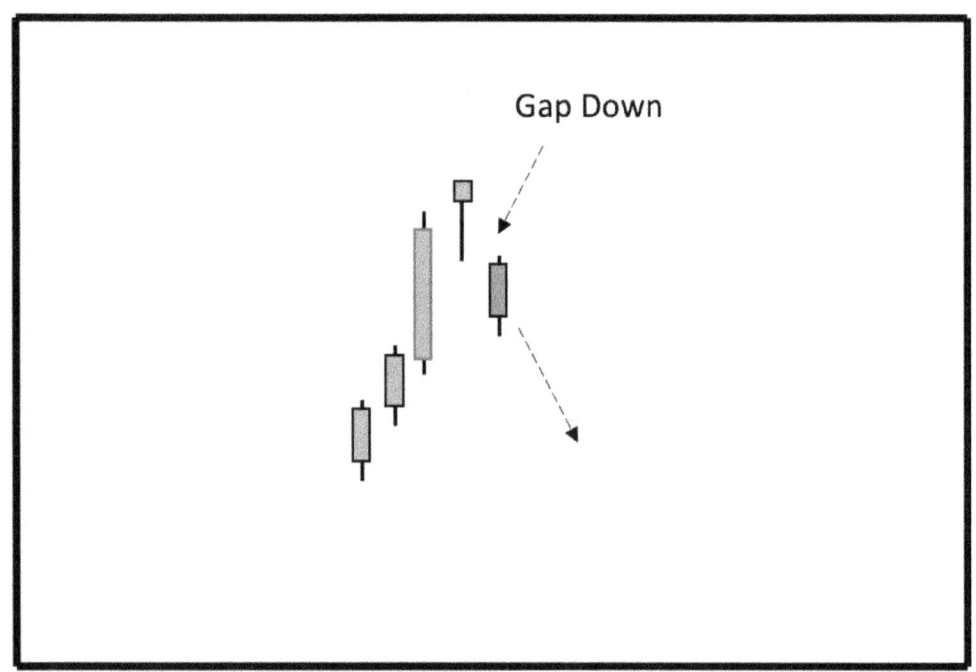

How to Trade Gap Down After Hanging Man Signal

The Hanging Man pattern is originally a bearish reversal pattern that suggests a potential downtrend. It reflects market sentiment by highlighting the strength of sellers and the weakness of buyers. Gaps, on the other hand, symbolize pressure or strength in the market. While many traders typically wait for a second candle after the Hanging Man before going short, the Gap Down After Hanging Man Signal is an exception. Since the Hanging Man itself is a bearish reversal pattern, the presence of a gap indicates a strong downtrend is imminent. Traders seize this opportunity and strategically wait to profit from the upcoming downtrend until the charts indicate otherwise. Setting trigger points at various levels allows for profit-taking as the trend progresses, but it's crucial to closely monitor the market and anticipate changes.

#65 - Gap Down After Shooting Star

This pattern emerges after a prolonged uptrend, indicating a loss of momentum for the bulls. The Shooting Star forms at the peak of the extended rally. On the subsequent day, there is ongoing buying activity, but the price declines. If the closing price is higher than the opening price, a green real body is formed. If the closing price is lower, a red body is formed. The wick of the Shooting Star is at least twice the size of the real body.

Figure 65: Gap After Shooting Star

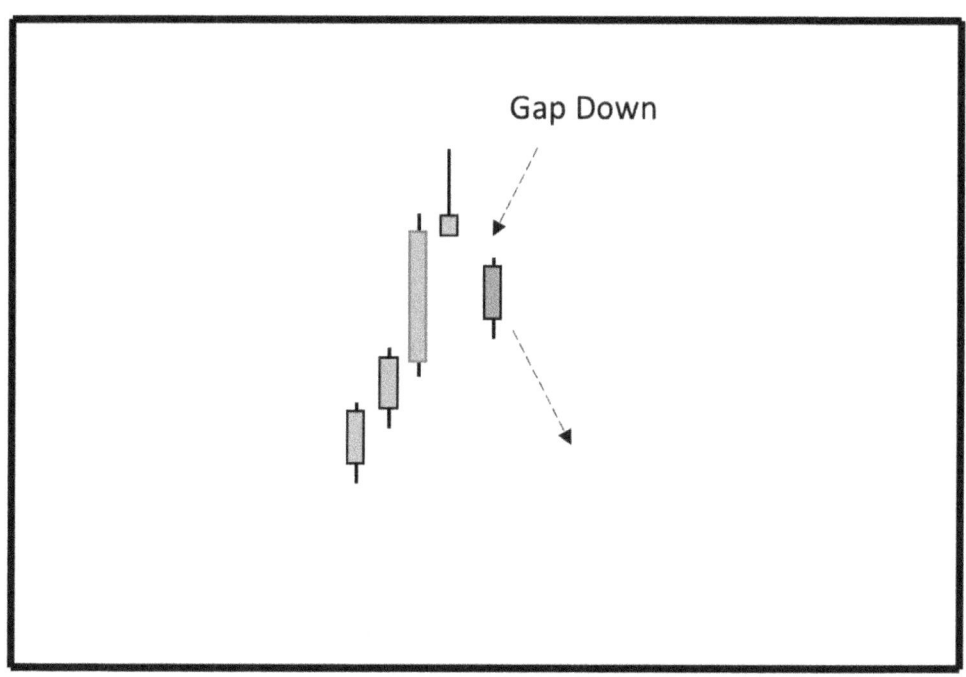

How to Trade Gap After Shooting Star

The Shooting Star is a bearish candlestick pattern that typically appears at the end of an uptrend, signaling the takeover of sellers and a potential downward price movement. When combined with a gap, this pattern confirms the strength of the subsequent downtrend. Traders often wait for the next candle after a Shooting Star to assess the market. If it is a bearish candle, they choose to sell. However, if it is a bearish candle with a gap, as seen in the mentioned case, it provides sufficient confirmation to sell without excessive hesitation.

#66 - Gap Down Bullish Engulfing Signal

This pattern, known as a significant reversal indicator, is called a Bullish Engulfing Signal. It appears after a prolonged downtrend, with immediate buying action taking place. The candlestick has a minimal downside wick. The Bullish Engulfing Signal is formed when the price makes a strong recovery, surpassing the previous day's body. The significance of the signal is heightened when there is a notable gap down followed by immediate buying activity.

Figure 66: Gap Down Bullish Engulfing Signal

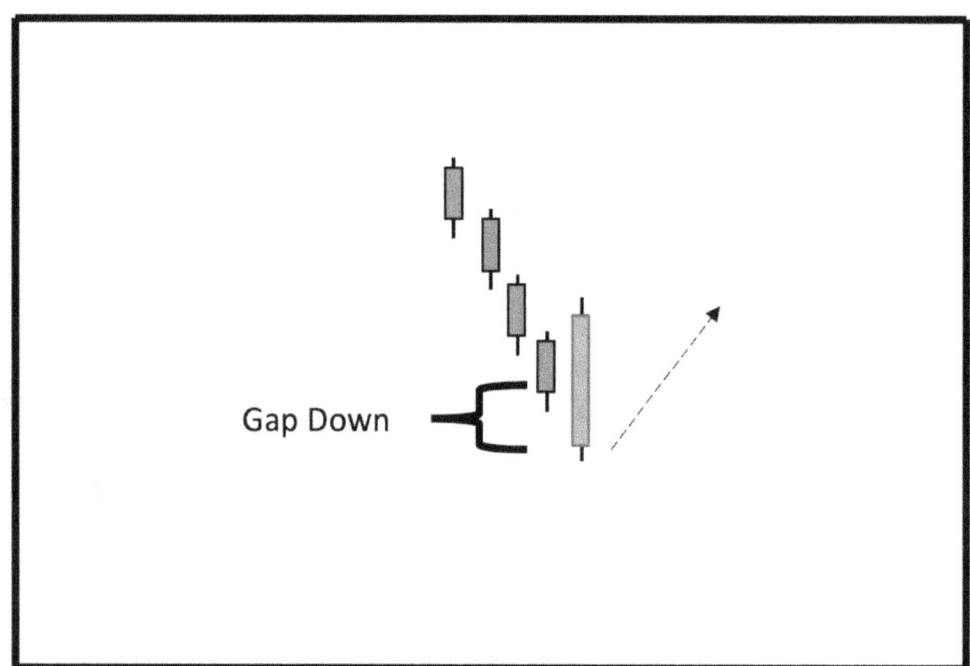

How to Trade Gap Down Bullish Engulfing Signal

One significant characteristic of the Bullish Engulfing Signal is that it consists of a bullish candle that completely engulfs the body of the preceding bearish candle. Additionally, it is often (if not always) preceded by four bearish candles, further enhancing the potential for a reversal. The presence of a gap indicates a significant shift in investor sentiment, causing the Bullish Engulfing candle to open lower than the previous day's close. Traders capitalize on this opportunity by initiating buy trades. To mitigate risk, it is advisable to place a stop loss at the opening of the Bullish Engulfing candle.

#67 - Gap Down Doji Bottom

This pattern occurs following an extended downtrend. The Gap Down Doji is a highly profitable pattern that indicates sellers attempting to exit at the bottom. The gap down serves as a signal that the bottom has been reached and suggests an imminent price reversal to the upside.

Figure 67: Gap Down Doji Bottom

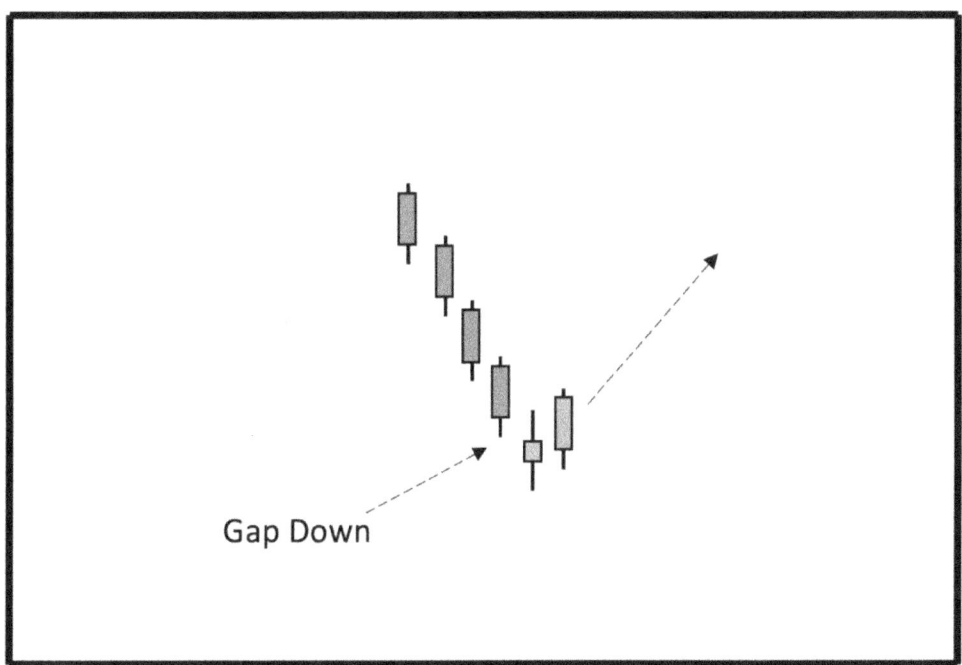

How to Trade Gap Down Doji Bottom

This is a bullish reversal pattern that typically experiences a 2.5% rise within approximately ten days, particularly evident in daily charts, resulting in around a 50% performance. Despite the indication provided by this candlestick pattern, it is important to exercise caution when trading with it. Specifically, pay attention to both the color of the Doji and the subsequent candlestick. In the example above, a red (or black) Doji suggests a weakening of selling pressure, and the size of the gap between the Doji and the opening of the next candlestick reflects the influence of buyers in the market. Skilled traders recognize these situations as opportunities to initiate long positions while setting a stop loss slightly below the Doji.

#68 - Gap Down Hammer at Bottom

After an extended downtrend, sellers start to feel uneasy, resulting in a gap down followed by a hammer signal. This pattern indicates that sellers are attempting to exit at the bottom while buyers are entering the market. When additional buying occurs after the hammer signal, it signifies a significant shift in sentiment, indicating a strong reversal in price direction.

Figure 68: Gap Down Hammer at Bottom

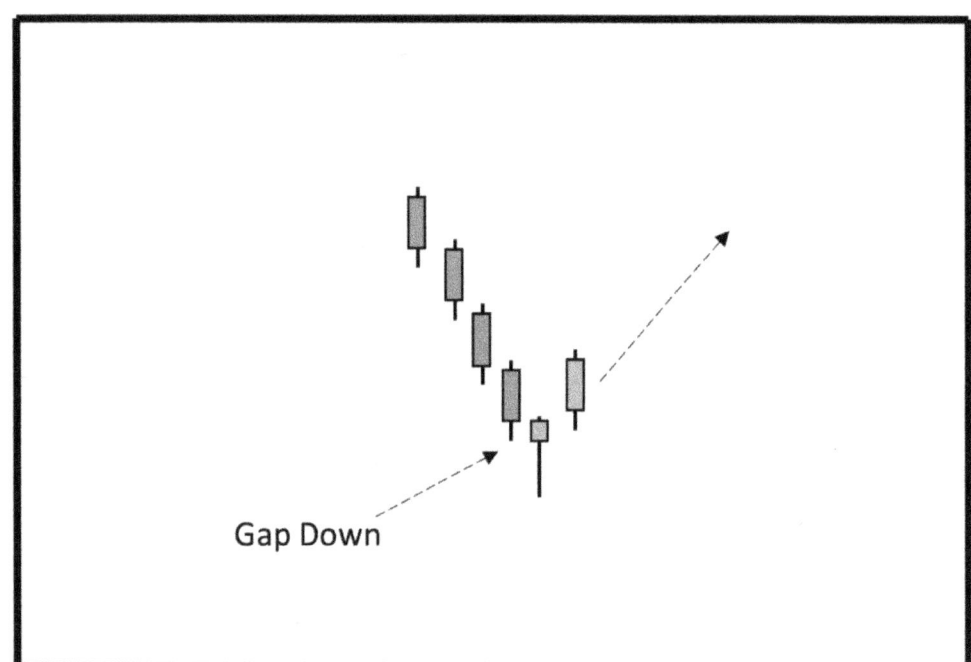

How to Trade Gap Down Hammer at Bottom

The presence of a hammer at the bottom is indicative of a loss of momentum in sellers' sentiment. However, the gap between the hammer and the previous bearish candle represents a temporary struggle between buyers and sellers, with the buyers ultimately gaining the upper hand. Although they were unable to generate a significantly bullish candle, the subsequent candle confirms the strong sentiment of the buyers, leading to an uptrend. Traders can seize this opportunity to initiate long trades, but it is crucial to emphasize the importance of setting a stop loss. Placing a stop loss below the shadow of the hammer would be suitable in this case.

#69 - Gap Up After Bullish Harami

In this pattern, the Harami signifies a halt in selling activity following an extended downtrend. A Bullish Harami confirms a reversal when there is sustained buying activity on the following day. If there is a gap up from the Bullish Harami, it indicates that the downtrend has come to a halt and buying pressure has strengthened enough to initiate an uptrend.

Figure 69: Gap Up After Bullish Harami

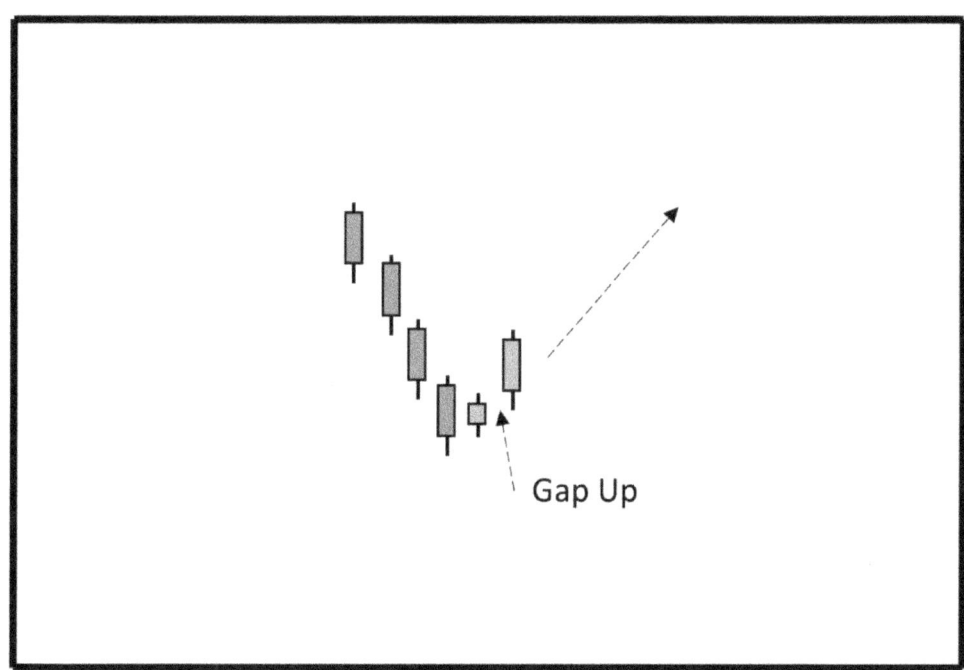

How to Trade Gap Up After Bullish Harami

There is little difference between trading the Gap Up after a Bullish Harami and the Bullish Harami itself. The distinguishing factor is the presence of a gap in the former and its absence in the latter. Similar to the regular Bullish Harami, the primary focus lies in the price rise. The Bullish Harami indicates a bullish reversal, making it a strong indicator of a bullish trend reversal. Many traders prefer to wait for the price to break the resistance trendline before triggering a buy signal. Combining the trendline break with the Harami can provide confirmation for this candlestick pattern. Wait for the price to break above the trendline before entering a trade and set your stop loss below the close of the last bearish candle.

#70 - Gap Up After Doji Bottom

A Doji appearing in an oversold position indicates indecision between bulls and bears, often serving as a precursor to a trend reversal. A gap up following the Doji suggests bullish tendencies. If a bullish candlestick subsequently forms, it signifies the emergence of an uptrend.

Figure 70: Gap Up After Doji Bottom

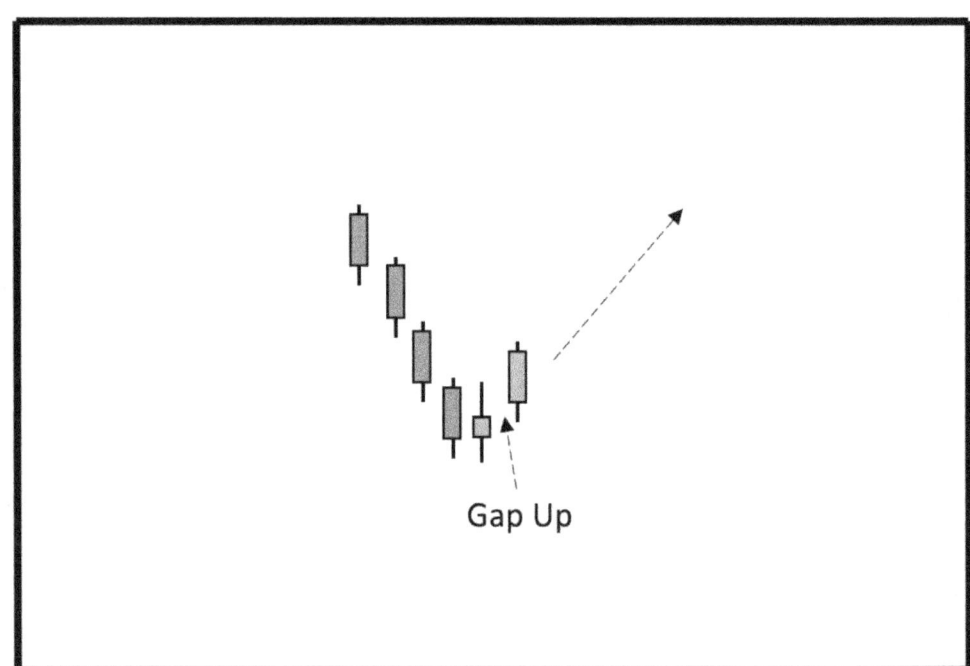

How to Trade Gap Up After Doji Bottom

A Doji Bottom typically occurs during a downtrend and reflects the indecisiveness of traders. To confirm this pattern, traders observe the candlestick that follows the Doji. A gap up after the Doji indicates that buyers have emerged victorious despite the market's indecision, signaling a strong uptrend to come. Traders have the option to buy either at the appearance of the Doji Bottom or wait for the subsequent candle. More skeptical traders may prefer to wait for a second candle after the gap to ensure it is not a false spike.

#71 - Gap Up After Hammer at Bottom

The hammer pattern at the bottom is a bullish signal. It forms when the market becomes oversold, with prices opening and moving lower in a downtrend. The color of the hammer can be either red or green. When price begins to move back up, it indicates buying activity and further validates the hammer signal.

Figure 71: Gap Up After Hammer Bottom

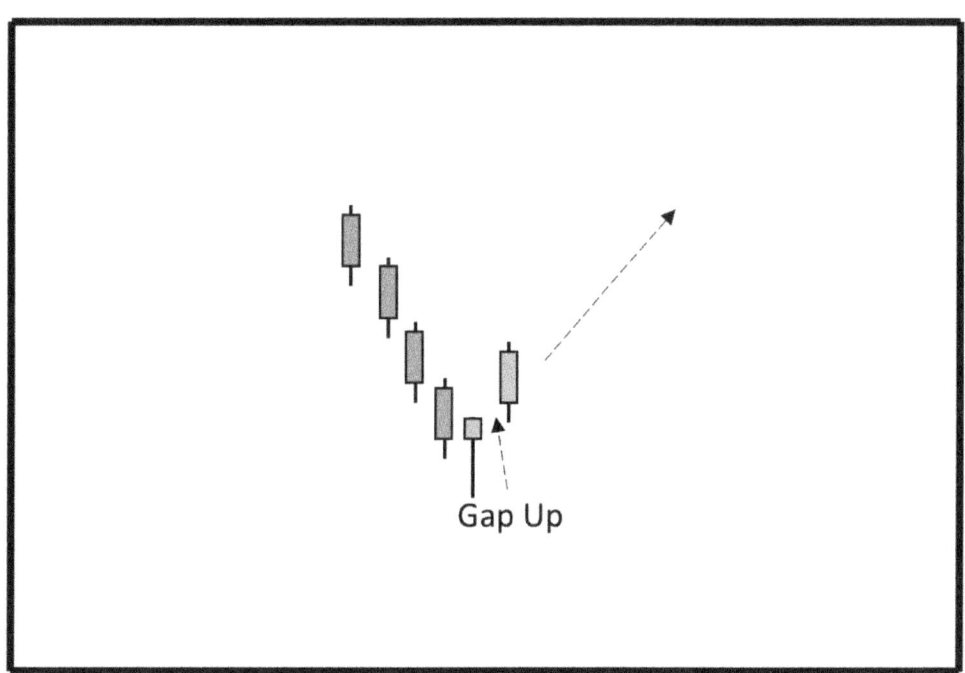

How to Trade Gap Up After Hammer at Bottom

The presence of a hammer at the bottom alone indicates an upcoming bullish trend, causing anticipation among buyers and dampening sellers' enthusiasm. If, as in this case, a gap follows the hammer, it signifies that buyers have taken control of the market with significant force and will likely continue driving the price upwards. In such a scenario, set your resistance line at the top of the bearish candle preceding the hammer, and place your stop loss at the bottom of the hammer. While you may consider waiting for a second candle for confirmation, doing so would mean potentially missing out on profits.

#72 - Gap Up at Bottom After Inverted Hammer

This pattern occurs within a downtrend and indicates some buying activity, as represented by the inverted hammer. The wick of the candle moves up into the body of the previous day's red candle, but not entirely. A gap up in price indicates aggressive buying and initiates a powerful rally.

Figure 72: Gap Up at Bottom After Inverted Hammer

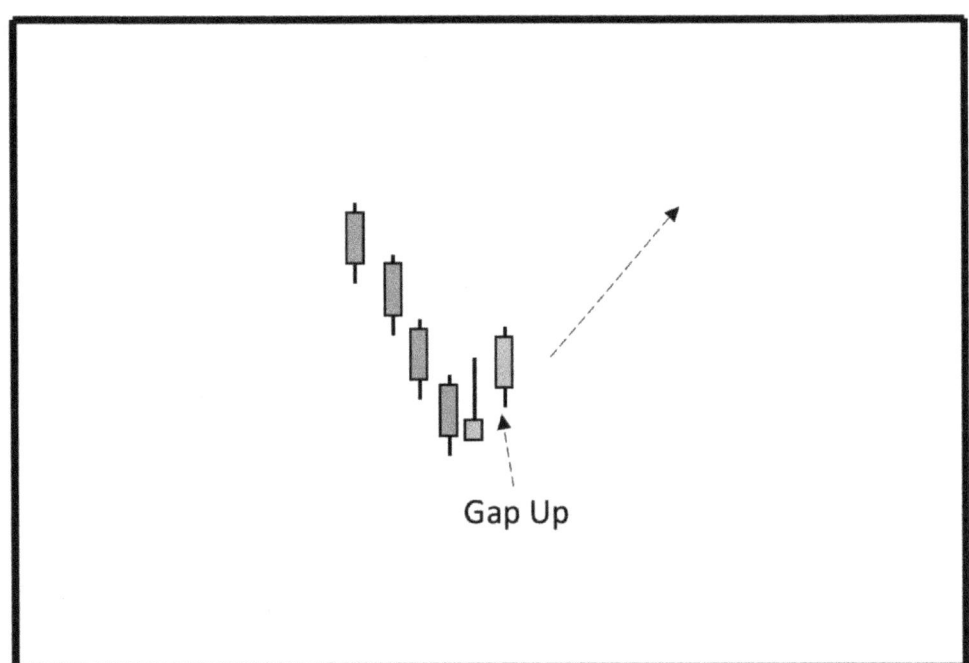

How to Trade Gap Up at Bottom After Inverted Hammer

An inverted hammer is a potential reversal indicator that typically appears at the bottom of downtrends. It signifies a struggle between buyers and sellers, with buyers gaining momentum. The presence of a gap highlights the aggressive buying behavior that has taken over the market, resulting in the victory of buyers in the struggle. This shift in sentiment leads to an increase in buying activity as the trend progresses. As shown in the figure above, you can place a resistance line above the opening of the bearish candle preceding the inverted hammer and wait for a price break, which often coincides with the occurrence of a gap.

#73 - Gaps With Windows

One of the most powerful technical indicators is a gap. A gap occurs when there is no trading in the current time frame that overlaps with any previous trading range. An upward gap at the bottom of a trend signifies buyers' intention to establish their position above the previous trading range. Conversely, a downward gap from the top indicates sellers' desire to exit their position, causing the price to fall below the previous trading range. Utilizing gaps in combination with candlestick signals enhances the potential for profitable trades. These gaps typically occur in lower time frames, such as minute charts.

Figure 73: Gaps or Windows

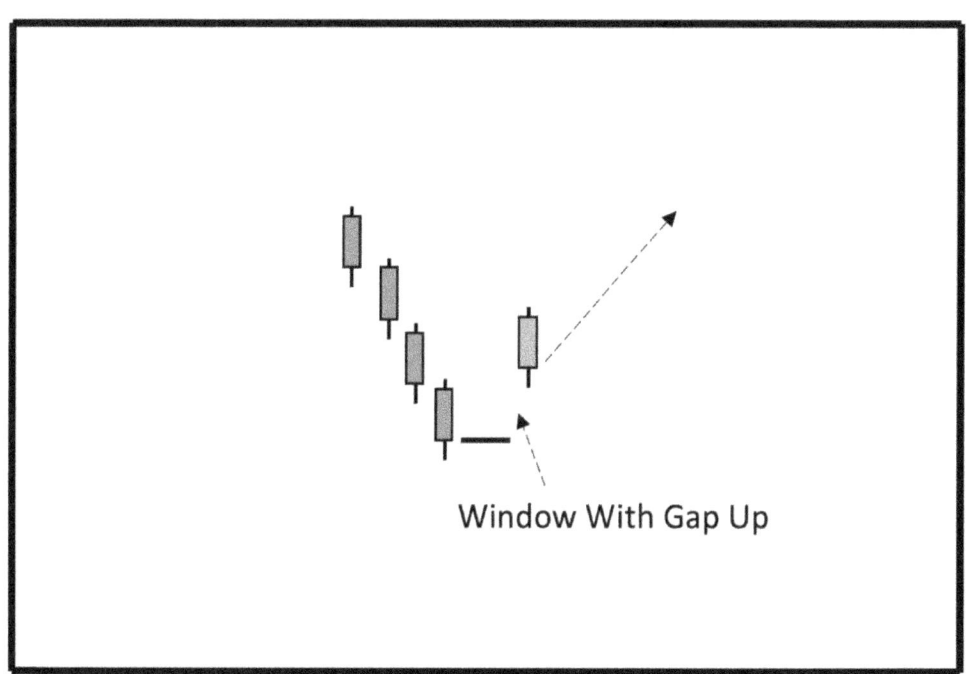

Window With Gap Up

How to Trade Gaps or Windows

One of the key characteristics of the Gaps or Windows pattern is its versatility, particularly the use of its resistance as price targets and its support as initial stops. A window can indicate a trend continuation, allowing traders to maintain their buy or sell trades, or a trend reversal, signaling traders to exit their positions. It can also suggest that a trend is nearing its end, helping traders anticipate its conclusion. Regardless of the scenario, it's important to note that in windows, the gap always fills before the price continues its movement. For instance, if you come across a chart with a significant upward gap, be aware that the price will likely decline to fill that gap before resuming its uptrend. This provides traders with an opportunity to anticipate the trend continuation and potentially achieve higher profits.

#74 - Hammer

Some important features of the Hammer pattern are that the real body is located at the upper end of the range, and the color is not crucial. Additionally, the lower wick should be at least twice the length of the body, while the upper wick is either non-existent or very small. The confirmation of the Hammer signal occurs on the next trading day with a strong bullish day, and a higher likelihood of reversal is present if the lower wick is exceptionally long. This pattern aids traders in identifying the location of support and demand. Hammers are most effective when preceded by at least three consecutive declining candles.

Figure 74: Hammers

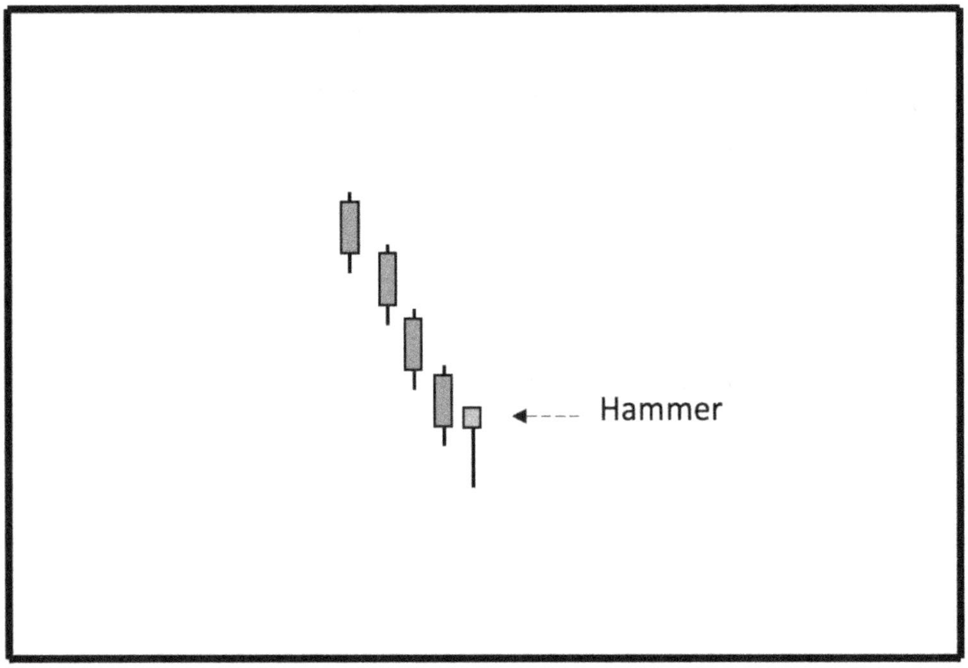

How to Trade Hammer

As a potential bullish reversal pattern, the Hammer indicates to traders that the market has reached its downward limit and a reversal is likely to occur soon. Traders analyze the candles preceding and following the Hammer to confirm the pattern. Once confirmed, a stop loss can be placed below the lower shadow of the Hammer or directly below the real body, depending on the aggressiveness of the upward price movement. The purpose of the stop loss is to manage risk, as there is no guarantee that the uptrend will continue despite the pattern confirmation. It's important to note that the Hammer pattern does not provide a specific price target, making the potential reward uncertain. Therefore, it is crucial to trade wisely and exercise patience.

#75 - Hanging Man

The Hammer pattern's lower wick should be at least twice the length of the real body. The real body of the pattern is positioned at the upper end of the trading range. If the body is red, it indicates bearish implications. This pattern typically lacks an upper wick or has a very small one. The confirmation of the signal occurs on the following trading day, usually with a red candle, as this pattern commonly appears at the top of uptrends. The longer the lower wick, the higher the chance of a reversal. The subsequent trading day determines whether prices will move higher or lower.

Figure 75: Hanging Man

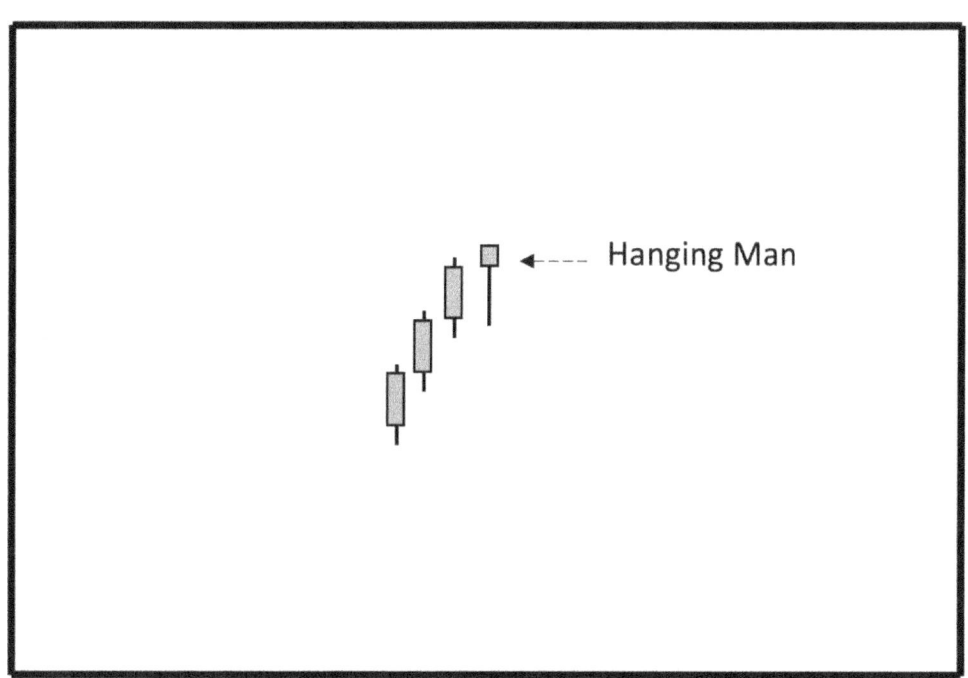

How to Trade Hanging Man Patterns

Bearish candles that follow Hanging Man patterns with longer shadows indicate a higher likelihood of prices moving downward, presenting investors with trading opportunities. Therefore, it is crucial to closely monitor the candlestick that follows a Hanging Man pattern. In the case of selling days as mentioned earlier, you might consider going short at the close of the bearish candle following the Hanging Man. Alternatively, for a more aggressive approach, you can sell at the open of the bearish candle or at the close of the Hanging Man itself. To manage risk, it is advisable to place a stop loss order slightly above the high of the Hanging Man.

#76 - Head and Shoulders Bottom

It is easiest to identify this pattern by using a bit of imagination. The pattern resembles a left and right shoulder with a head, where the head is higher than both shoulders. In this pattern, the left shoulder forms first during a downward trend. It's worth noting that there could be two or three shoulders on each side. The presence of more shoulders makes it easier to trade and predict the market direction. This pattern is excellent for identifying reversals from a downtrend and is commonly referred to as the Inverted Head and Shoulders.

Figure 76: Head and Shoulders Bottom

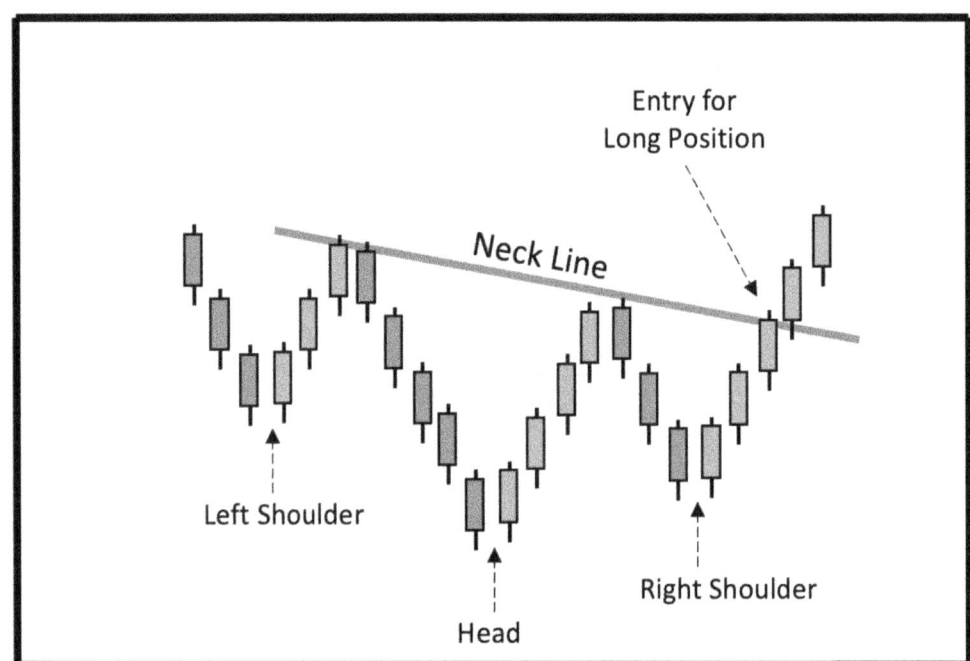

How to Trade Head and Shoulders Bottom

Since the Head and Shoulders pattern indicates the end of a downtrend and the beginning of an uptrend, it is advisable to consider taking a long position (buying) once the pattern is confirmed. It is important to note that confirming the pattern before entering a trade position is crucial. To confirm the Head and Shoulders Bottom, you need to establish a neckline resistance that connects the peaks between the head and the left and right shoulders. In the provided figure, the left neckline is higher than the right, but this may not always be the case. Sometimes, the necklines may be at the same level. The key to trading this pattern is to wait for the price to break above the neckline. Once that occurs, you can comfortably take a long position (buy). To manage risks, it is recommended to place a stop loss directly below the right shoulder.

#77 - Head and Shoulders Top

It is easiest to identify this pattern using a little imagination. The pattern will look like a left and right shoulder with a head. Remember, the head will be elevated above both shoulders. In this pattern, the left shoulder will form first in an upward trend. Note that there could be two or three of each shoulder. The more shoulders there are, the easier it is to trade and predict where the market is going. The pullback will often occur and requires the necessary patience to continue looking for this Head and Shoulders pattern to avoid a panic sell.

Figure 77: Head and Shoulders

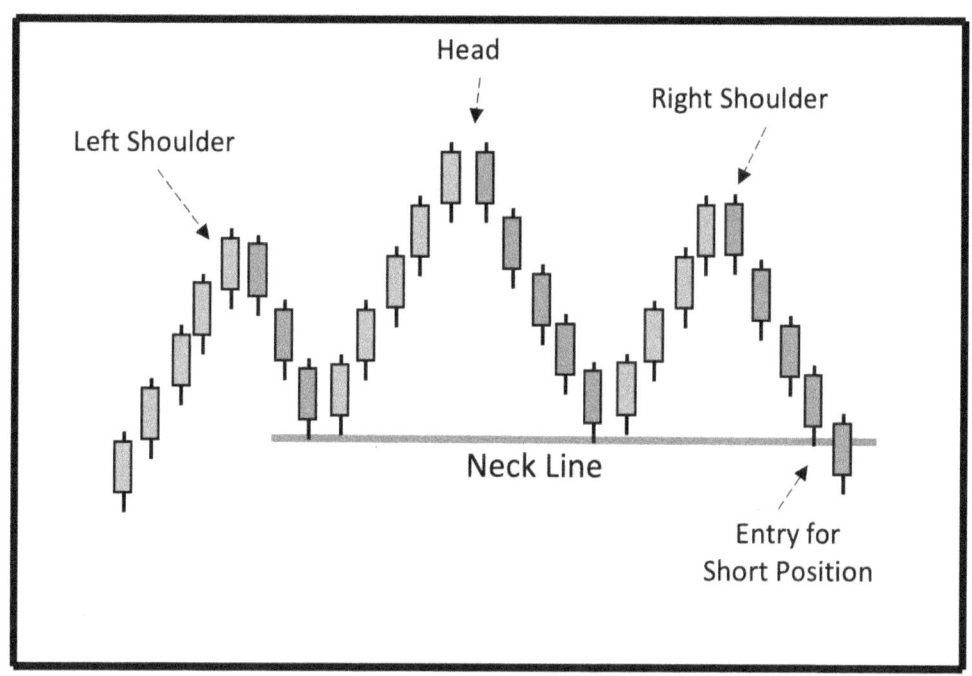

How to Trade Head and Shoulders

Knowing how the Head and Shoulders Top formation occurs, successfully trading it requires patience. It becomes valid when the bearish (red) candlestick closes below the neckline. At this point, there are two ways to proceed. First, you can open a sell (short) order immediately, placing your stop loss just above the peak of the last candlestick. Alternatively, you can wait for the price to retest the neckline before entering a short position. In this case, your stop loss should be placed above the resistance level. Note that the price only retests the neckline about 50% of the time, so it is advisable to go short after the neckline break. If there is a retest, you have an opportunity to add more positions. The take profit target can be either the lows (troughs) or the initial distance from the head to the neckline.

#78 - Homing Pigeon

This pattern is quite similar to the Harami, except that the color of the second candlestick is the same as that of the first candlestick. It consists of a two-candle formation in a prolonged downtrend. The real body of the first candle is longer than that of the second candle, and the open and close of the second candle occur within the range of the first candle. Additionally, the wick on the second candlestick does not need to stay within the body of the first candlestick. It is important to note that further confirmation is required for a change in trend.

Figure 78: Homing Pigeon

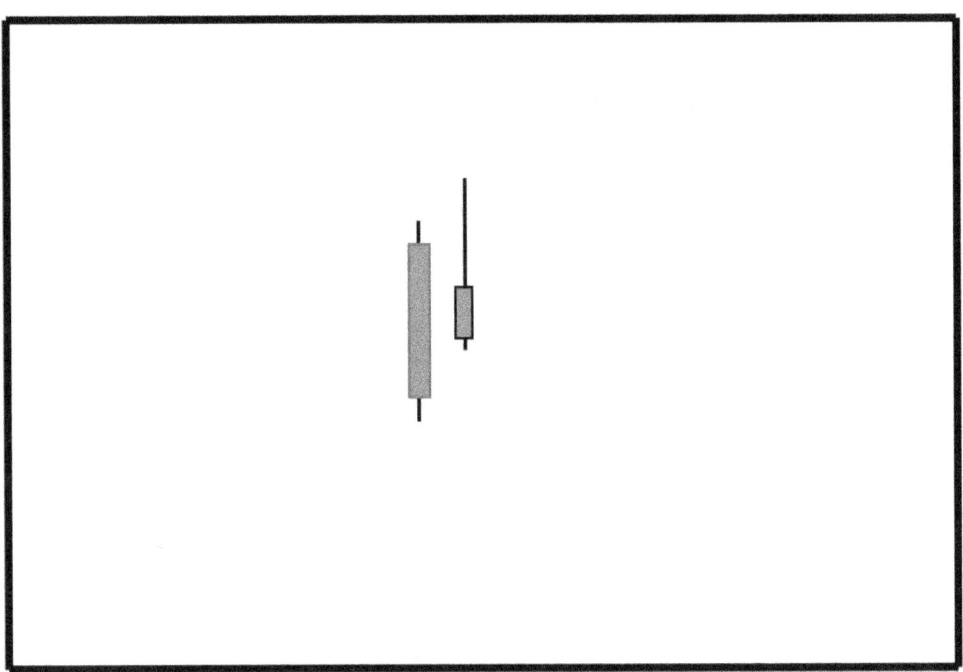

How to Trade Homing Pigeon Patterns

Before trading the Homing Pigeon pattern, it is important for you to confirm the pattern. With this pattern, traders pay attention to the third candle. In the case of a bullish Harami, the third candle should close above the high of the first candle, and in the case of a bearish Harami, it should close below. To reduce risk, place the stop loss at the lowest low of the first candle. It is best to use this pattern in conjunction with other technical analysis tools, such as other chart patterns   and   indicator   tools.

#79 - In The Neck Line

This is a two-candle pattern similar to the Meeting Line pattern. A long red candlestick is formed in a downtrend. The second candle closes at or slightly above the close of the first candle, and it gaps down from the first candle. The pattern represents a bearish continuation pattern that occurs at the end of a downtrend. Confirmation of this pattern occurs when the next candle closes below the closing price of the second candle.

Figure 79: In the Neck Line

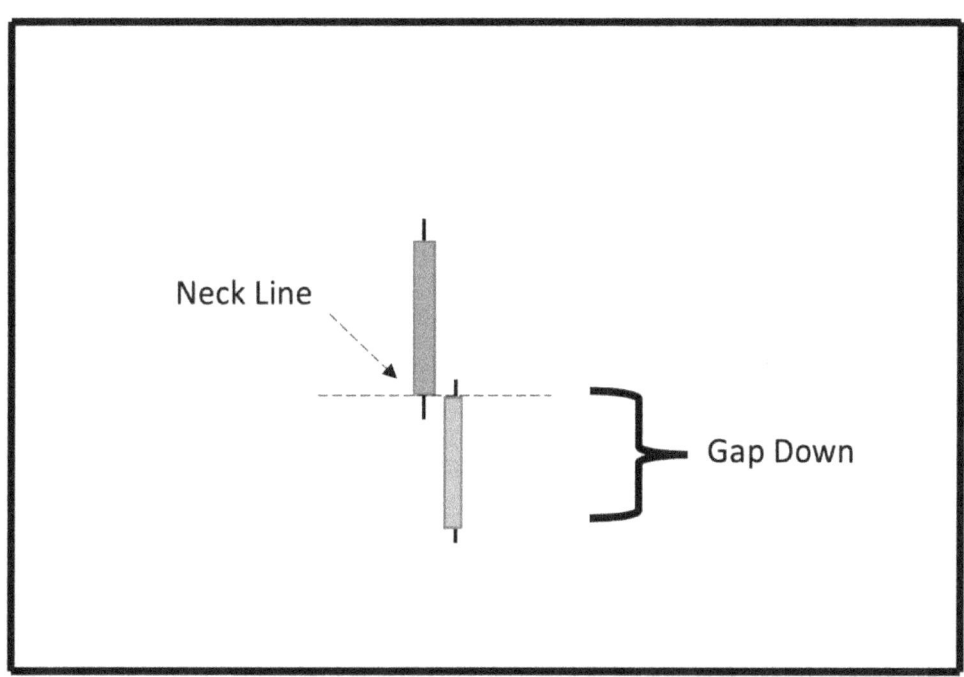

How to Trade In The Neck Line

This pattern indicates the strength of the bears in the market, suggesting that they will continue pushing the price down. To confirm this trend, pay attention to the candle on the third day. If it is red (or black), then the downtrend is likely to continue. In some cases, the price may experience a period of horizontal movement but will eventually resume the downward trend. Place a support line below the second candlestick and wait for price breaks, especially during horizontal movements. This pattern is similar to its counterpart, On The Neckline, so as a trader, it requires patience and keen   observation.

#80 - Inverted Hammer

The Inverted Hammer is a pattern characterized by an upper wick that is at least two times the length of the real body, with the real body positioned at the lower end of the trading range. The lower wick is typically very small or non-existent. To confirm the Inverted Hammer, the following day needs to have a strong, bullish candle. The potential for a reversal is higher when the upper wick is significantly longer. When the next day opens higher after a gap down from the previous day's close, it sets up for a stronger reversal. If the Inverted Hammer occurs after a prolonged downtrend, it is considered bullish.

Figure 80: Inverted Hammer

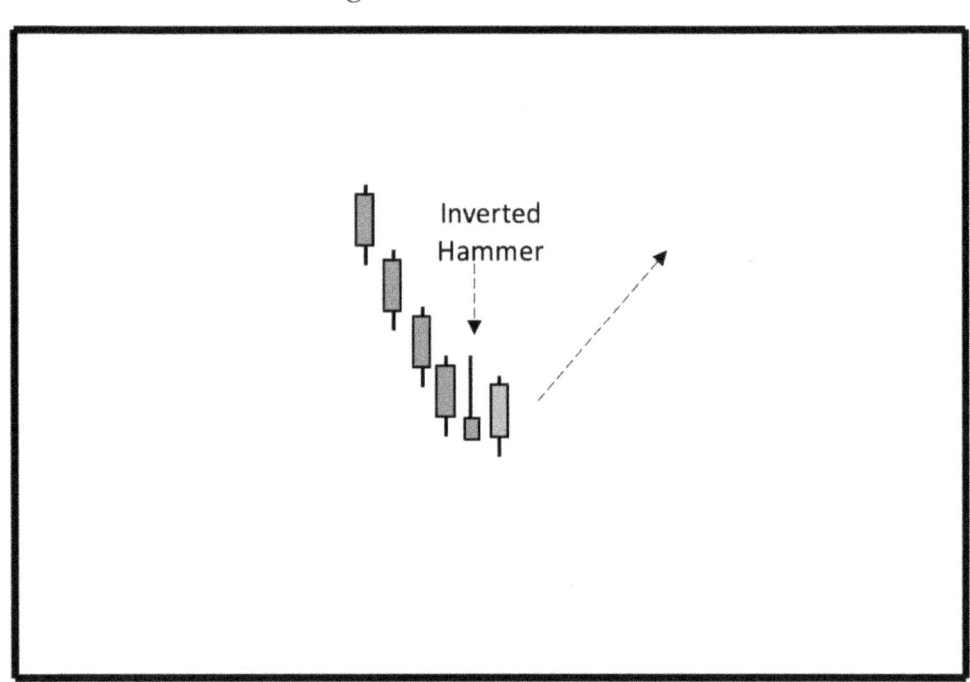

How to Trade Inverted Hammer

The Inverted Hammer is a candlestick pattern that occurs at the end of a downtrend, indicating a potential reversal as the bulls attempt to push the price higher but fail to maintain strength. A strong bullish candle following the Inverted Hammer suggests a possible strong uptrend. Pay attention to whether it forms around a Fibonacci retracement level. To trade this pattern, place a buy stop order one or two pips above the high of the Inverted Hammer and set a stop loss order below the Inverted Hammer, typically around two to five pips. For the profit target, use the nearest swing high point. While the Inverted Hammer is easily identifiable on a chart, trading it requires patience as the reversal may not occur until one or two subsequent candles.

#81 - Harami

The Harami is considered a significant candlestick signal and is commonly observed in trading. It consists of two candles: one larger bullish or bearish candle and one smaller bullish or bearish candle. The nature of each candle determines whether the Harami is bullish or bearish, as well as its position on the chart. In a bullish Harami, a large bearish candle is followed by a smaller bullish candle, while the opposite is true for a bearish Harami. The Harami is a reversal pattern that requires an understanding of trends to be effectively utilized.

Figure 81: Harami

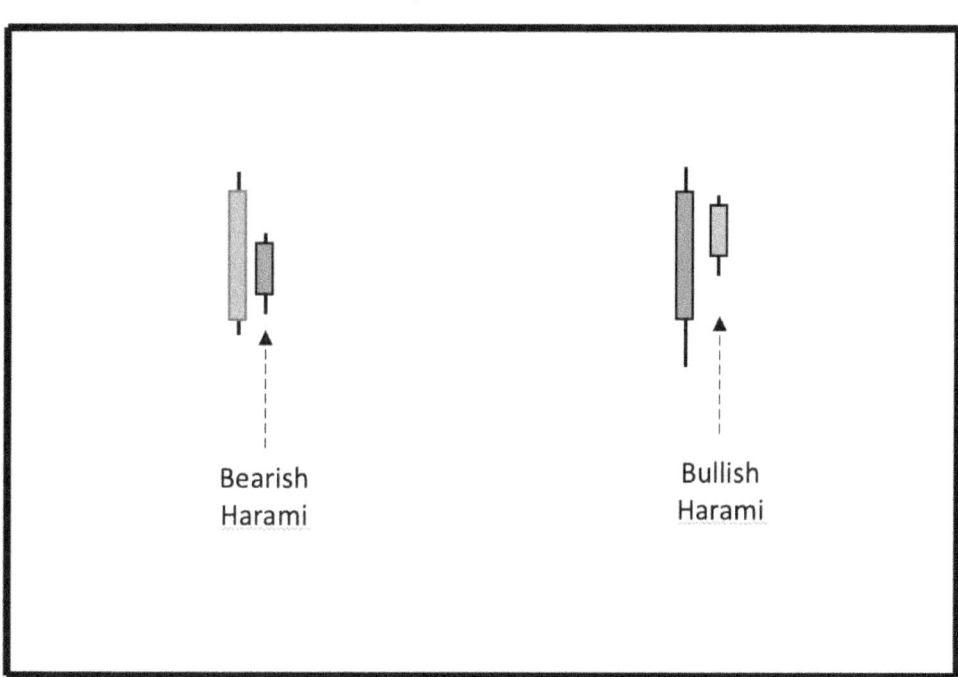

How to Trade Harami

Trading the Harami is a simple process. Start by drawing a downward resistance trendline on the open of the previous day's candle or the close of the candle before that. Then, wait for the price to break above this trendline. The combination of the trendline break and the Harami pattern creates a potential signal for a trade. Many traders choose to wait for the candlestick that follows the bullish or bearish Harami before entering a trade. This approach adds an additional confirmation before taking action.

#82 - Jay Hook Pattern

The Jay Hook Pattern occurs after a robust uptrend, characterized by a substantial percentage move that exceeds the current market trend. Once sell signals emerge, the trend experiences a pullback, the magnitude of which depends on the buy signals. Subsequently, a new uptrend unfolds when buying signals emerge. Indecisive candles found in this pattern may include Dojis, Small Hammers, and Bullish Engulfing Signals. These candles reflect uncertainty or potential reversals in the market.

Figure 82: Jay Hook

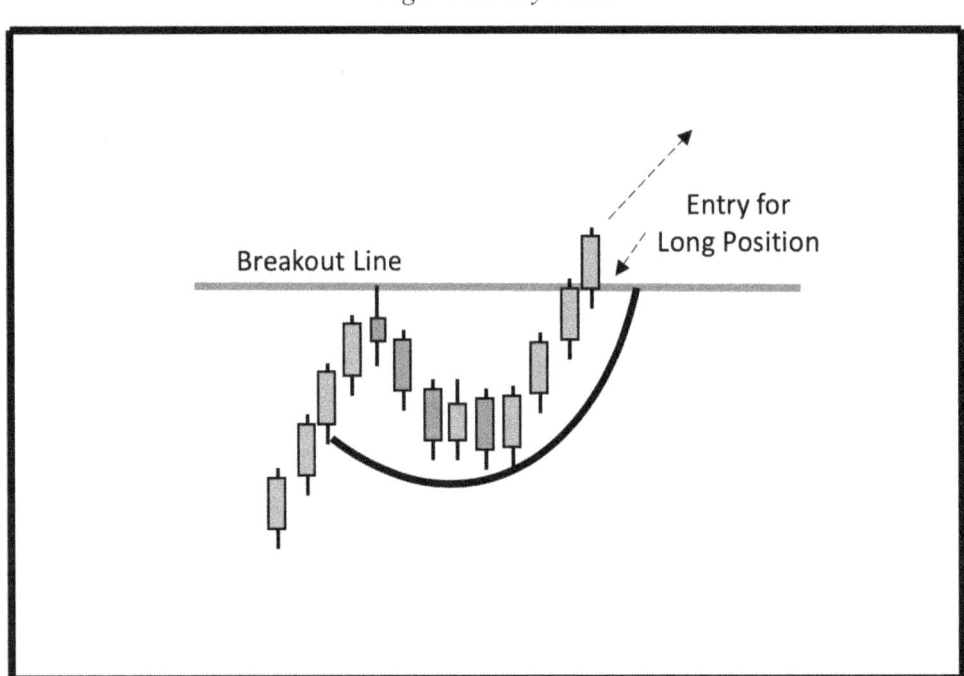

How to Trade Jay Hook Pattern

Now that you understand when and how the Jay Hook Pattern is formed, it is crucial for you to know how to take advantage of it and benefit from it. The presence of indecisive candles suggests that selling pressure is diminishing, signaling the potential for the Jay Hook Pattern. To mitigate downside risk, it is advisable to take profit when the first sell signal appears during the initial uptrend. This is because there is no guarantee that a 20-60% retracement of the pullback will not occur. The key to profiting from this pattern is to monitor the chart for flattening downtrend pullbacks, as they often indicate more uptrends and potential buy signals.

#83 - Kickers

In this pattern, the opening prices of the first and second days are identical, and the price moves in the opposite direction from the opening price. Kickers are typically formed due to unexpected news before or after trading hours. The trading range of the previous day does not retrace the price, and more significant price reversals tend to result in longer real bodies. This candlestick pattern is useful for traders in determining which party controls the market trend.

Figure 83: Kickers

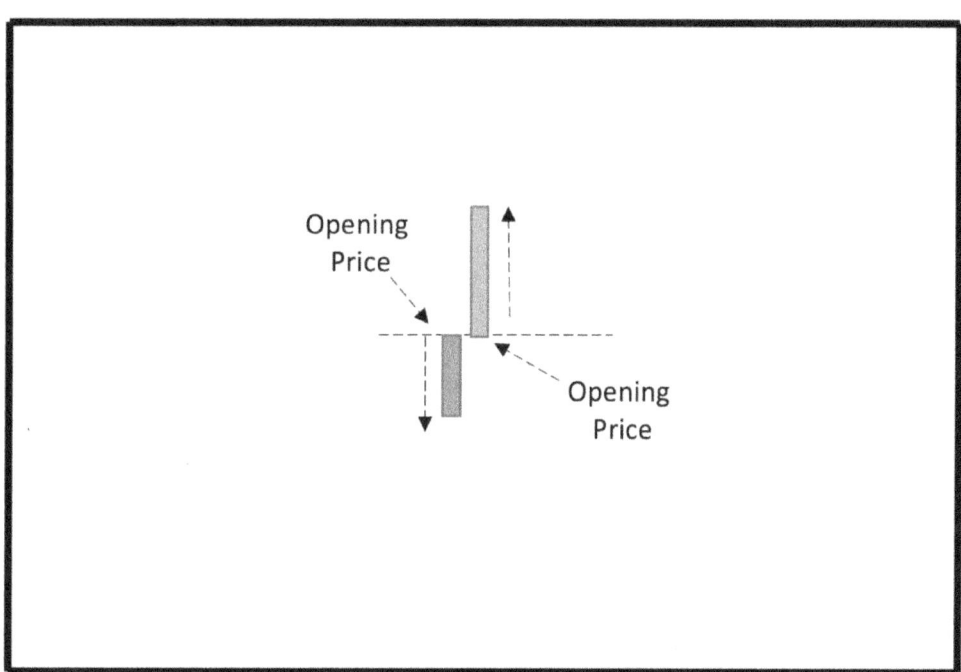

How to Trade Kickers

The Kickers pattern is widely recognized as one of the most reliable reversal patterns. Traders who are keen observers of this pattern have been able to make prompt and informed trading decisions. Those who are familiar with the Kickers pattern understand the importance of trading immediately upon its identification. On the other hand, those who choose to wait for pullbacks may end up regretting their decision. As a rare pattern that serves as a highly reliable indicator of traders' sentiment, it would be unwise to overlook its appearance on any chart, particularly in overbought or oversold markets.

#84 - Ladder Bottom

This pattern occurs at the conclusion of a downtrend and is characterized by four consecutive red candlesticks. Each red candlestick closes lower than the previous day. On Day 4, the candlestick closes at a low but opens and trades higher throughout the day. On Day 5, the candlestick opens higher than the opening price on Day 4 and continues to trade upwards, eventually closing higher than the range of the last three days. It is worth noting that this pattern is relatively uncommon.

Figure 84: Ladder Bottom

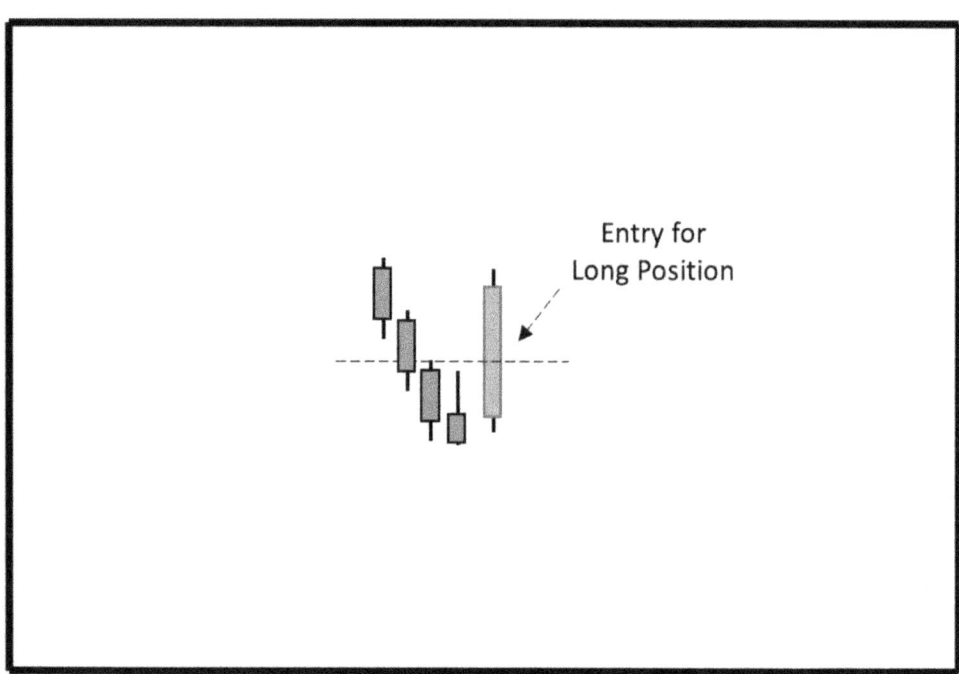

How to Trade Ladder Bottom

The occurrence of the Ladder Bottom pattern indicates a gradual loss of momentum in the downtrend. This pattern consists of four bearish candles followed by one bullish candle, with the last bearish candle being an Inverted Hammer. It is important to pay attention to this candle as it signals the potential for a market reversal, with bulls taking control. Confirmation should be awaited from the fifth bullish candle. It is worth noting that this pattern is both uncommon and unreliable in predicting reversals, but when it does make accurate predictions, they tend to be exceptional. Therefore, caution should be exercised when trading based on the Ladder Bottom pattern.

#85 - Long Shadow

The Long Shadow pattern, also referred to as a wick or tail, occurs when a candlestick is elongated to display the opening and closing prices within a specific timeframe. The highest and lowest prices are represented by the shadows. There are two types of long shadows: the Long Upper Shadow and the Long Lower Shadow. Among these, the Long Upper Shadow is easier to identify. A key characteristic of the Long Shadow is that it is always twice the size of the real body. Additionally, the Long Shadow can be either bullish (green or white) or bearish (red or black) in color.

Figure 85: Long Shadows

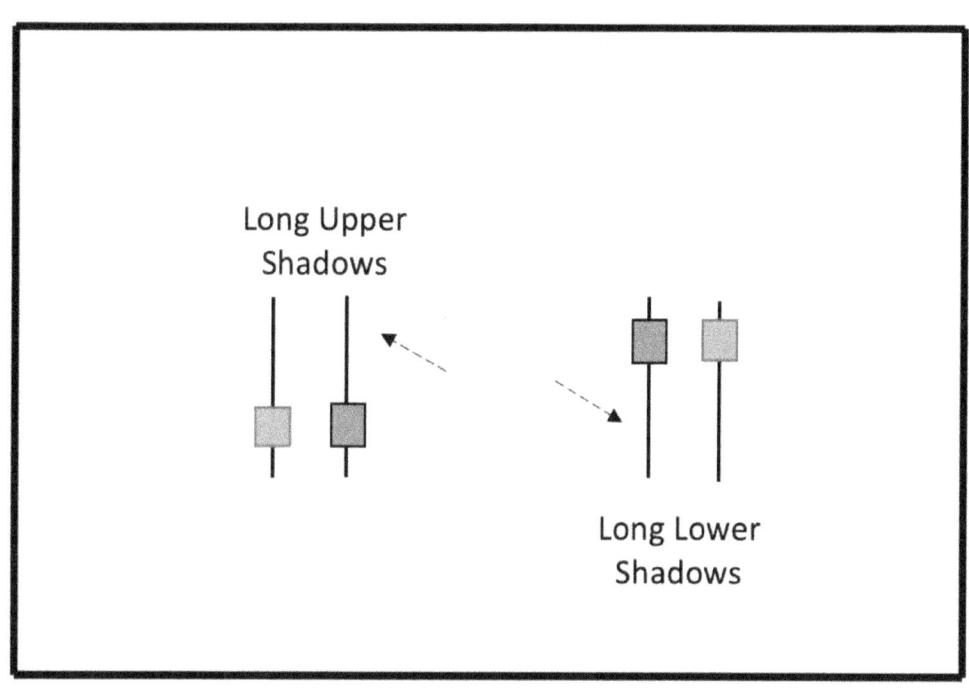

How to Trade Long Shadow

Traders generally view the Long Shadow as a bullish signal, although its significance can vary depending on its position on the chart and the characteristics of the shadow. Long Lower Shadows are typically associated with an upcoming uptrend, particularly when they appear at the bottom of an ongoing downtrend. On the contrary, Long Upper Shadows indicate a potential downtrend, especially when observed at the peak of an ongoing uptrend. To effectively trade the Long Shadow pattern, it is important to wait for confirmation by observing the candle that follows. Once confirmed, enter your trade position and set a stop loss at the lowest low (for a Long Lower Shadow) or highest high (for a Long Upper Shadow) to manage risks effectively.

#86 - Longhorn Bottom

Any Texan knows the distinct appearance of a Longhorn! This pattern consists of three candlesticks and is easily recognizable. It forms a cup and handle formation, resulting in a low throwback percentage of 30%. If identified early, this pattern can lead to average profits of around 30% on a daily chart. It's important to note that the Longhorns in this pattern do not have to be evenly sized.

Figure 86: Longhorn Bottom

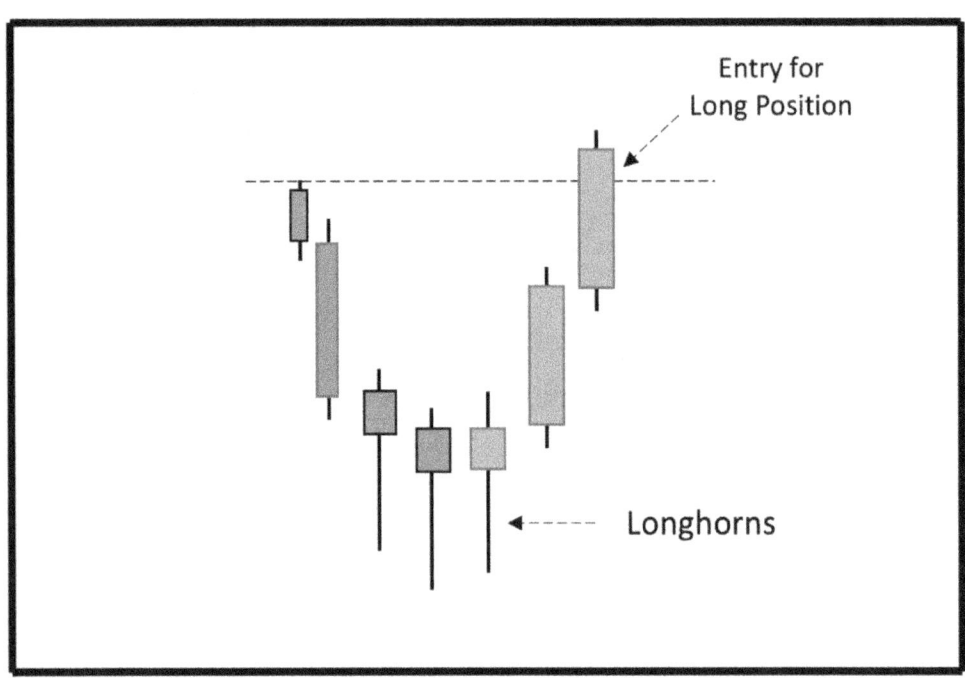

How to Trade Longhorn Bottom

When trading the Longhorn Bottom during uptrends, it is important to be vigilant for potential reversals. Additionally, there are two other factors to consider: the length of the horns and the volume of the breakout. Tall horns typically perform better than short horns, and horns accompanied by heavy breakout volumes tend to yield better results. Furthermore, horns that exhibit a lighter right side but a more pronounced left spike are known to outperform. To confirm the pattern, it is crucial to wait for the price to close above the highest high within the pattern before entering a position. Alternatively, you can place a buy stop slightly above that price to initiate a trade.

#87 - Marubozu

This pattern serves as a tool for traders to gauge market sentiment during specific periods, and it only occurs when the market closes without any retracement. The Marubozu is characterized by a single candlestick, making it relatively straightforward to identify. There are three variations of the Marubozu, each having both a bullish and bearish form. These include the full Marubozu, which lacks any wicks; the open Marubozu, featuring a bullish candle with a minimal upper wick and a bearish candle with a minimal lower wick; and the close Marubozu, consisting of a bullish candle with a small lower wick and a bearish candle with a small upper wick.

Figure 87: Marubozu

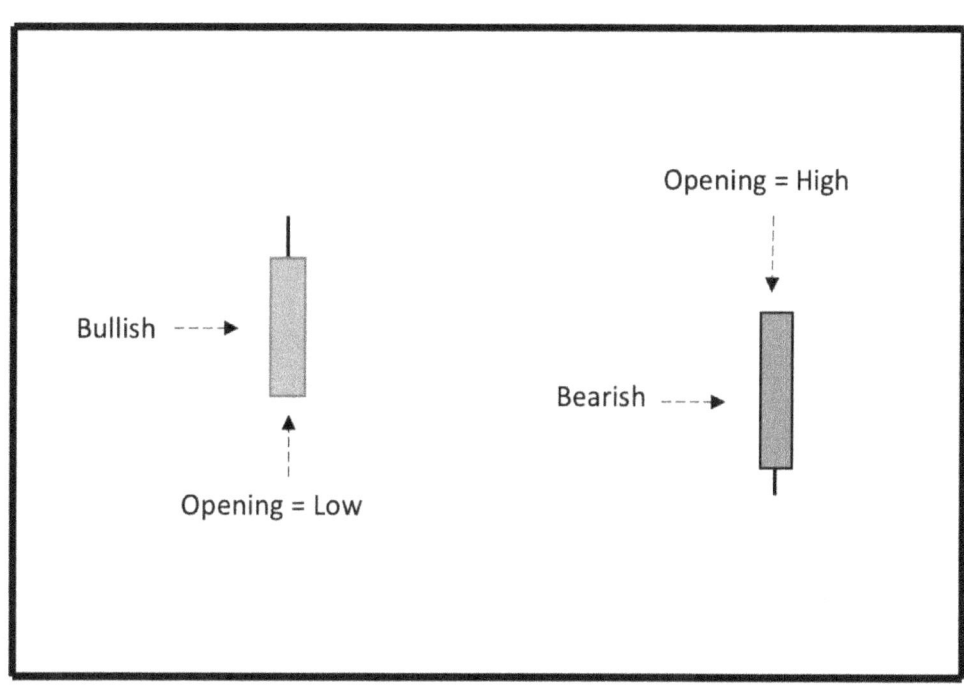

How to Trade Marubozu

When trading the Marubozu pattern, it is important to understand the unique meaning associated with each of the three types. For instance, if there is a bullish Marubozu at the end of a downtrend, it indicates a potential reversal, and you should consider taking a buy position. Conversely, if a bearish Marubozu appears at the end of a downtrend, it suggests that the downtrend is likely to continue, and maintaining a sell position is advisable. In the case of a bullish Marubozu at the end of an uptrend, it implies a potential trend continuation, whereas a bearish Marubozu indicates a likely reversal. It is crucial to note that confirmation is necessary, and observing the candles that follow the Marubozu is recommended. If the subsequent candle confirms the trend, then you can proceed with your trading decision.

#88 - Mat Hold

This pattern is similar to the rising three methods and bears resemblance to the Upside Gap Two Crows. However, it differs in that the red candlestick on candle 3 penetrates the body of the preceding large green candle. Following candle 3, an additional red candlestick forms, dipping slightly further into the body of candle 1's green candle. On candle 5, there is a gap up, and the closing price surpasses that of all previous candle within the pattern. This pattern indicates that the trend has not stalled and is considered a stronger continuation pattern compared to the rising three methods.

Figure 88: Mat Hold

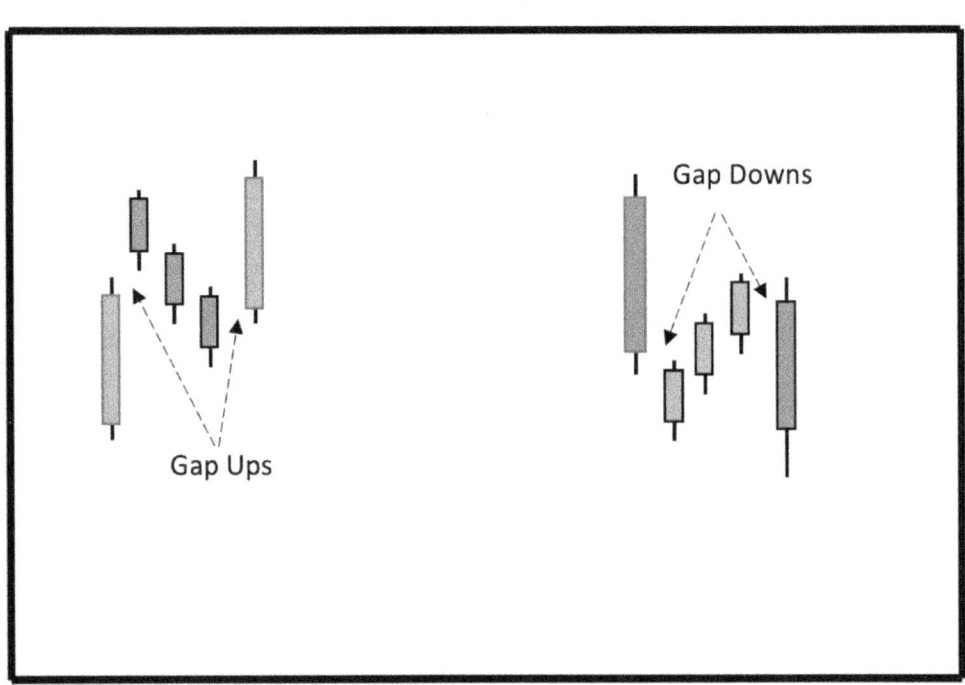

How to Trade Mat Hold Pattern

When trading the Mat Hold pattern, it is crucial to carefully observe its formation to avoid mistaking a bullish Mat Hold for a bearish one. Surprisingly, some traders do make this mistake. The key to successfully trading this pattern is to exercise patience and wait for breakouts. If the price breaks out in a bullish direction, the bullish trend is likely to continue. Conversely, if a breakout occurs in the opposite direction, a reversal is imminent. To manage risk, consider placing your stop loss below the opening of Candle 1. While the Mat Hold pattern is rare yet reliable, it is wise to exercise caution and confirm the signal using other technical analysis tools.

#89 - Matching High

The Matching High candlestick pattern is a bearish reversal pattern that occurs at the conclusion of an uptrend. This pattern consists of two candles, with the first candle being bullish. In some cases, the first candle may close with an upper shadow, while in other instances, it may not. However, the notable characteristic of this pattern is the second candle. The second candle, also bullish, opens slightly above the opening price of the previous candle and closes at the exact same price level as the first candle, regardless of whether it has an upper shadow or not.

Figure 89: Matching High

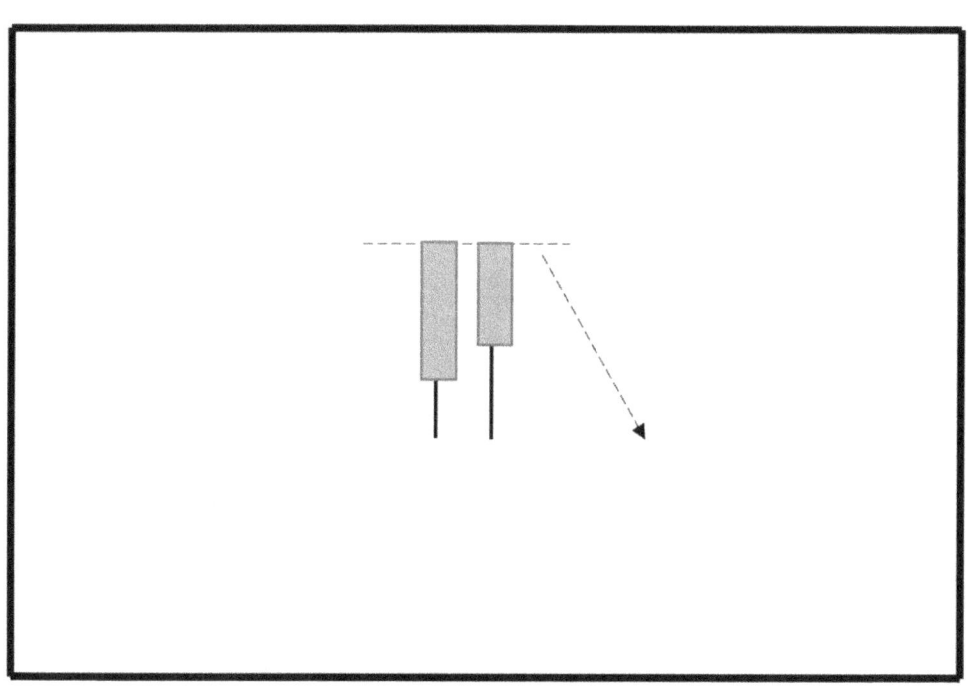

How to Trade Matching High

The Matching High is a bearish reversal pattern that exclusively appears at the conclusion of an uptrend. Given its potential for misinterpretation, confirmation is essential. Pay close attention to the subsequent candle to validate the pattern. Another method of confirmation is to establish a support zone at the opening of the second candle and wait for breakouts below that level. When the following candle breaks below the support line, it serves as an entry point for a sell trade. To effectively manage risks, consider placing your stop loss order just above the closing price of both candles.

#90 - Matching Low

This pattern shares similarities with the Homing Pigeon, with the key difference being that both candles in the pattern close at the same low. It typically occurs after a prolonged downtrend and signifies a potential bottoming out of the market. Both candles have bearish real bodies, and the first candle may or may not have a lower shadow. Similar to the Matching High pattern, the second candle is a crucial distinguishing feature. It opens slightly below the previous candle's opening and closes at the exact same price level as the first candle, regardless of whether it has a lower shadow or not. However, additional confirmation is necessary to validate the possibility of an uptrend.

Figure 90: Matching Low

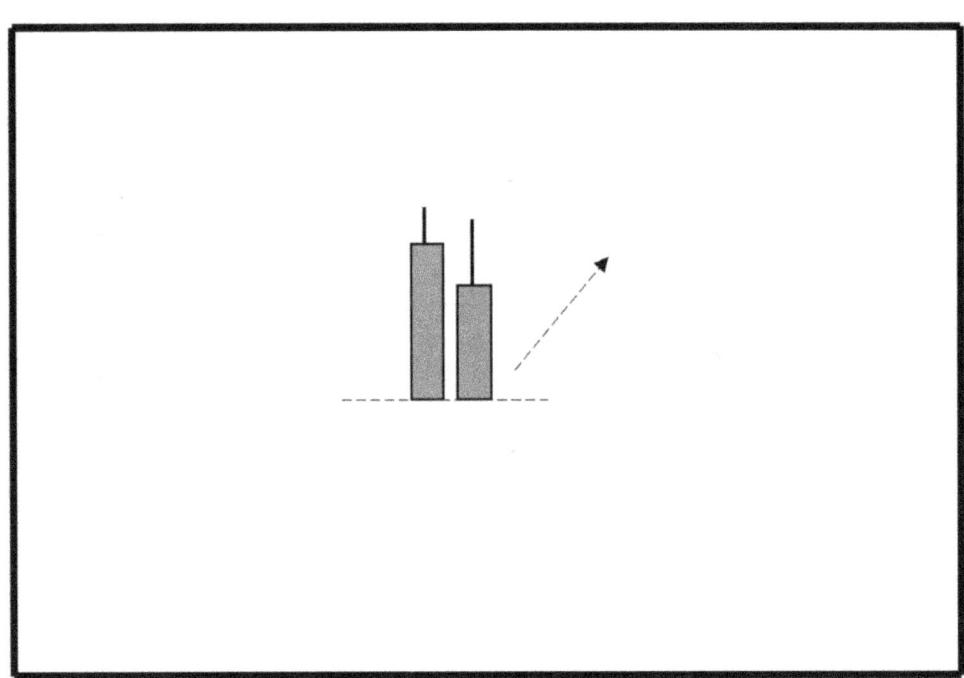

How to Trade Matching Low Pattern

The Matching Low is a bullish reversal pattern that exclusively occurs at the conclusion of a downtrend. Due to its similarity to the Homing Pigeon pattern, confirmation is crucial. Pay close attention to the subsequent candle to validate the pattern. Another method of confirmation is to establish a resistance level at the opening of the second candle and wait for breakouts above that level. Once the following candle breaks above the resistance line, it serves as an entry point for a buy trade. To effectively manage risks, consider placing your stop loss order just below the closing price of both candles. Trading this pattern follows similar principles to its counterpart, but in reverse.

#91 - Meeting Lines

The Meeting Lines pattern, also known as Counterattack Lines, occurs when two candlesticks with opposite colored real bodies have the same closing price. The first candlestick is of the same color as the preceding trend. The pattern continues with a gap that aligns with the trend, represented by the second candlestick. On candle 2, the candlestick color is opposite to that of candle 1, but both candlesticks have elongated bodies. A more significant reversal pattern is indicated by longer bodies, suggesting a stronger potential reversal in the trend.

Figure 91: Meeting Lines

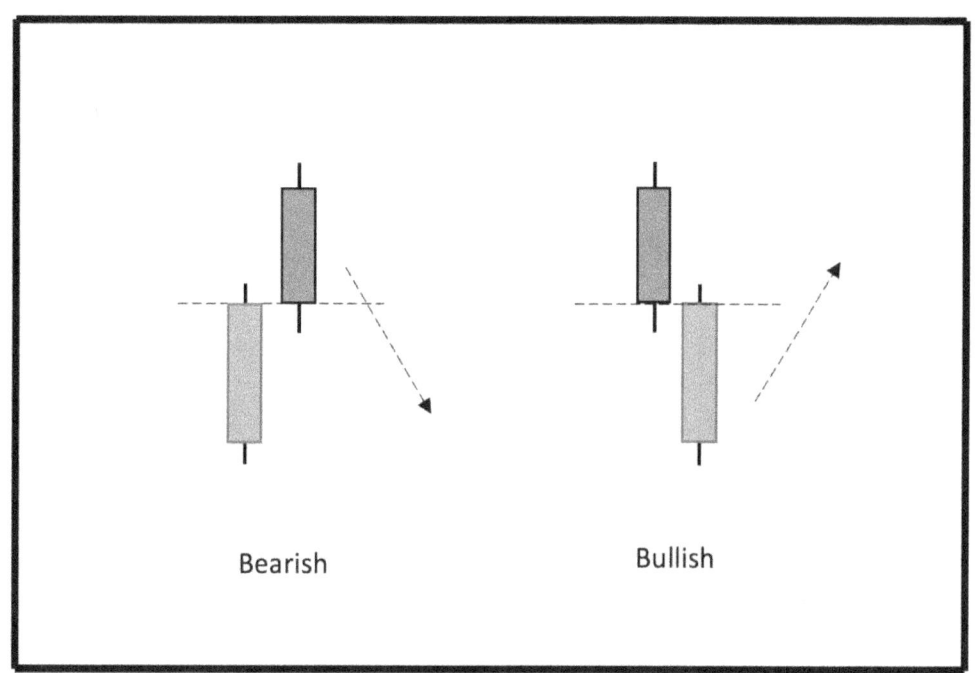

Bearish   Bullish

How to Trade Meeting Lines Pattern

The Meeting Lines pattern represents a stalemate between bullish and bearish forces, signaling a potential bullish reversal. However, confirmation of this pattern is necessary. This can be achieved by drawing a resistance line above the most recent closing price. If the price breaks above this resistance line, it confirms the bullish reversal. To manage risk, consider placing a stop loss order at the last low. If the price retraces in the bearish direction, the stop loss will be triggered upon detection. Always remember to trade in the direction of the breakout for optimal   results.

#92 - Morning Star

The Morning Star chart pattern emerges within a noticeable downtrend. The first candlestick has a red body, aligning with the ongoing trend, while the second candlestick indicates indecision. On the third candlestick, bullish tendencies are observed, with the closing price ideally reaching at least halfway up the red candle. The strength of the reversal is intensified by longer red and green candles. The presence of a gap between the first and second candlestick further enhances the likelihood of a reversal. Additionally, price increases on the third candlestick often offset the losses witnessed on the first candle.

Figure 92: Meeting Lines

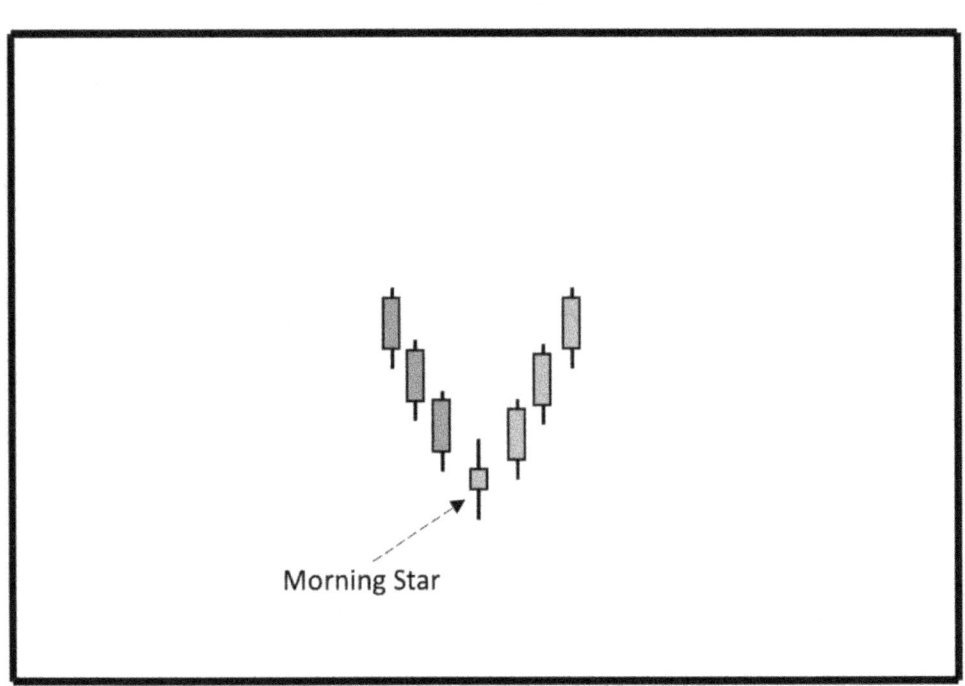

How to Trade Morning Star

Apart from its easy identification, the Morning Star pattern is simple to apply to a price chart. Its appearance indicates an imminent reversal of the current trend, specifically in the bullish direction. This presents traders with an opportunity to initiate long positions and hold them as the price continues to rise. Various strategies can be employed to enter a Morning Star trade, such as the breakout strategy. By placing a resistance level at the high of the first candle, traders can use it as a trade entry point as the price continues its upward trend. To manage potential losses, a stop loss order can be placed just below the low of the second candle in the Morning Star formation. This helps minimize losses in the event of a retracement, allowing for an   easier   exit   from   the   trade.

#93 - Moving Average Once Breached Will Act As Resistance

When a significant moving average is broken, it transitions from serving as support to functioning as resistance during any upward movement. During the testing of this breach, indecisive candlestick signals tend to appear. This pattern exhibits similarities to the situation where a moving average acts as support after being breached.

Figure 93: Moving Average Once Breached Will Act as Resistance

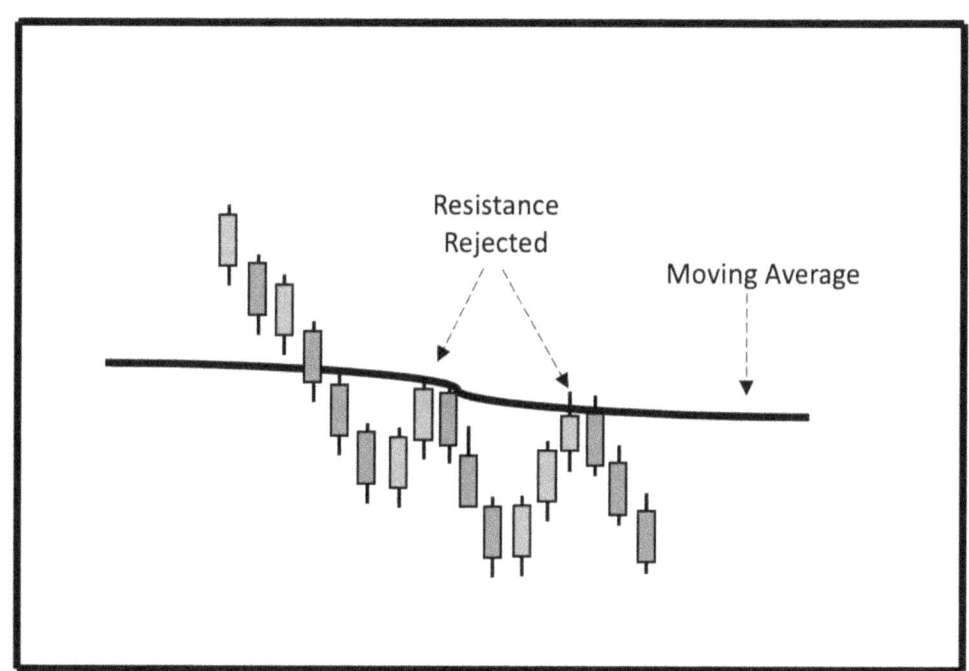

How to Trade Moving Average Once Breached Will Act As Resistance

The fascinating aspect of the Moving Average as Resistance Once Breached is its dynamic nature, which is influenced by price action. This quality makes it valuable for identifying potential trend reversals or continuations. By appropriately configuring a moving average, such as a ten and 20-period EMA on a daily chart, you can determine an uptrend when the price consistently remains above the moving average. In this scenario, holding a buy position until the price crosses back below the moving average allows for exiting the trade and adjusting sentiments. There is no strict rule regarding which moving average to use, so experimentation is necessary to find the most effective one for individual trading preferences.

#94 - Moving Average Once Breached Will Act As Support

This pattern initially functions as a resistance, but once a moving average is breached, it transitions to acting as a support level. Prices retrace and test the original level before resuming their upward movement. By utilizing candlestick signals, it becomes possible to promptly identify investors' actions following the breach of the level.

Figure 94: Moving Average Once Breached Will Act as Support

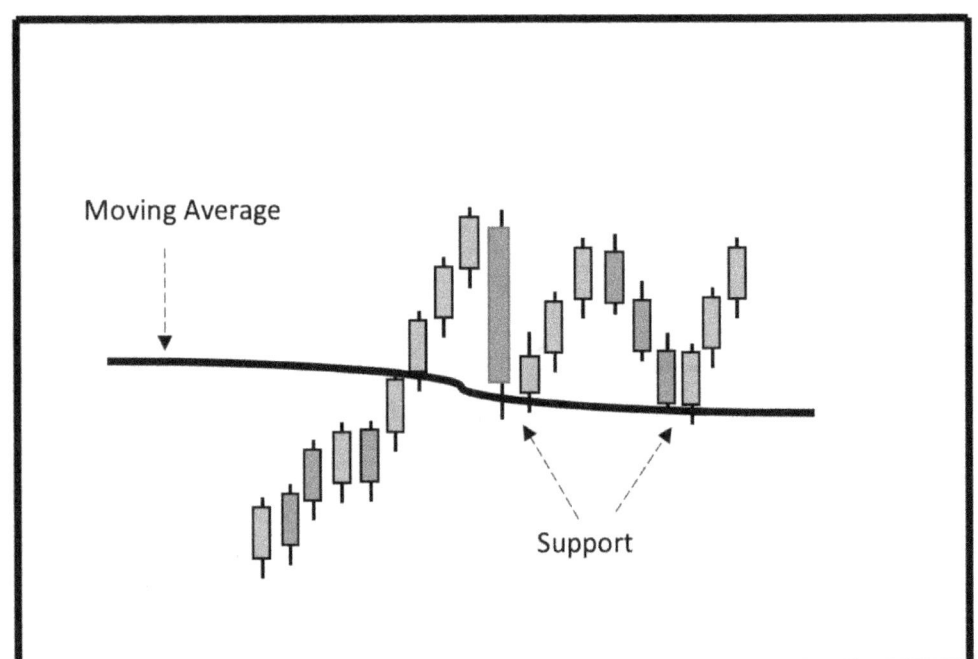

How to Trade Moving average once breached will act as support

The intriguing aspect of the Moving Average as Support Once Breached is its dynamic nature, which is influenced by price action. This quality proves beneficial for price action support, as a properly configured moving average can provide clear insights into potential trend reversals. For instance, applying a 50-period SMA to a daily chart allows for identifying a downtrend when the price consistently remains below the moving average. In this scenario, maintaining a sell position until the price crosses back above the moving average enables the trader to exit the trade and adjust their sentiments. There is no strict rule regarding the choice of moving average; experimentation is necessary to determine the most effective one for individual trading preferences.

#95 - Moving Averages Act As Price Magnets

In this pattern, prices typically find support at one major moving average and are often pulled towards the next major moving average. Candlestick signals can reveal the dynamics at play at the major moving average level and provide insights into the signals that occur at the second target area.

Figure 95: Moving Average Act as Price Magnets

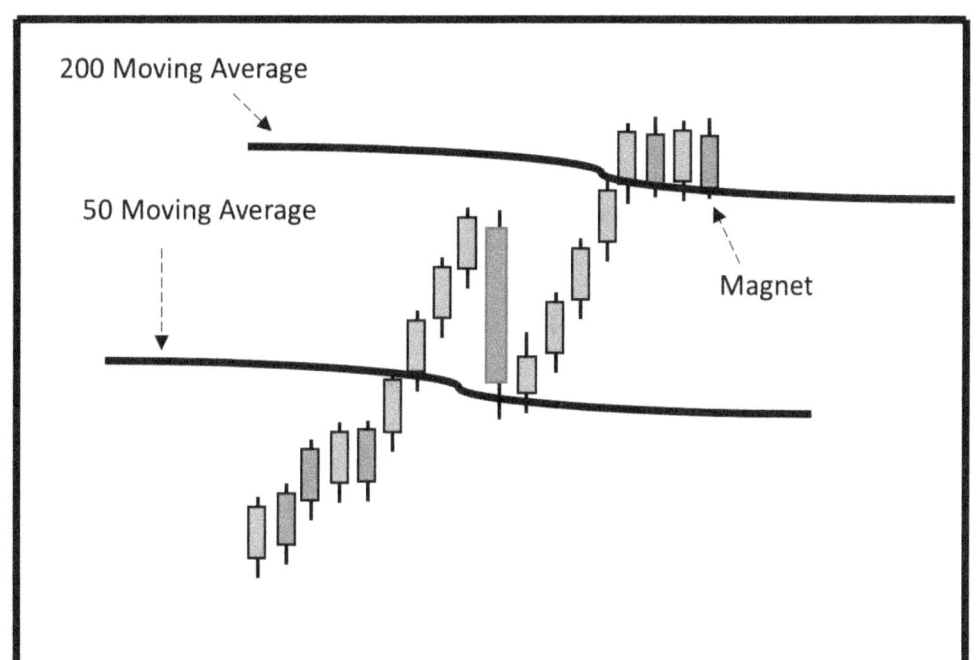

How to Trade Moving Averages Act as Price Magnets

To maximize the effectiveness of this indicator and pattern combination, it is important to wait for the price to become excessively stretched in a specific direction. In situations where the price briefly touches the lower moving average before resuming its upward movement, you can set a buy limit order slightly above the high of this turning point. Although the likelihood of a retracement is low, it is still prudent to exercise caution by placing a stop-loss order below the low of the first bullish candle following the bearish ones. To confirm the validity of this pattern, it is advisable to wait for the price to break above the high of the initial bearish candle. Once this occurs, a bullish continuation can be expected with a higher level of certainty.

#96 - Moving Averages

Moving Averages serve as support and resistance indicators. The two primary moving averages commonly used are the 50-day simple moving average (SMA) and the 200-day SMA. These moving averages are employed for portfolio analysis. When combined with candlestick signals, they form a powerful analytical tool. One popular moving average often used in conjunction with candlestick patterns is the Exponential Moving Average (EMA).

Figure 96: Moving Average

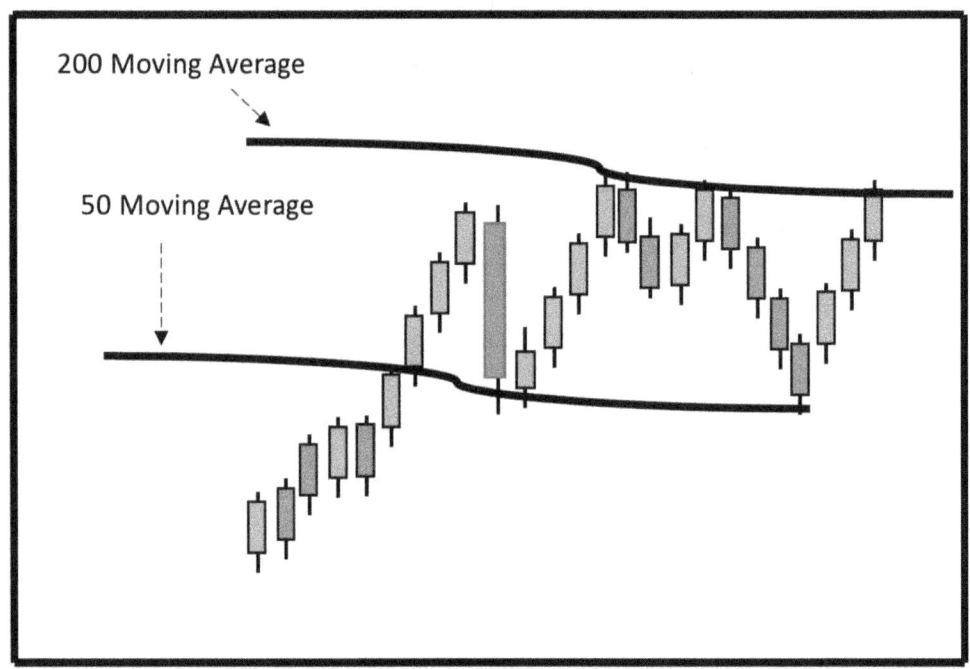

How to Trade Moving Averages

Trading candlestick patterns alongside technical indicators like the Moving Average can be both intriguing and rewarding. These indicators provide additional context to candlestick formations, enhancing their interpretability. It's important to note that the chosen length for a moving average corresponds to the number of days it represents. Moving averages assist in identifying the initiation and conclusion of trends. Commodities that close above the selected length are considered bullish, while those closing below are deemed bearish. By applying both the 50-day and 200-day moving averages to your candlestick chart, you gain deeper insights into price action. However, it is crucial not to overcomplicate things and to have a sound understanding of technical analysis tools like the moving average to maximize their effectiveness.

#97 - Multiple wicks to the downside

This pattern occurs following a prolonged downtrend. Downward wicks signify a shift in investor sentiment. In this pattern, the wicks extend beyond the previous trading range, typically formed by Dojis, Spinning Tops, and Hammer Signals. A price gap up or a bullish candle indicates a change in indecisiveness, resulting in a robust rally.

Figure 97: Multiple Wicks to the Downside

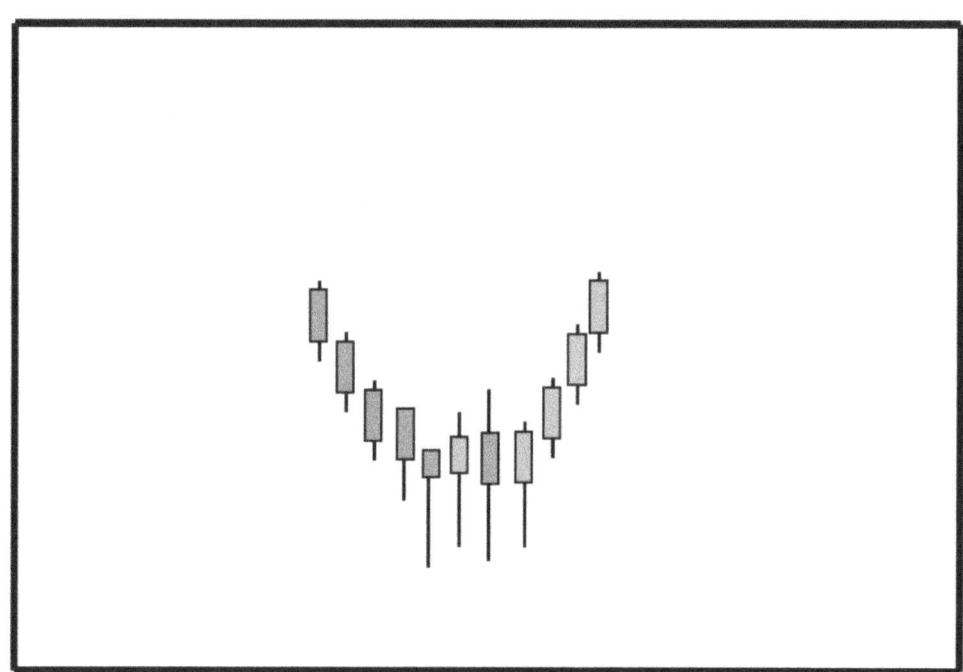

How to Trade Multiple Wicks to the Downside

A notable characteristic of this candlestick pattern is its clear indication of a reversal in direction. Wicks are often considered as potential reversal signals, and having a series of wicks at the end of a trend greatly increases the likelihood of a strong reversal. When trading the Multiple Wicks to the Downside pattern, it is important to consider the overall trend in addition to the candlestick pattern alone. The longer the wick, the higher the probability of a reversal, similar to the concept of a long shadow. As this pattern can be somewhat ambiguous, determining the optimal trade entry can be challenging. However, observing consecutive candles following the multiple wicks can serve as a strong indicator. The key to trading this pattern lies in patiently waiting for the subsequent candles to confirm the reversal.

#98 - On the Neck Line

This pattern bears a resemblance to the Meeting Line pattern, wherein Day 2 fails to reach the close of candle 1 but reaches its low. It entails the formation of a long red candlestick during a downtrend, with candle 2 opening lower than candle 1's close. The On the Neckline pattern is a bearish continuation pattern that can occur during a pullback or at the conclusion of a downtrend. Many traders perceive this pattern to be more dependable than its counterpart, the In the Neckline pattern.

Figure 98: On the Neck Line

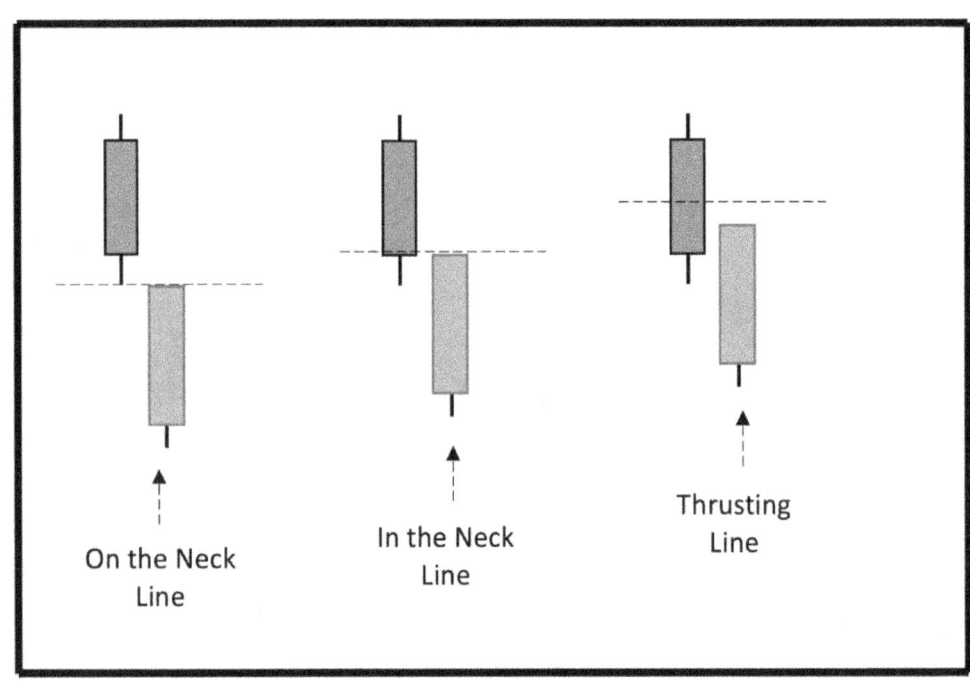

How to Trade On the Neck Line

Similar to the In the Neckline pattern, the On the Neckline pattern also signifies the strength of bearish sentiment in the market. This suggests that sellers will continue to exert downward pressure on the price. To confirm this trend, observe the candle on the third day; if it is red (or black), then the downtrend is likely to persist. While there may be instances of sideways movement, the overall trend is expected to continue downward. Place a support line below the second candlestick and wait for price breaks, particularly during periods of horizontal movement. Given its resemblance to the In the Neckline pattern, it is crucial for traders to exercise patience and careful observation to avoid mistaking one pattern for the other.

#99 - Piercing Pattern

body. There is a clear downtrend, and at the end of the trend, a long red candle is formed. On candle 2, the opening price is lower than the closing price of candle 1, and the green candlestick closes more than halfway up the red candlestick. The strength of the reversal increases with the length of the red and green candles, and a more significant reversal is observed when there is a larger gap down from the previous day's trading.

Figure 99: Piercing Pattern

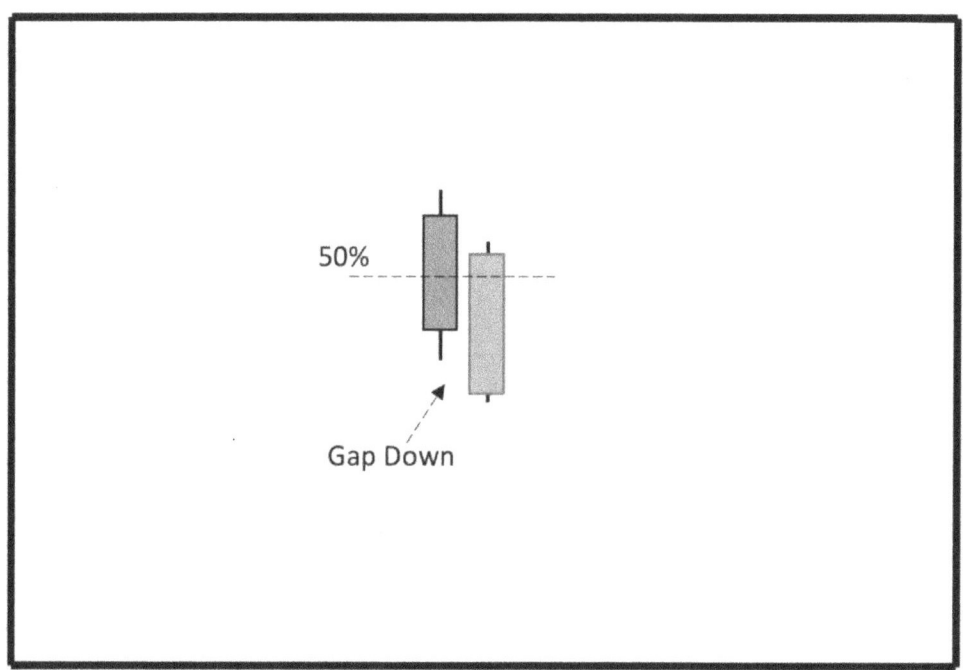

How to Trade Piercing Pattern

This pattern serves as an indicator of potential bullish reversals and is relatively straightforward to trade. The key to trading this pattern lies in paying close attention to two factors. Firstly, observe the breakaway gap, which occurs when two bullish candles appear, with the second candle opening higher than the closing price of the first. Secondly, position your support level just above the open of the first bearish candle and wait for the price to break above this support. Note that sometimes the price may gap away, while other times it may not. However, once you understand how to capitalize on this pattern, you will have no difficulty adapting to either scenario. It is always advisable to use other technical indicators to confirm the signals of this pattern, ensuring you maximize its effectiveness.

#100 - Pipe Bottom

This pattern bears resemblance to the Longhorn pattern, so it is important to exercise caution and avoid confusing the two. Throwbacks occur approximately 50% of the time, so it is advisable to be cautious of panic sales. Additionally, this pattern may exhibit similarities to the Head and Shoulders pattern. Early profits from this pattern typically average around 35%. It is a two-candlestick pattern that appears at the bottom of a bearish trend. The first candle is a Doji, and the second candle can be either a Hammer or a Dragonfly Doji.

Figure 100: Pipe Bottom

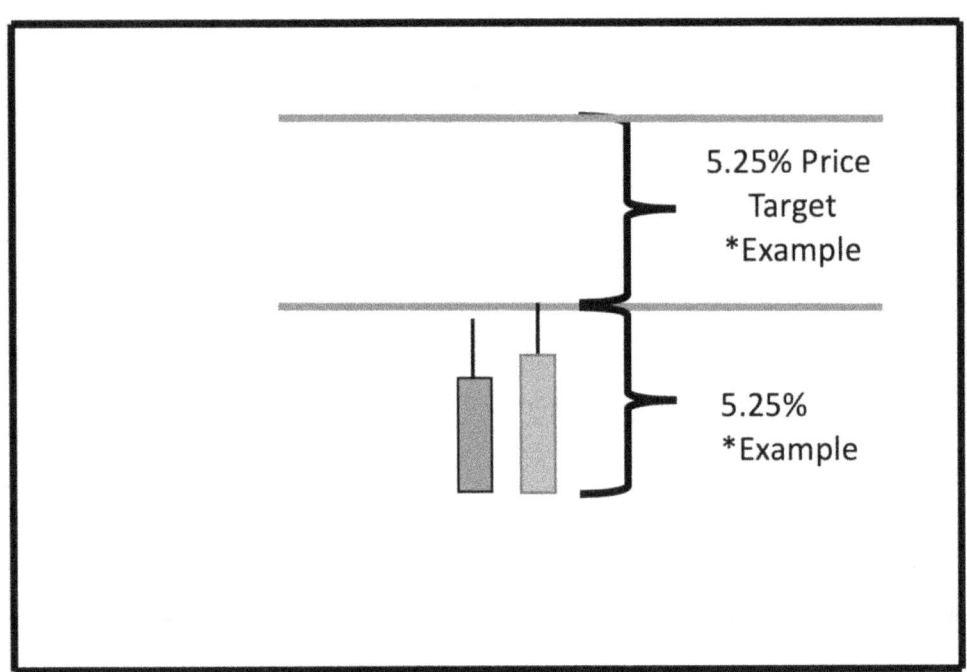

How to Trade Pipe Bottom

The Pipe Bottom candlestick pattern is a reliable indicator of trend reversal, typically occurring at the end of a downtrend. Traders can take advantage of this pattern by going long in anticipation of the reversal. To confirm the pattern, it is important to wait for the close of the bullish candle. Once the price breaks above this close, the pattern is validated, and it is an opportune time to enter a trade. When it comes to profit targets, one approach is to measure the distance between the pattern's high and low, and then add it to the highest point to determine the initial price target. Since the trend is likely to extend beyond this point, the same measurement can be used for subsequent price targets to maximize profitability with the Pipe Bottom candlestick pattern.

#101 - Pipe Top

Caution should be exercised not to confuse this pattern with the Longhorn pattern, as they share similarities. Pullbacks are known to occur approximately 30% of the time. Additionally, this pattern may resemble the Head and Shoulders pattern. Recognizing this pattern early can help protect profits. It is a two-candlestick pattern that typically appears at the top of a bullish trend. The first candle is a Hammer, followed by the second candle, which forms a Doji.

Figure 101: Pipe Top

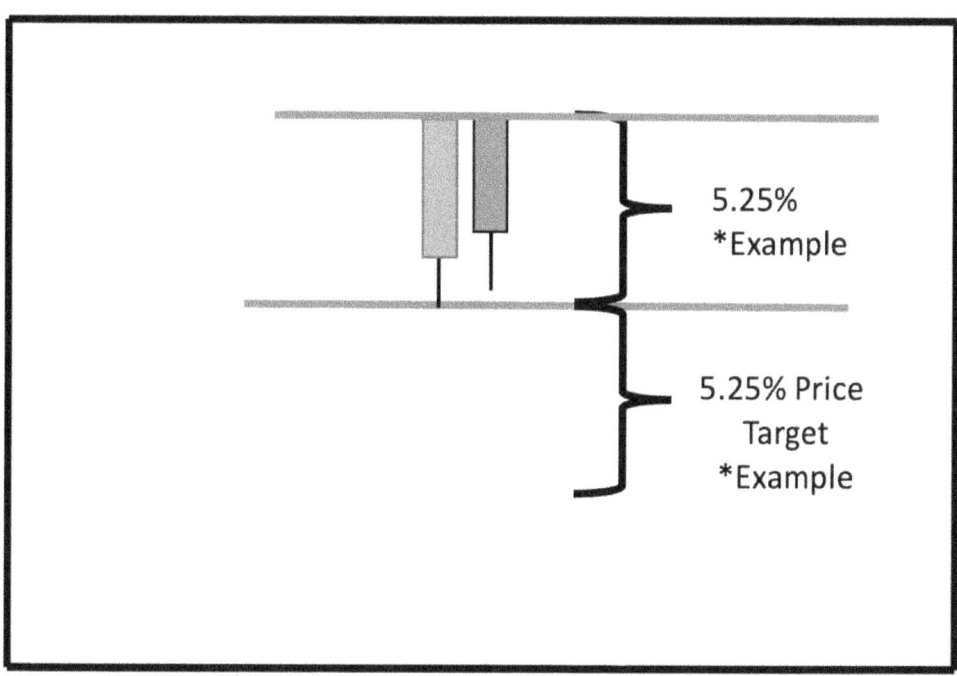

How to Trade Pipe Top

Trading the Pipe Top pattern follows a similar approach to the Pipe Bottom pattern, with reversed conditions. This pattern occurs at the end of an uptrend, providing an opportunity for traders to go short in anticipation of a reversal. To confirm the pattern, wait for the open of the longer bullish candle, and when the price breaks below this open, the pattern is validated, signaling a trade position. When setting profit targets, measure the distance between the pattern's high and low, and add it to the lowest point to establish the initial price target. Since the trend is likely to extend further downward, use the same measurement for subsequent price targets to maximize profitability with the Pipe Top candlestick pattern.

#102 - Pullback

A pullback is a common occurrence in a bearish market and presents an opportunity to generate quick profits. It is a key strategy that works well following a bearish breakout, with average profits typically around 5%. Importantly, this pattern always trades in the opposite direction of the prevailing trend.

Figure 102: Pullback

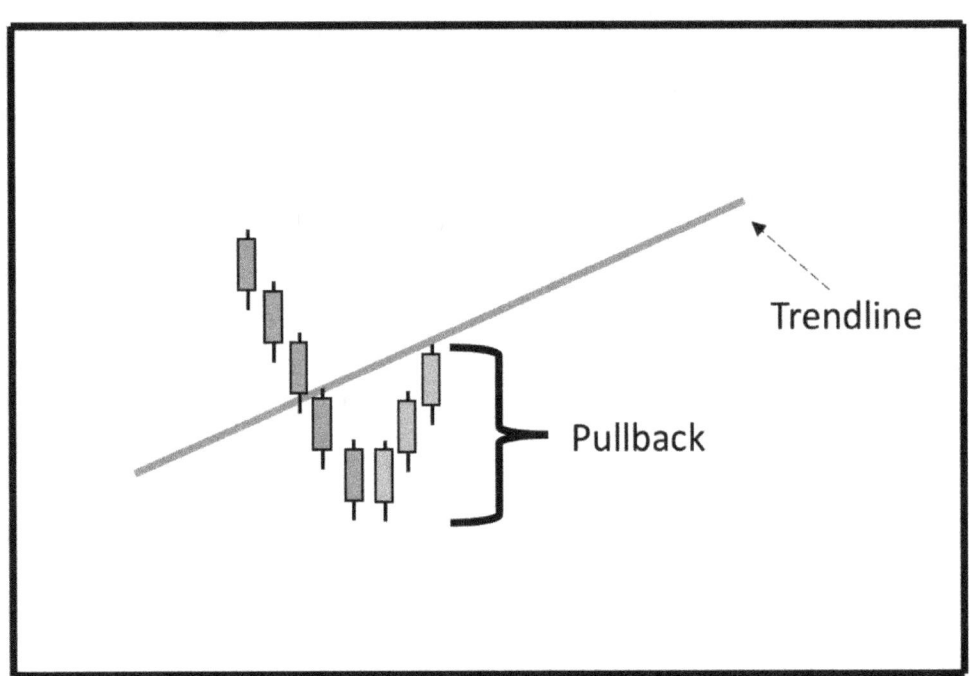

How to Trade Pullbacks

To effectively capitalize on trading pullbacks, it is crucial to identify a well-defined trend, enabling you to optimize profits while minimizing risks. Begin by identifying the trend and then switch to a timeframe that suits your trading preferences, preferably a lower timeframe. Next, locate the most recent high and low swings and draw a Fibonacci retracement between them. The objective is to enter a buy position within the 50% to 61.8% Fibonacci retracement area. Set your stop loss below the low swing area and place your take profit just above the last swing high. This strategy can help you make the most of pullback trading.

#103 - Rectangle Bottom

The bullish rectangle pattern is well-suited for trading purposes. The breakout typically occurs around 90% towards the beginning of the rectangle, regardless of whether it is a bullish or bearish trend. Pullbacks are observed approximately 60% of the time, while throwbacks occur around 85% of the time. These statistics can provide valuable insights when analyzing and trading the bullish rectangle pattern.

Figure 103: Rectangle Bottom

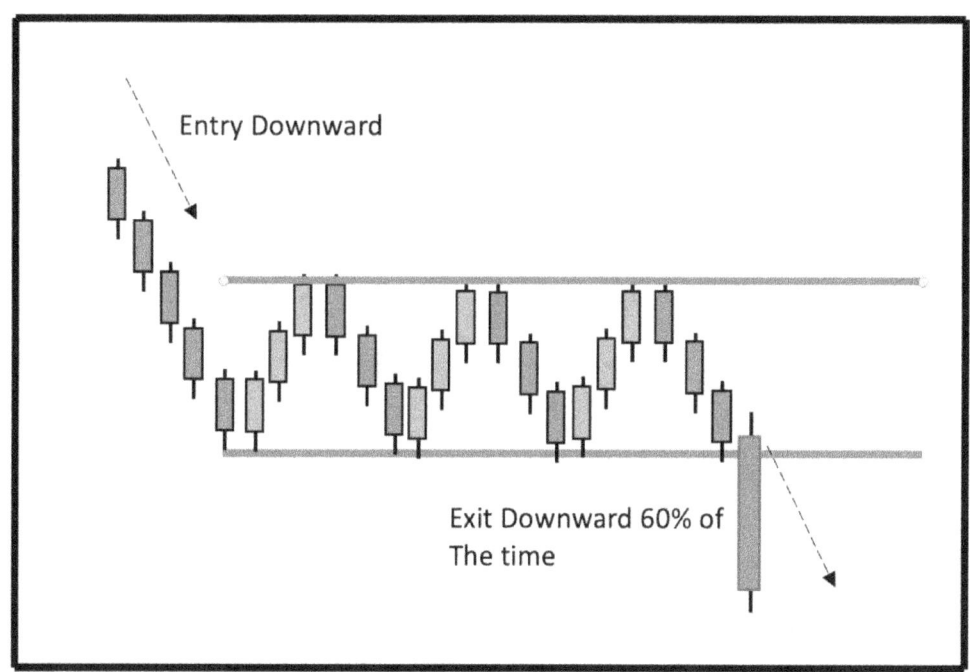

How to Trade Rectangle Bottom

When trading the Rectangle Bottom pattern, one of the primary tasks is to identify the existing trend. Draw support and resistance lines by connecting the highs and lows that form within the rectangle and wait for breakouts in the direction of the original trend. Before trading with the Rectangle Bottom pattern, confirm that there are no larger patterns in play. Determining the height of the rectangle can assist in establishing a price target for the breakout. While the pattern is generally reliable, it is advisable to use other technical indicators for added safety and   confirmation.

#104 - Rectangle Top

The bullish rectangle pattern is highly suitable for trading purposes. The breakout typically occurs around 80% towards the beginning of the rectangle, regardless of whether it is a bullish or bearish trend. Pullbacks are observed approximately 50% of the time, while throwbacks occur around 65% of the time. The support and resistance levels within the rectangle are relatively easier to identify compared to other breakout patterns. Moreover, this pattern can be implemented flexibly across various markets, making it a versatile tool for traders.

Figure 104: Rectangle Top

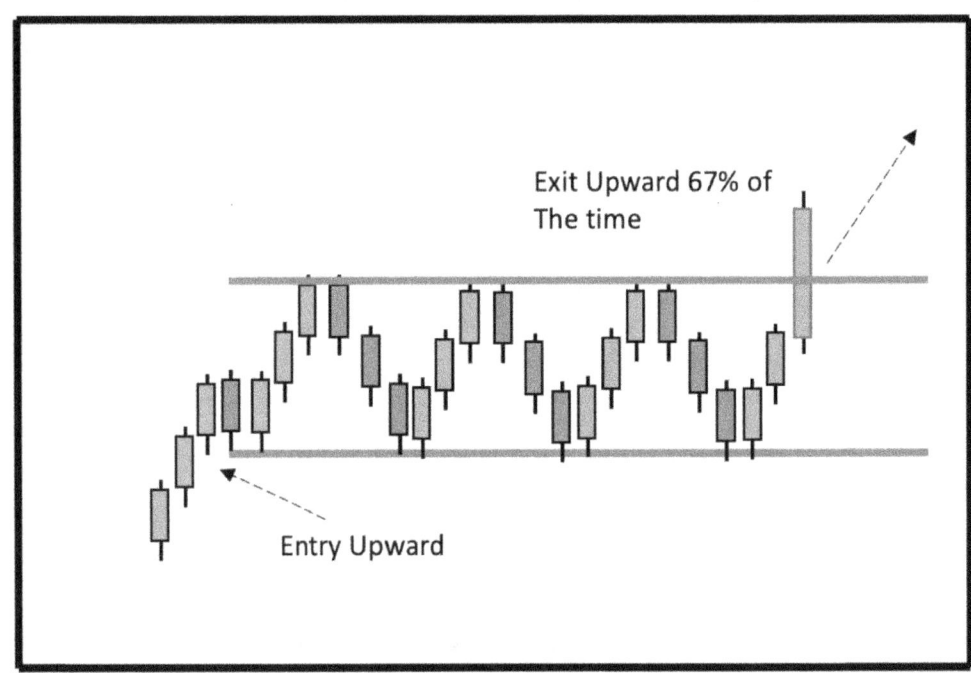

How to Trade Rectangle Top

When trading the Rectangle Top pattern, one of the primary tasks is to identify the existing trend. Draw support and resistance lines by connecting the highs and lows that form within the rectangle, and wait for breakouts in the direction of the original trend. Before deciding to trade with the Rectangle Top pattern, ensure that there are no larger patterns in play. Determining the height of the rectangle can greatly assist in establishing a price target for the Rectangle Top breakout. It is important to consider these factors when utilizing this pattern in your   trading   strategy.

#105 - Reverse Symmetrical Triangle

The 3x5 index card pattern is relatively easy to identify. It is characterized by three correction waves occurring at five different intervals. An essential aspect of this pattern is to recognize it promptly, as it signifies a diverging trendline. Notably, the lows within this pattern are higher than the highs, providing a key distinction. Traders should be attentive to these features when spotting and utilizing the 3x5 index card pattern in their analysis and decision-making processes.

Figure 105: Reverse Symmetrical Triangle

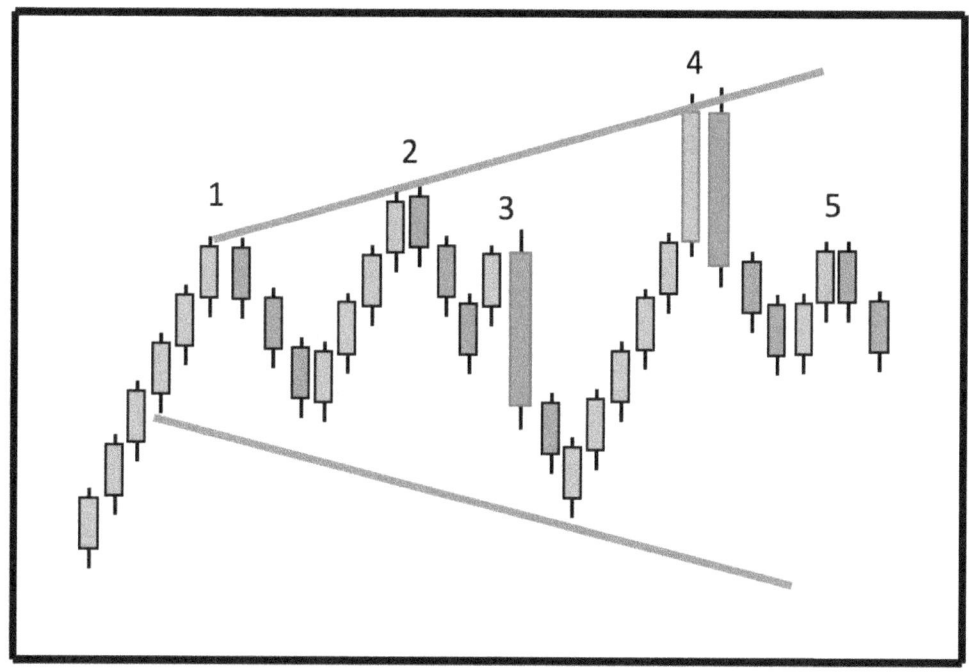

How to Trade Reverse Symmetrical Triangle

While the price may appear confined within this pattern, it is important to recognize that it cannot remain constrained indefinitely, making a breakout highly probable in either direction. Traders typically keep an eye out for such breakouts. However, it is not always advisable to enter trades immediately after the confirmation of this pattern. It is generally recommended to wait for a pullback and retest of the market. This approach allows for better timing of trade entry by observing the emergence of reversal patterns like the Engulfing pattern or the Hammer. Given the market's uncertain nature, implementing a trailing stop loss with a 50MA can be beneficial. This strategy helps manage risk and safeguard against sudden market fluctuations.

#106 - Rising Three Method

The Rising Three Method is a bullish continuation pattern that can be spotted in trading. It consists of a long bullish candlestick, followed by three smaller bearish candlesticks that are contained within the range of the first candlestick, and finally, another long bullish candlestick that exceeds the high of the first candlestick. This pattern indicates that after a brief consolidation, the uptrend is likely to continue. Traders can identify this pattern by looking for the specific candlestick formation and analyzing the candlestick sizes and their relationship to each other. It is important to note that confirmation and additional technical analysis should be used before making any trading decisions based on the Rising Three Method.

Figure 106: Three Method

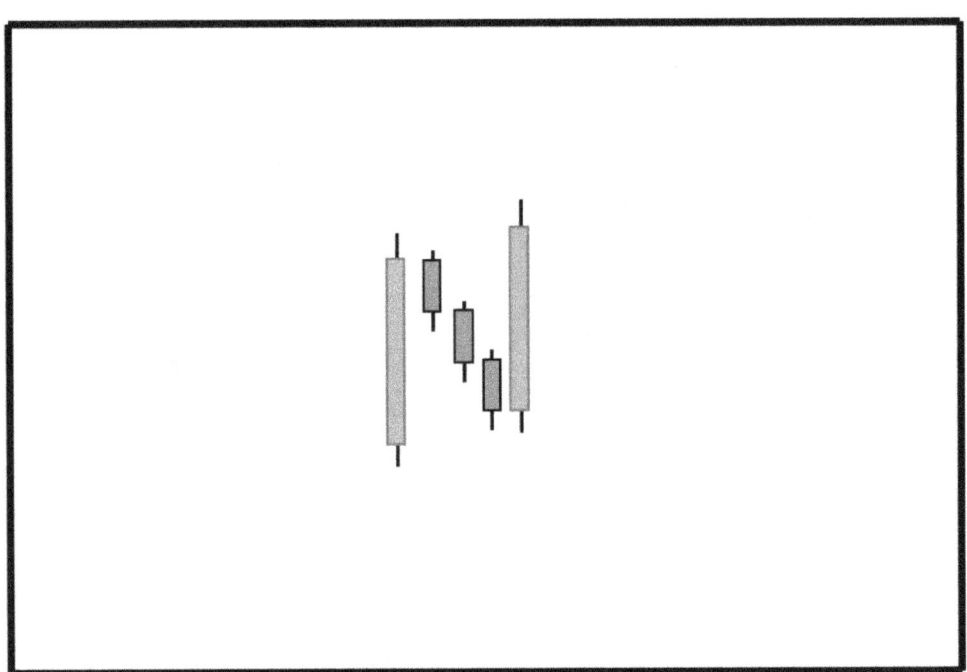

How to Trade Rising Three Method

Trading this candlestick pattern is similar to trading the Falling Three Method. It is a bullish continuation pattern that can be confusing if not properly understood. To enhance understanding and confirmation of this pattern, it is advisable to incorporate technical indicators such as the Relative Strength Index (RSI) and Moving Average line on the chart. These indicators can help validate the continuation of the trend. In many cases, the price of the commodity corrects itself, especially when the RSI indicates oversold conditions. Even if this correction does not occur immediately, it is likely to happen eventually. To confirm the pattern, plot a trendline above the bullish candles and wait for breakouts in the downward direction. Alternatively, waiting for the formation of the candle after the fifth one can provide a safer approach. If this candle is bearish, the pattern continuation is inevitable. However, if it is bullish, a reversal may be imminent.

#107 - Running Flat

This pattern consists of two 3-correction waves followed by a 5-wave Elliott Wave. All waves in this pattern follow the Elliott Wave rules. Because the start and end of this pattern are at or near a +/-3% margin, it makes for a fairly easy opportunity to trade and generate good profits. This is a rare pattern, so it is much better to check for a configuration of the 3-3-5 subwave.

Figure 107: Running Flat

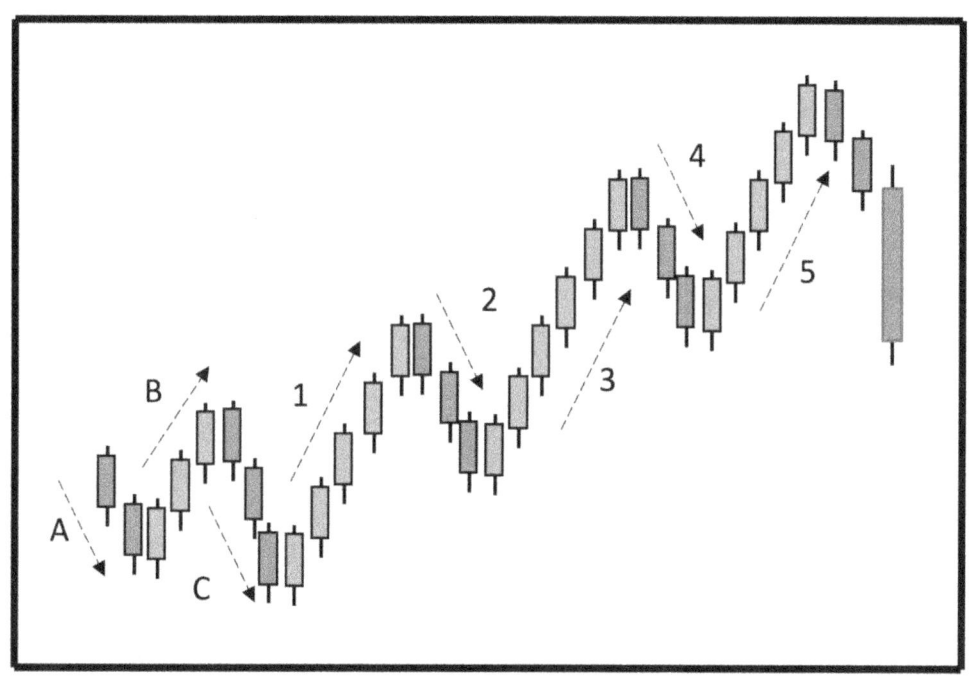

How to Trade Running Flat

As rare as this candlestick pattern is, it is also a complex pattern to identify, confirm, and trade. The key to identifying and confirming this pattern is to count the number of waves using the subwave configuration 3-3-5. A different combination indicates that it is not the same pattern. The ABC rules guide this candlestick pattern for confirmation, where Wave B reverses beyond the starting point of Wave A, and Wave C reverses before the end of Wave A. This pattern is both rare and risky, requiring a great deal of patience from traders.

#108 - Scoop Pattern

This pattern resembles an ice cream scoop. It has an extended flat trading period consisting of indecisive signals like the Doji, small Hammers, and Star formations that never break out of a narrow range. The flat trading period serves as a signal for a potential scoop pattern. The Scoop is formed by a few days of selling, followed by bullish candles and small buy signals that bring the trading up to the handle level, forming the Scoop. Once the price rises above the handle, an extended period of uptrend continues.

Figure 108: Scoop Pattern

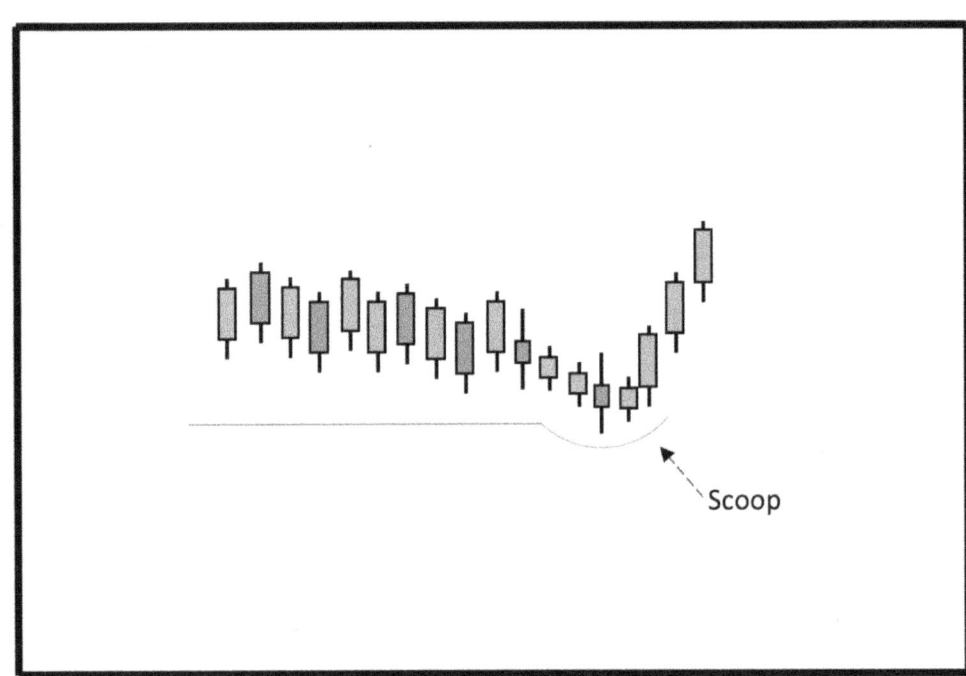

How to Trade Scoop Pattern

This candlestick pattern begins with strong market indecision, but it is important to keep an eye out for a rise in prices, particularly those that surpass the handle of the Scoop pattern. To confirm this pattern, you can set a resistance level above the indecisive candles that form the handle of the scoop and patiently wait for the price to break above the resistance line. Once this occurs, it is likely that the trend will continue in the bullish direction. The rise in price is driven by traders who are attracted to the brief decline that forms the Scoop, anticipating its subsequent rise. Placing a stop-loss order below the candle with the lowest low can help manage potential losses.

#109 - Separating Line

This pattern is a trend continuation pattern. For a bullish separating lines pattern, it must occur within an uptrend with a long bearish (red or black) candle as its first candle. This is followed by a long bullish (green or white) candle with a pullback. The pattern shows a pullback indicated by a long red candle, and on candle 2, the price opens at the same level as candle 1, except it has no lower wick and moves in the opposite direction of the first candle but closes higher. The separating line pattern is the exact reverse of the meeting line pattern.

Figure 109: Separating Line

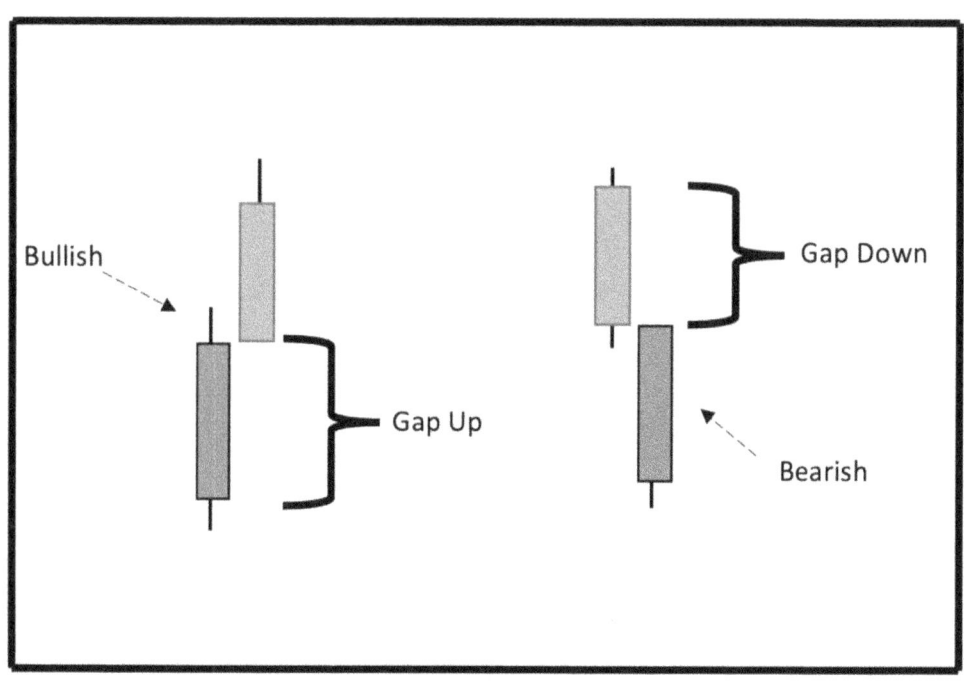

How to Trade Separating Line

Although the bears struggle to take control of the market, they lack the force to drive it further down and initiate a reversal. Due to this and other reasons, the Separating Line pattern is relatively easy to identify and trade. To manage risk, it is advisable to place a stop loss at the opening of either candle to account for potential retracements, although they are unlikely. The appearance of the bullish candle indicates that the bears have lost their grip on market control, increasing the likelihood of a continuation in the bullish trend. While this candlestick pattern is easy to identify on a price chart, it rarely occurs. It is essential to confirm the pattern before trading by patiently observing the candle that follows the second bullish candle.

#110 - Shooting Star

The Shooting Star formation occurs when there is minimal movement in the trading period, and the open, low, and close prices are roughly the same. The upper wick should be at least twice the length of the real body. The color of the real body is not significant, but it should be positioned at the lower end of the trading range. There is either no lower wick or a very small one. To confirm the signal, additional trading days can be observed, such as a solid candle or a gap down with a lower close on the following day. A longer upper wick indicates a higher potential for a reversal. In this pattern, a stronger reversal is possible if there is an upward gap from the previous day's close and the Shooting Star signal opens lower. A blow-off day may occur when there is significant volume on a Shooting Star day.

Figure 110: Shooting Star

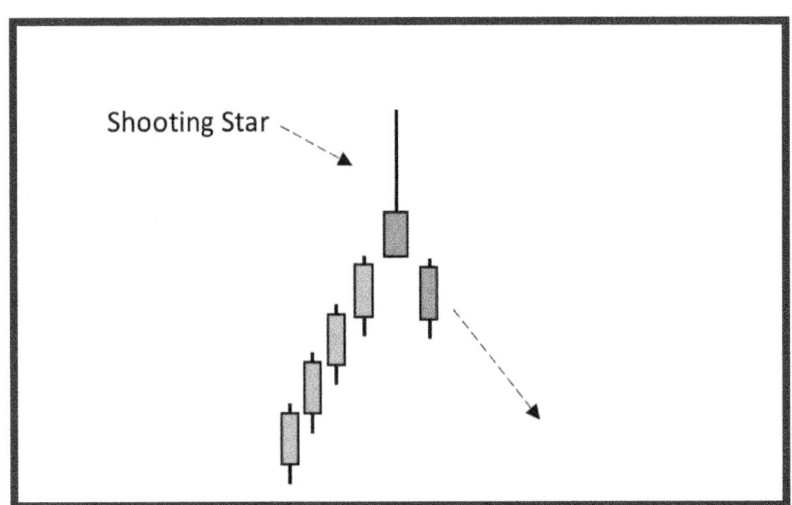

How to Trade Shooting Star

Depending on its position on the price chart, the Shooting Star candlestick pattern can indicate a bullish or bearish reversal. Therefore, the key to trading this pattern is to identify it and trade in the opposite direction of the current trend. If the Shooting Star appears at the top of an uptrend, it suggests a potential short (sell) position, whereas in a downtrend, it may signal a long (buy) position. As one of the most reliable candlestick patterns, the Shooting Star can be highly profitable if utilized correctly. The reliability of the pattern increases with more preceding bullish candles. It's important to note that the candle following the Shooting Star is crucial as it confirms the pattern and signals traders to take a short position (sell). To ensure certainty, set a resistance level above the wick of the Shooting Star, which can also serve as a stop-loss zone.

#111 - Side by Side White Line

This pattern occurs during an uptrend. The Side by Side White Line pattern is characterized by two adjacent green candlesticks following a gap up from the previous day's candlestick. This formation indicates a temporary pause or a stalemate in the market. When all three candlesticks in the pattern are green, it suggests a bullish signal, whereas if all the candles are red, it indicates a bearish signal. On candle3, the opening and closing prices are near those of candle 2.

Figure 111: Side by Side White Line

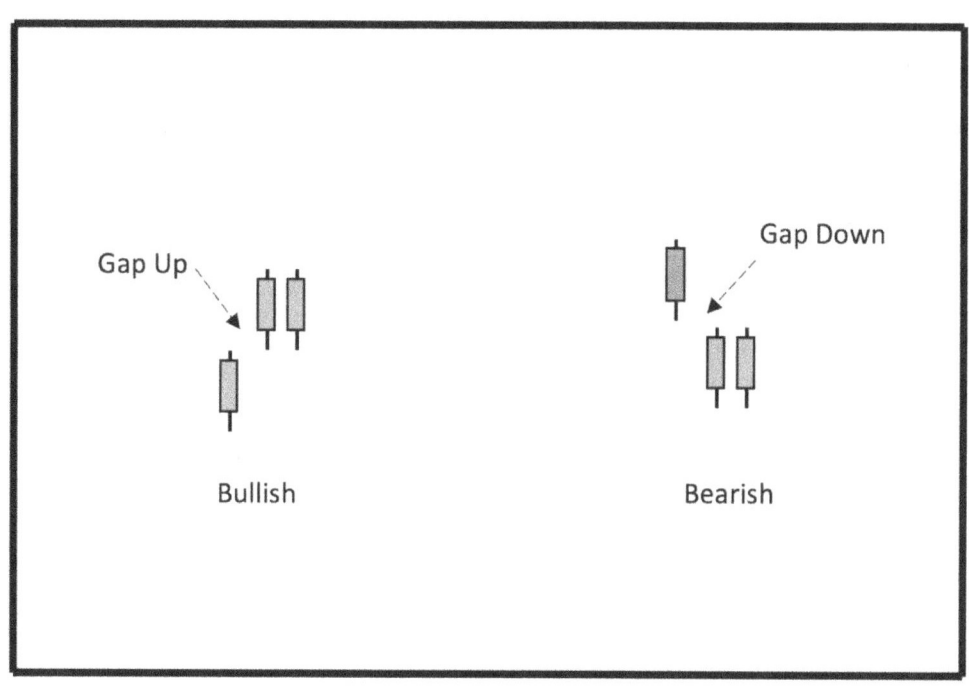

How to Trade Side by Side White Line

Depending on the placement of the Side-by-Side White Line pattern, it can indicate either a bullish or bearish continuation, with taller twin candles typically generating stronger patterns. While the pattern may sometimes lack clarity, it is generally regarded as a robust bullish indicator. However, like many technical analysis tools, the Side-by-Side White Line pattern requires confirmation before initiating a trade. This confirmation can come in the form of a higher close or another gap. To manage risk, consider placing a stop loss at the closing price of the last candle preceding the gap. This can help alleviate any concerns and provide a level of protection.

#112 - Spikes

This pattern, if it can even be classified as one, is highly prevalent in the cryptocurrency market. Spikes in price action are associated with higher levels of risk but can also generate quick profits. It is recommended to set profit targets of less than 2% when trading these spikes. Such price movements often occur following the dissemination of false news, which triggers panic among certain traders.

Figure 112: Spikes

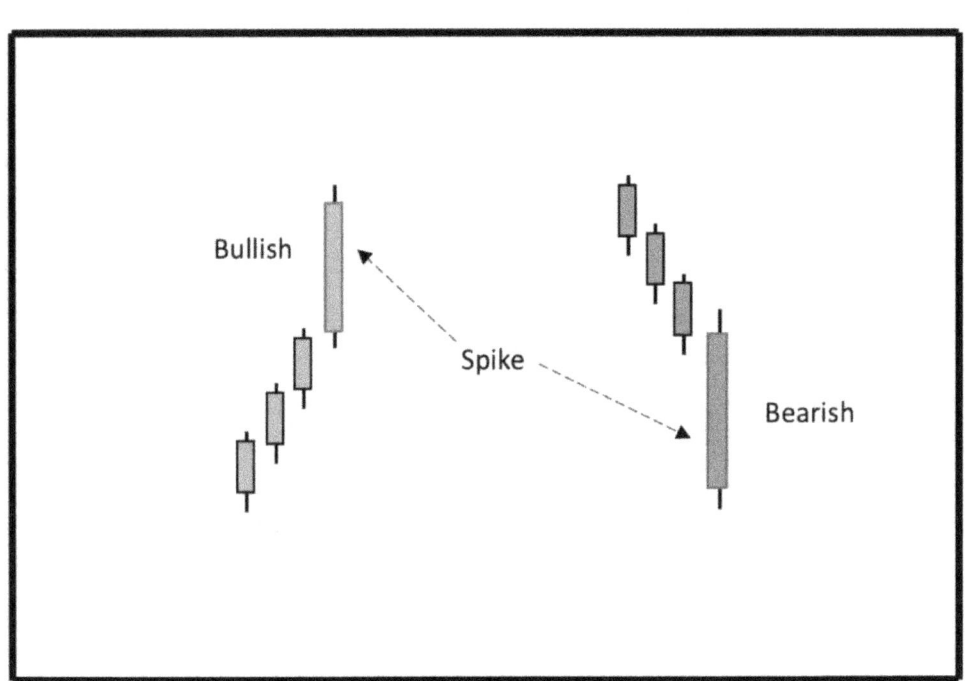

How to Trade Spikes

Spikes come in various types, and your ability to identify them determines the potential profitability. Certain spikes are known to reverse a trend, and traders who can recognize this type of spike can anticipate the formation of a new trend in the near future. Other spikes create a ranging market trend, providing traders with an opportunity to anticipate a breakout in either direction. The key to trading spikes lies in understanding support and resistance levels, as well as analyzing fundamental data such as market news. It is crucial to remember that information plays a vital role in successfully trading spikes, as it helps inform your trading direction.

#113 - Stick Sandwich

The Stick Sandwich pattern is composed of two red candlesticks with a green candlestick in between. In this pattern, the closing prices of the candlesticks on Day 1 and Day 3 are identical, indicating a level of support in the price. The Day 3 candlestick completely engulfs the Day 2 candlestick and closes at the same level as Day 1, suggesting a high likelihood of a trend reversal. As this pattern is not specific to a particular direction, it can indicate both bearish and bullish signals. Traders who utilize this pattern focus on Day 3 for further insights and confirmation.

Figure 113: Stick Sandwich

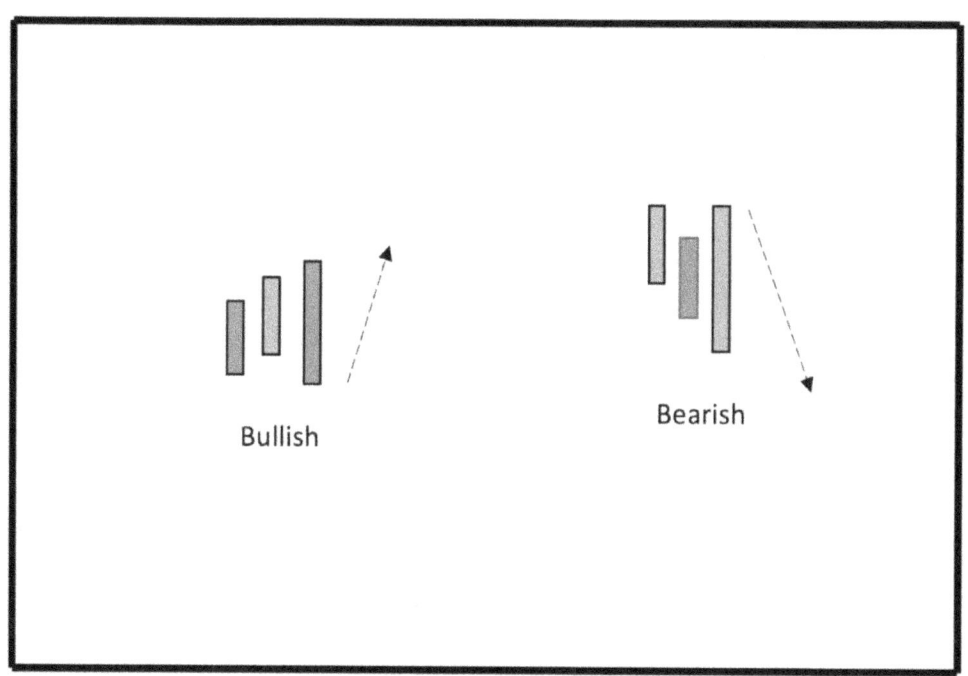

How to Trade Stick Sandwich

One important aspect to consider when trading the Stick Sandwich pattern is the color of the candles, as it determines whether the pattern is bullish or bearish. In a bearish Stick Sandwich, the middle candle is red, sandwiched between two green candles (as shown in the figure above). Conversely, in a bullish Stick Sandwich, the middle candle is green, surrounded by two red candles. To profit from the bearish Stick Sandwich pattern, it is advisable to wait for the price to break below the low of the third candle before entering a position. Similarly, for the bullish pattern, wait for the price to break above the high of the third candle before taking a position.

#114 - The Breakaway

Whether bullish or bearish, the Stick Sandwich pattern signifies a trend acceleration. The pattern begins with a long candle that reflects the existing trend, which remains unchanged until the fifth candle. The only potential variation is the color of the candle on candle 3. By the fourth candle, the trend starts to lose momentum and undergoes a reversal on candle 5, indicated by a candle of the opposite color to that of candle 4. This trend persists until the gap from Day 2 is closed.

Figure 114: Breakaway

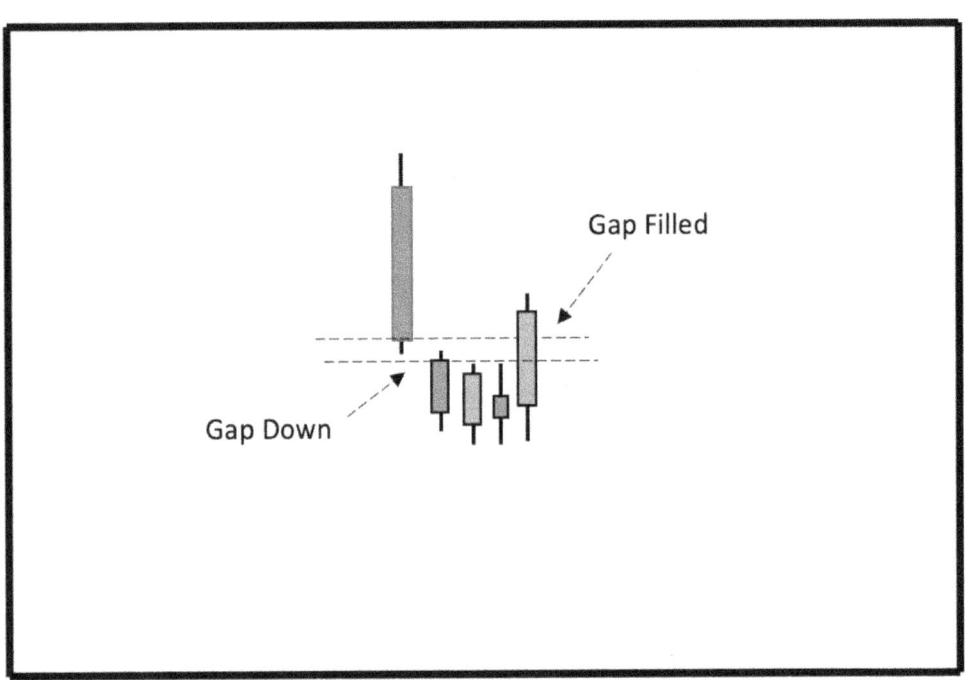

How to Trade The Breakaway

This pattern is often regarded as a bullish reversal candle, but in many cases, trading in the bearish direction proves to be more profitable. The breakaway pattern can be complex to trade, but once understood, it offers significant profit potential. Since the effectiveness of the breakaway pattern can vary depending on timeframes and charts, it is crucial to combine it with other technical analysis tools and strategies. Utilizing a chart tool to gather relevant data and determine the most likely breakout direction is essential. Trading blindly without proper analysis can result in substantial losses and should be avoided.

#115 - The Falling Three Method

This pattern is essentially the opposite of the Rising Three Method, occurring within a downtrend. The Falling Three Method starts with a long red candlestick, followed by a sequence of smaller candles that gradually rise. Typically, between two and five counter-trend candle can be observed, with three being the most common. Importantly, none of these candle close higher than the open of the initial long red candlestick, including the wick. The final candle of the pattern should open below the body of the previous uptrend candle and close below the closing price of the initial red candlestick from candle1.

Figure 115: Falling Three Method

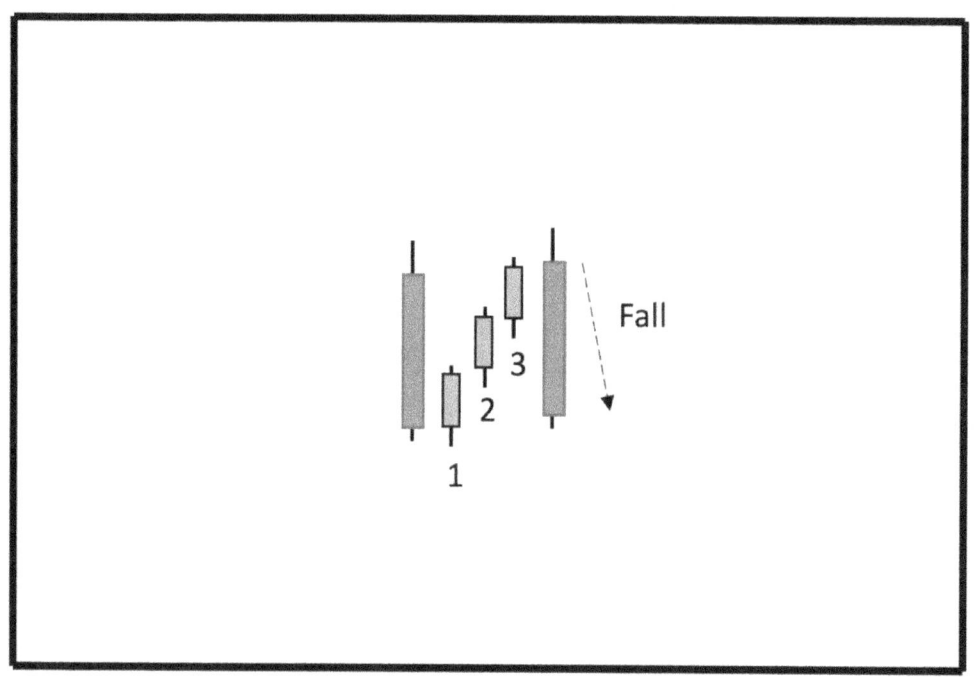

How to Trade The Falling Three Method

This pattern is a bearish continuation pattern that can be confusing if not properly understood. It is advisable to supplement the chart with technical indicators such as the RSI and Moving Average line to confirm the pattern. These indicators can help determine if the trend is indeed continuing. In many cases, the price of the commodity corrects itself, especially when the RSI indicates oversold conditions. Even if this correction doesn't occur immediately, it is likely to happen eventually. To confirm the pattern, draw trendlines above and below the bullish candles and wait for downward breakouts. Another approach is to wait for the formation of the candle after the fifth one. If it is bearish, the pattern continuation is likely; if it is bullish, a reversal may be imminent.

#116 - The Rising Method

This pattern is an extension of the Rising Three Method pattern. It typically consists of three to six indecisive days characterized by Dojis or Spinning Tops, indicating sellers' uncertainty. The final pullback candlestick should not close below the open of the last bullish candlestick, signaling a potential continuation of the upward trend. After the final day, the trend typically resumes its upward trajectory.

Figure 116: The Rising Method

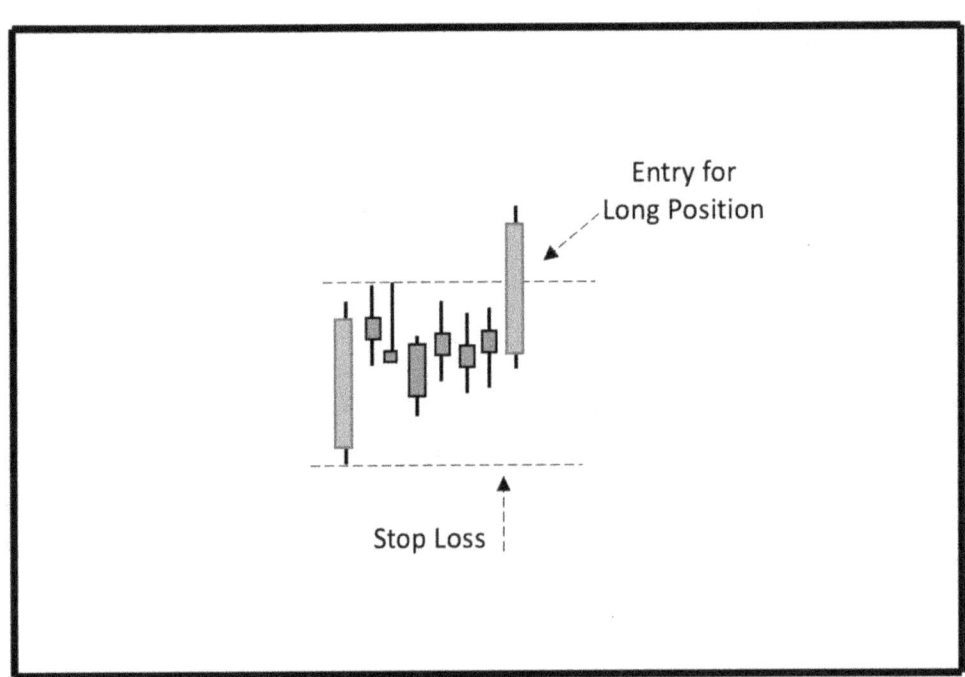

How to Trade the Rising Method

Trading this pattern is similar to trading the Rising Three Method. It is advisable to utilize technical indicators such as the RSI and Moving Average line on the price chart to confirm the pattern. This helps to determine if the trend is indeed continuing. Similarly to the Rising Three Method, plotting a trendline above and below the bearish candles and waiting for upward breakouts can be effective. To further ensure safety, wait for the formation of the candle after the second bullish candle. If it is bullish, the pattern continuation is likely, but if it is bearish, a reversal may be imminent.

#117 - Three Black Crows

This pattern derives its name from its resemblance to three crows perched and looking down. It typically appears following a robust uptrend, signaling an anticipation of lower prices. Each candlestick in the pattern should close near its daily low. Furthermore, each day's opening price should fall within the real body of the previous day's trading. The pattern consists of three consecutive red candlesticks with similar lengths.

Figure 117: Three Black Crows

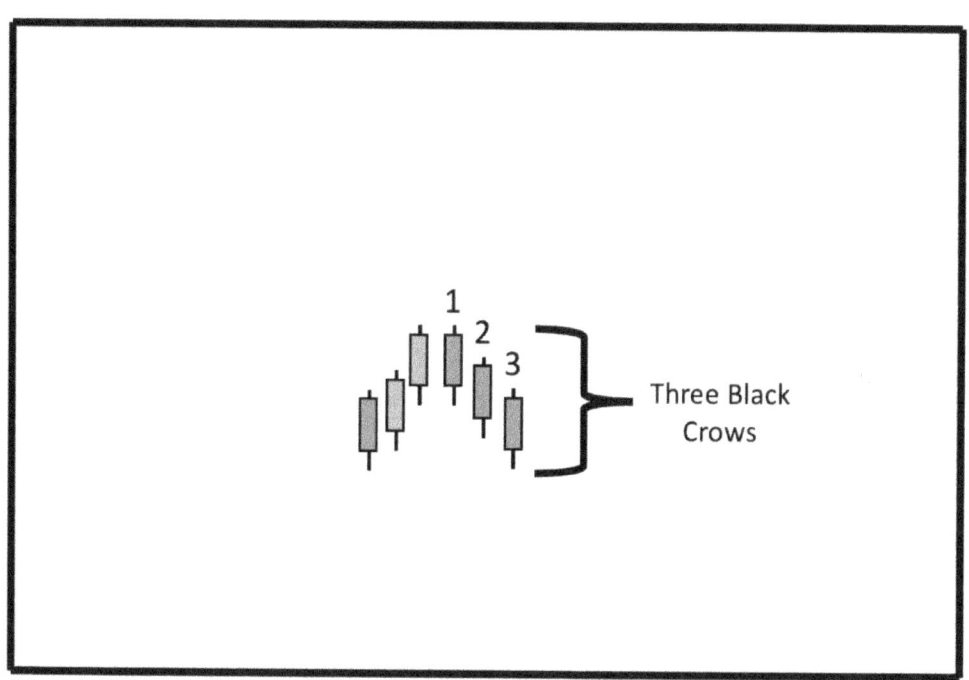

How to Trade Three Black Crows

The Three Black Crows pattern is typically a bearish reversal pattern that provides traders with an opportunity to initiate short trades or exit long positions. It is worth noting that this pattern can also appear within a downtrend, making it particularly advantageous for swing traders. On its own, the pattern indicates a 51% probability of a price decline. In many instances, the Three Black Crows pattern extends into the bearish three-line strike pattern. One challenge you may encounter is pullbacks, which can be managed through the use of stop losses. This allows you to prepare for increased volatility before entering the market at its peaks.

#118 - Three Identical Crows

The Three Identical Crows pattern occurs following a robust uptrend. It consists of three consecutive red candlesticks with similar lengths. Each day's trading opens at the close of the previous day, and the closing price is near the day's low. This pattern also serves as a bearish reversal signal and bears resemblance to the Three Black Crows pattern.

Figure 118: Three identical Crows

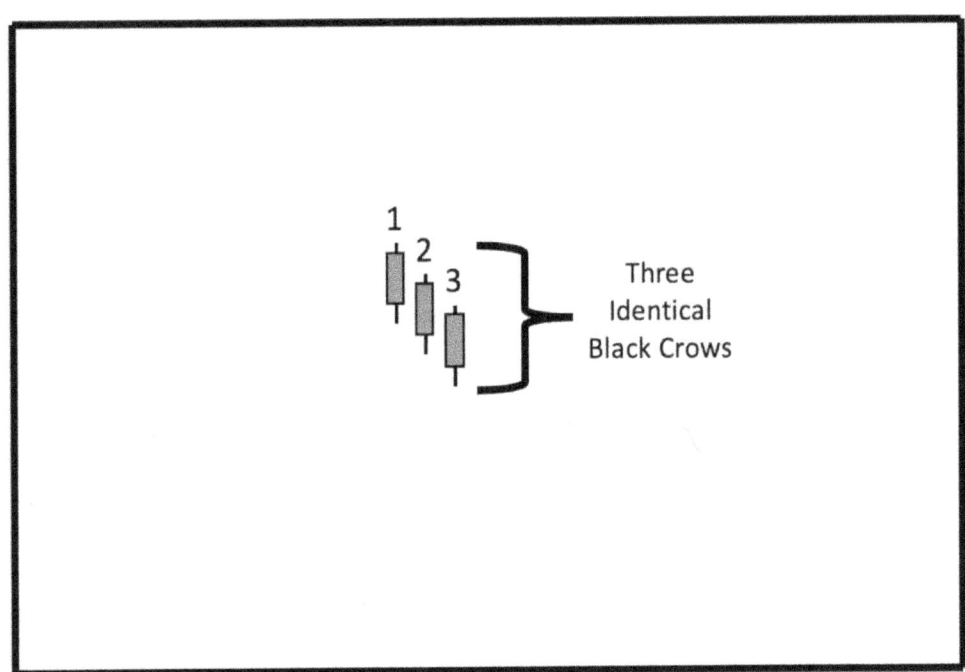

How to Trade Three Identical Crows

This pattern is indicative of a battle between bulls and bears, typically occurring when the market is in a range between support and resistance levels. When this pattern appears during an uptrend, a downward breakout is expected, followed by a quick recovery. It is crucial to closely monitor price volumes as they provide insights into market performance. Additionally, be alert for breakouts below the 50-trading day Moving Averages, as they often result in the strongest performances. In certain cases, the market may consolidate after the Three Identical Crows pattern before resuming its bearish trajectory.

#119 - Three Inside Up and Three Upside Down

This is a three-day pattern known as the Harami pattern. The most significant aspect of this pattern is the Harami body, which has a color opposite to that of the long candle day. Additionally, on Day 3, the closing price is higher than the opening price of Day 1. If the pattern occurs during a downtrend, it is considered bullish. Conversely, if the pattern appears during an uptrend, it is considered bearish.

Figure 119: Three Inside Up and Three Upside Down

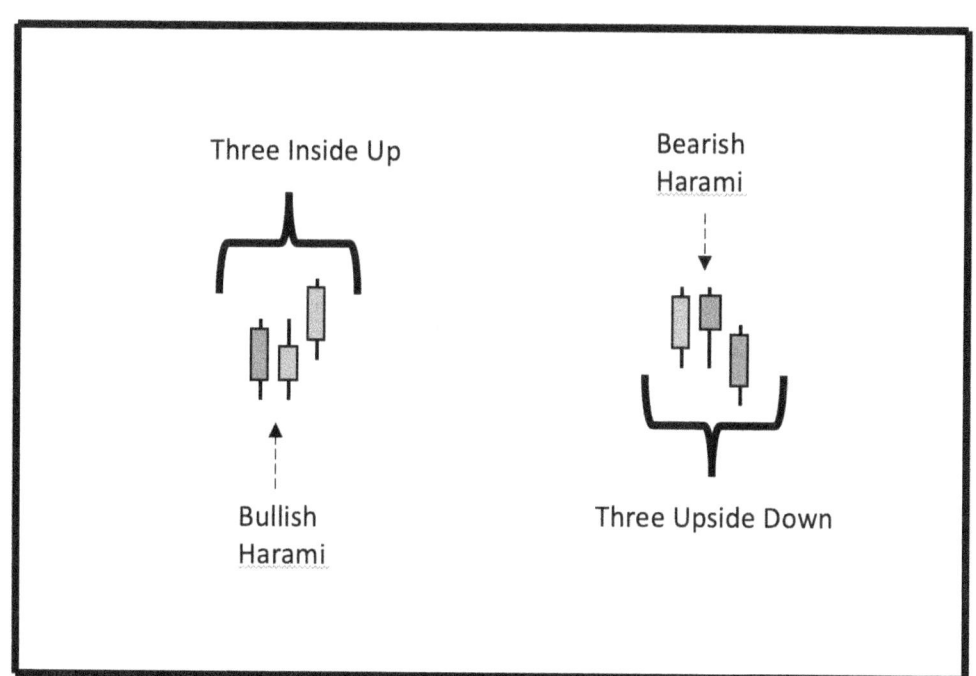

How to Trade Three Inside Up and Three Upside Down Pattern

Although the Three Inside Up pattern can occur in both uptrends and downtrends, the underlying principle remains the same. In the depicted scenario, despite the bears dominating the market, the bulls manage to stage a rally and seize control. The second bullish candle illustrates their ability to drive the price higher. Additionally, a Three Inside Up pattern with a longer second candle indicates a stronger trend reversal. While the third candle provides confirmation, many traders prefer to wait for a fourth candle, a gap up, or other forms of confirmation before entering a trade position. Using additional technical analysis tools can help instill confidence in your decision-making process.

#120 - The Rising Three Method

This pattern is a robust continuation pattern comprising five candles. The initial three candles depict a three-day pullback, with the requirement that their closing prices cannot be lower than the open of the preceding large bullish candle. On the final day, the bulls open the price and drive it above the close of the last bullish candlestick. This pattern indicates a strong likelihood of another uptrend. The closer the proximity of the candlesticks, the more significant the pattern becomes.

Figure 120: Three Inside Up and Three Upside Down

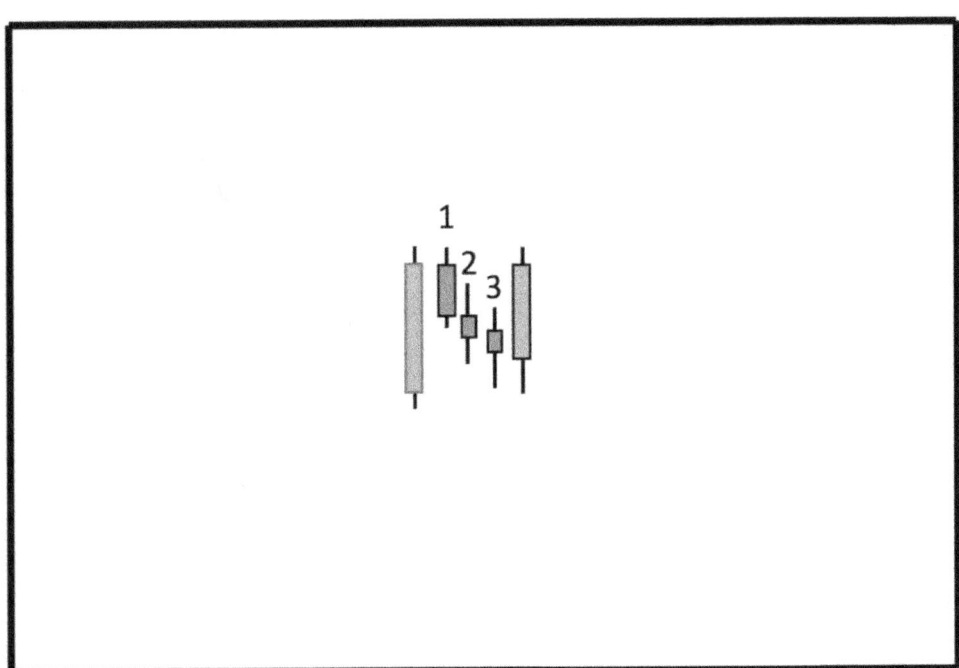

How to Trade Three Rising Method

This pattern can be confusing without a proper understanding. To confirm the pattern, it is advisable to use technical indicators such as the RSI and Moving Average line on the chart. These indicators can help determine if the trend is truly continuing. In most cases, the price of the commodity tends to correct itself, particularly when the RSI indicates overbought conditions. This correction may not happen immediately but is likely to occur eventually. To further confirm the pattern, plot a trendline above and below the bearish candles and wait for breakouts in the upward direction. Another cautious approach is to wait for the candle after the fifth one to form. If it is bullish, the pattern continuation is highly likely, but if it is bearish, a reversal may be imminent.

#121 - Three Stars in the South

The decrease in momentum of the trend is visually apparent in this pattern. The Advance Block pattern serves as the opposite signal to this pattern. In the Advance Block pattern, the final day of the downtrend features a long red body, and there is some buying activity indicated by the presence of a wick. Another notable characteristic is its resemblance to a Hammer candlestick pattern. On Day 2, there is a reduction in selling momentum, with a shape similar to Day 1 but on a smaller scale. Day 3 displays a Marubozu candlestick with no wick, and it falls within the trading range of Day 2. If the day following this pattern is bullish, it suggests the end of the downtrend.

Figure 121: Three Stars in the South

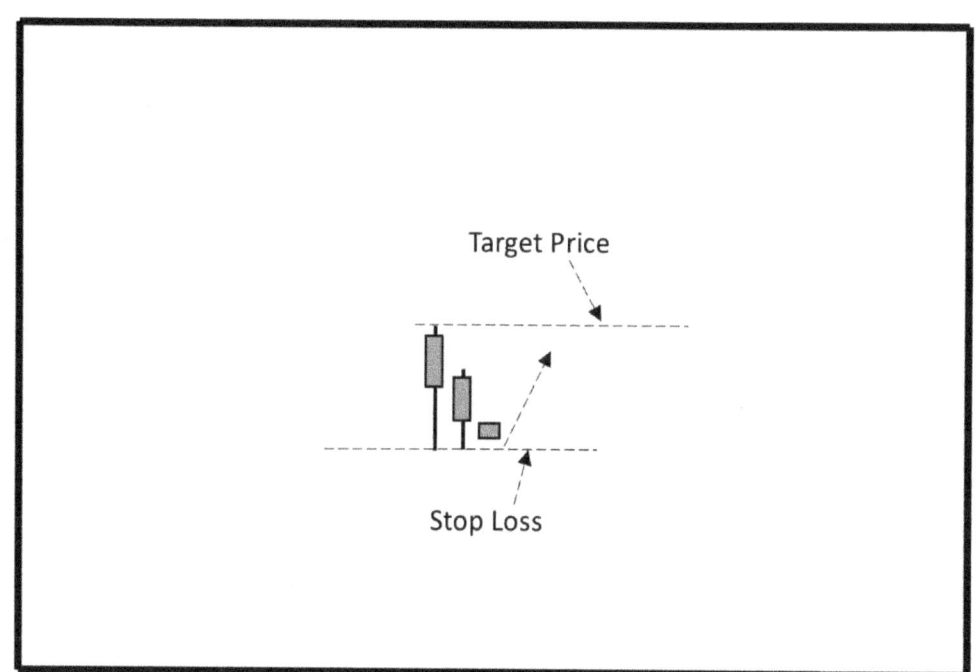

How to Trade the Three Stars in the South

This is a bullish reversal candlestick pattern that typically occurs at the end of a downtrend. It signifies a weakening of bearish strength and control in the market, indicating a potential bullish reversal. Traders can seize the opportunity to capitalize on this reversal by taking appropriate positions, and you should consider doing the same. This pattern is considered rare in trading, often referred to as a "lucky break." However, it is crucial to exercise caution. Place a resistance level at the midpoint of the last black body. If the price crosses above this level, it confirms the bullish reversal.

#122 - Three White Soldiers

This pattern is also referred to as the Advancing Three White Soldiers. The Three White Soldiers pattern indicates a robust market reversal. It consists of three consecutive green candlesticks, with the opening prices of Day 2 and Day 3 lower than the previous day's closing price. These candles close with new highs. Day 2 and Day 3 candles open within the body of the previous day's candle. The presence of very small wicks suggests a significant shift in the market. This pattern serves as the opposite of the Three Black Crows pattern.

Figure 122: Three White Soldiers

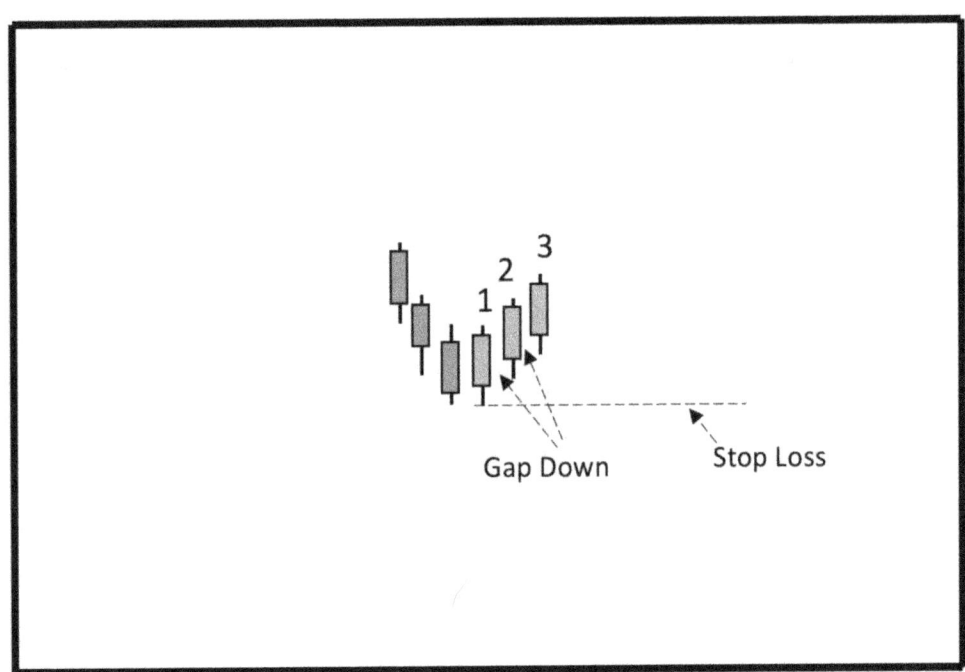

How to Trade Three White Soldiers

The Three White Soldiers pattern typically emerges following a downtrend, signaling the loss of control by bears and the reclaiming of control by bulls. The three consecutive bullish candles indicate that not only have the bulls regained control but they have also initiated an upward price movement. Long-term traders tend to benefit the most from this pattern, especially when it occurs at the conclusion of a robust downtrend. Although rare, once identified, this pattern can yield substantial profits. The key to capitalizing on this pattern is to trade in the direction of the bullish reversal.

#123 - Three Line Strike

This pattern is also known as the Fooling Three Soldiers. It is a variation of the Three White Soldiers pattern that appears within an uptrend. The Fooling Three Soldiers pattern occurs when, during a defined trend, Day 4 opens higher but then retraces and closes below the open of the first green candlestick. This retracement represents a brief resting period that takes place within a single day. Additionally, there are two types of the Three Line Strike pattern: the Bullish Three Line Strike and the Bearish Three Line Strike.

Figure 123: Three Line Strike

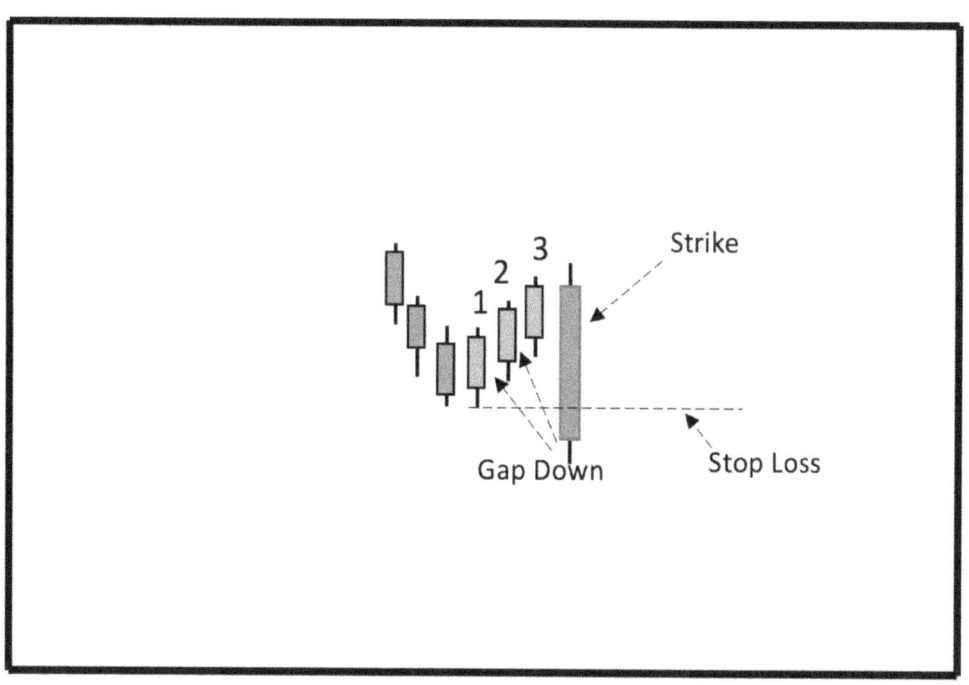

How to Trade Three Line Strike

The displayed Three Line Strike pattern signifies the dominance of bulls in the market. The pattern showcases a strong uptrend characterized by three consecutive bullish candles, demonstrating a consistent price progression. The presence of a bearish candle interrupts the previous progress, indicating a potential reversal pattern. Therefore, it is crucial to pay attention to the candle that follows the significant bearish or bullish candle. When trading this pattern, it is essential to prioritize risk management. With an 85% accuracy rate, this pattern proves to be quite reliable.

#124 - Thrusting

This candlestick pattern bears resemblance to the "on the neck" or "in the neck" patterns. It begins with a long red candlestick during a downtrend, followed by Day 2 which opens with a gap down from Day 1. The distinguishing factor of this pattern is that the real bodies are typically larger compared to the "on the neck" or "in the neck" patterns. Additionally, Day 2 closes slightly below the middle of Day 1's candlestick. Overall, this pattern indicates a bearish continuation pattern.

Figure 124: Thrusting

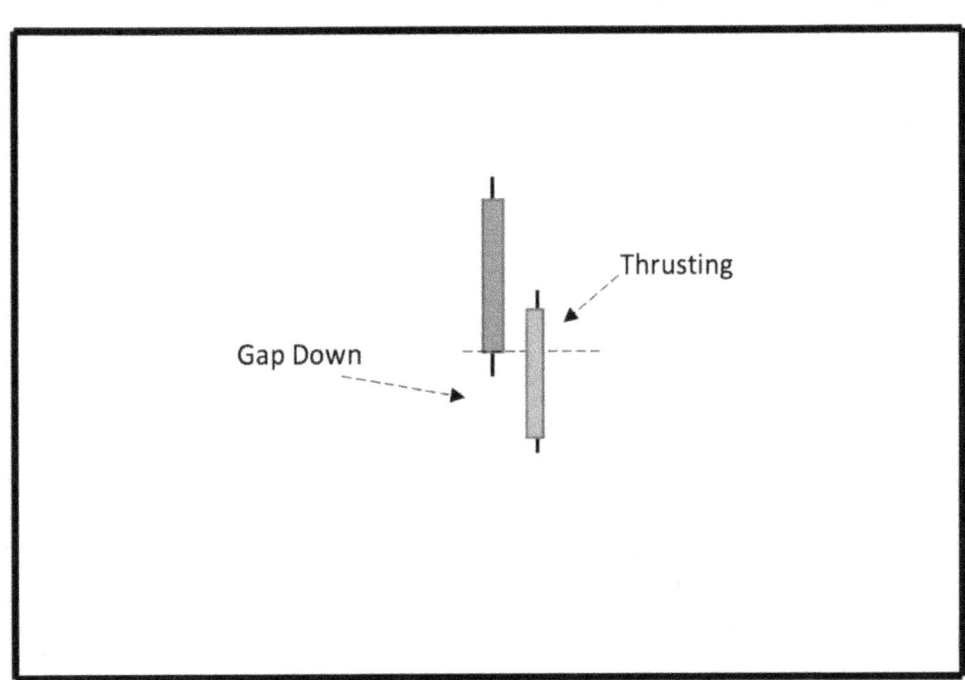

How to Trade Thrusting Pattern

In this pattern, the bulls make an attempt to intervene and seize control of the market but ultimately fail, indicating their lack of strength to initiate a trend reversal. Traders may anticipate a bullish reversal, only to be disappointed as the trend continues in the bearish direction. However, statistical data suggests that bullish reversals are more prevalent in the Thrusting pattern. Therefore, it is crucial to exercise patience and observe the third candle, and possibly the fourth, to confirm this pattern. Due to the inherent uncertainty, it is advisable to utilize other technical analysis tools for a comprehensive analysis before engaging in trading based on this pattern.

#125 - Trading Price Channels

This pattern occurs when trendlines can be drawn parallel to the top and bottom of the candlesticks. As two sets of parallel trendlines emerge, they become easily noticeable for chart followers. This pattern proves advantageous for investors as it enables them to identify market sentiment as the trendlines take shape. It is worth noting that this pattern can consist of up-trending, flat, or down-trending lines, making it applicable across various market conditions rather than being specific to a single trend.

Figure 125: Trading Price Channels

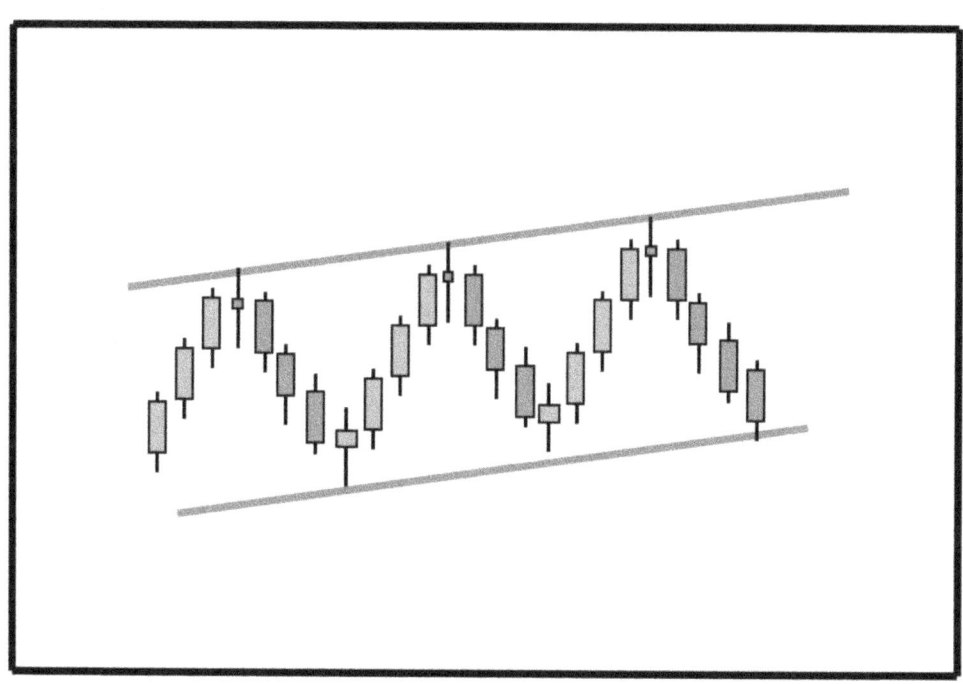

How to Trade Price Channels Pattern

Price Channels are considered one of the most effective methods for traders to profit from their trades, and they are also among the simplest chart patterns to understand. The primary advantage lies not in the Price Channel itself, but in the subsequent breakout. This breakout is what traders should actively watch for. To confirm a breakout, it is necessary to establish resistance and support lines above and below the price action, respectively. Price channels are not permanent, and a breakout is inevitable. However, traders can also capitalize on various trading opportunities that arise within the Price Channel. Price Channels are commonly observed in longer timeframes and can persist for days or weeks. Therefore, while waiting for a breakout, it is advisable to benefit from the trends within the larger trend.

#126 - Tri Star

The Tri Star pattern is a relatively uncommon formation that holds significant importance as a reversal indicator. It consists of three consecutive Doji candles. On Day 2, there is a gap either above or below the candles of Day 1 and Day 3. The length of the wicks is not excessively long. The larger the gap from the previous day's close, the stronger the potential for a reversal. Additionally, a high trading volume on any of the signal days enhances the likelihood of a substantial reversal. It is worth noting that the presence of gaps is not necessary for the shadows in this pattern.

Figure 126: Trading Price Channels

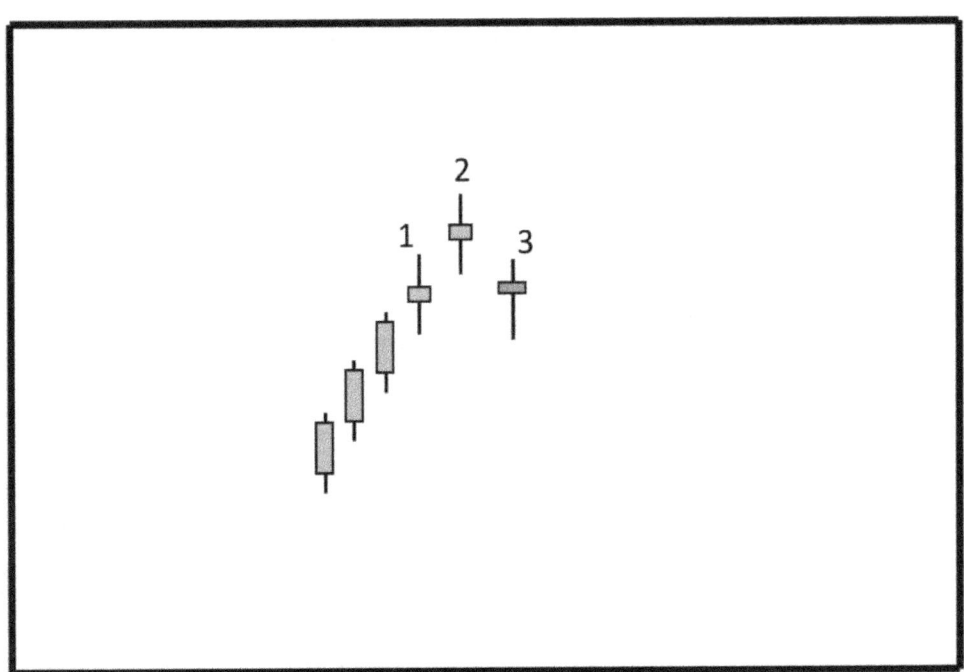

How to Trade Tri Star

The diminishing size of the candlestick bodies, particularly the first two Dojis, indicates a weakening trend and a shift in trader sentiment. Bullish traders exercise caution upon encountering the first Doji, while the second Doji prompts them to prepare for potential trade positions. The Tri Star pattern can manifest as either bullish or bearish, appearing at the conclusion of an upward or downward trend. Regardless of the trend direction, the same trading principle applies. To effectively trade this pattern, it is advisable to initiate a sell position at the close of the second Doji, with a stop-loss order set at the open of the same candle. The stop-loss order plays a crucial role in safeguarding against potential price increases rather than decreases.

#127 - Tweezer Bottom

The Tweezer Bottom pattern is characterized by two long wicks that extend below the trading range. An important feature of this pattern is that the lows are either identical or very close to each other at the bottom of the trading range. This indicates a robust level of support and signifies that buyers are growing more assertive in the market. The Tweezer Bottom pattern is considered a potent signal for a trend reversal.

Figure 127: Tweezer Bottom

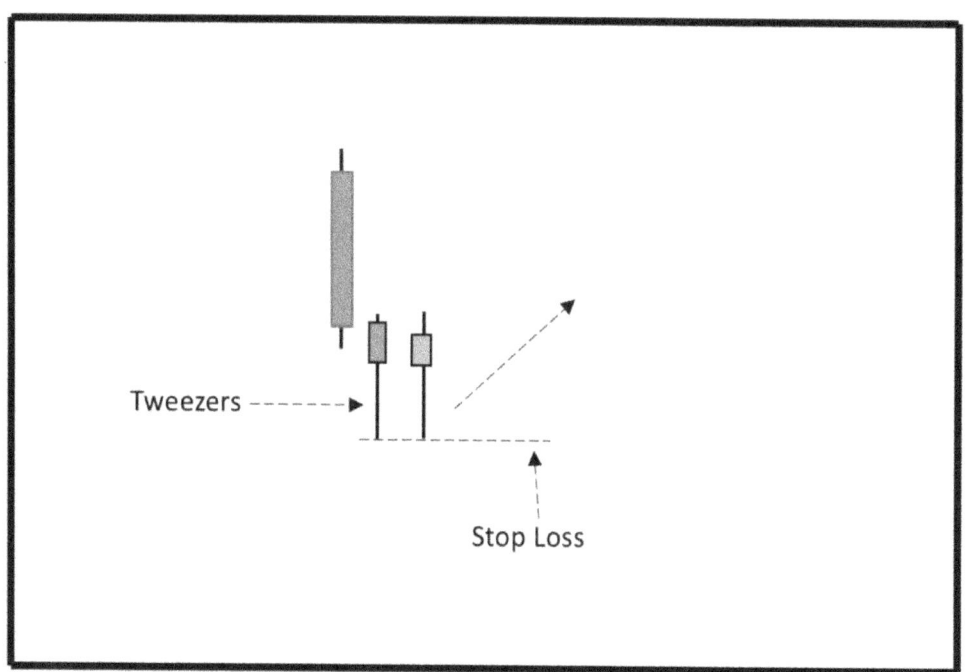

How to Trade Tweezer Bottom

The Tweezer Bottom is a reversal pattern that effectively illustrates the shift in sentiment from bears to bulls. Referring to the provided figure, it is advisable to position a resistance line just above the last candle with a substantial real body and wait for a breakout to transpire above this resistance level. Similarly, it is recommended to set the stop-loss order at an equal distance from the Tweezer as the resistance, ensuring risk management in the event of a retracement in the bearish direction. It is crucial to note that the utilization of other technical analysis tools is essential before employing this pattern for trading purposes.

#128 - Tweezer Top

This pattern is characterized by two upward-extending wicks at the top of an uptrend. These wicks are either identical or very close in length. As buyers drive prices higher, sellers enter the market aggressively. Eventually, the price reaches a peak, forming a strong resistance level. The Tweezer Top is recognized as a bearish reversal pattern, with the highs being a notable feature of this pattern.

Figure 128: Tweezer Top

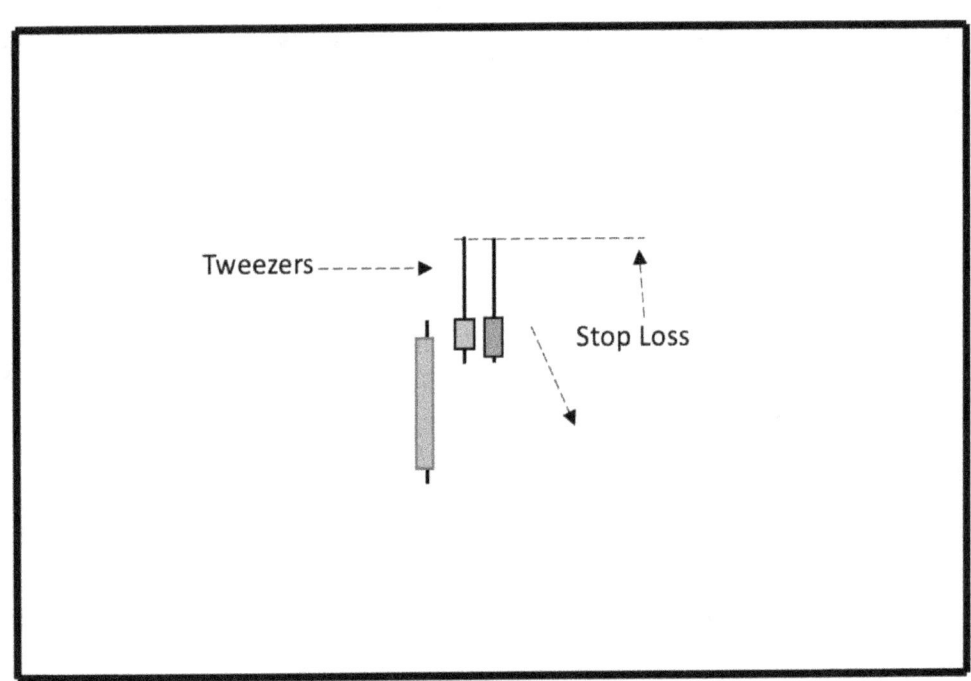

How to Trade Tweezer Top

The strength of the Tweezer Top pattern lies in the bearish candle within the formation. A longer Bearish Engulfing candlestick typically signifies a stronger reversal signal for the upcoming bars. This pattern indicates a decline in buyer sentiment and an increase in seller confidence. Referring to the provided figure, it is recommended to position a support line directly below the last candle with a significant real body and wait for a breakout to occur below this support level. Similarly, the stop-loss order should be set at an equal distance from the Tweezer as the support, ensuring risk management in case of a retracement in the bullish direction. It is crucial to note that the use of other technical analysis tools is necessary before employing   this   pattern   for   trading   purposes.

#129 - Two Crows

This three-day bearish reversal pattern is known as the Evening Star. It begins with a gap between a long green candle at the top of an uptrend and a small red candle on the second day. On the third day, the price opens within the body of the small red candle and fills the previous gap, closing within the range of the green candlestick. If the third day's close is more than halfway down the green candle, it forms the Evening Star pattern. This pattern bears resemblance to the Upside Gap Two Crows candlestick pattern.

Figure 129: Two Crows

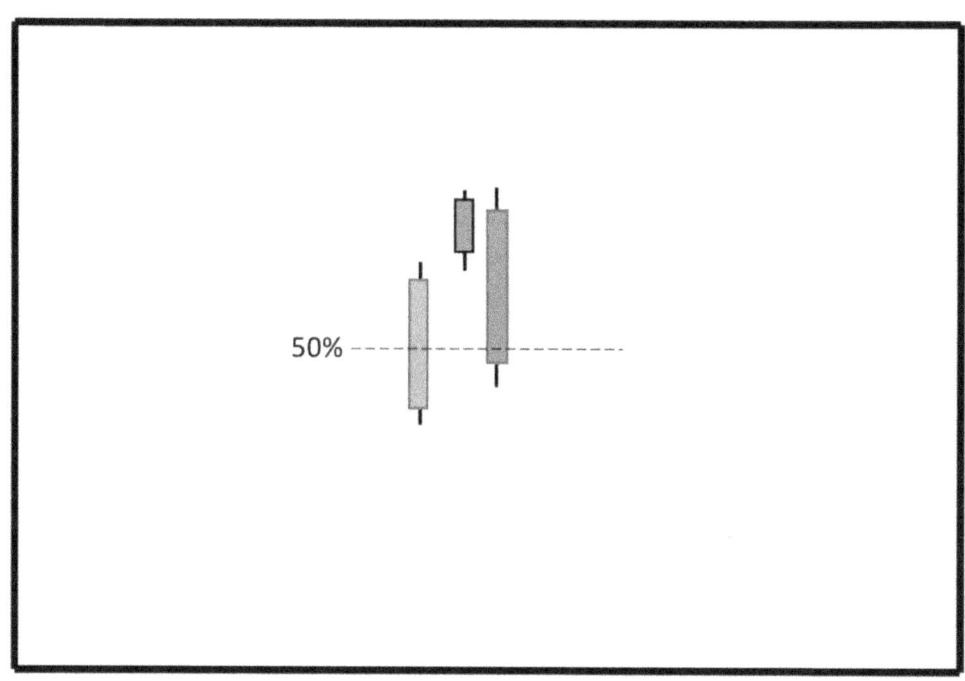

How to Trade Two Crows

This chart pattern is a rare occurrence that requires confirmation before it can be deemed a reversal. Without confirmation, it may simply be a temporary pause within an uptrend. The presence of a gap indicates the bulls' attempt to maintain pressure, but their momentum wanes. The two subsequent bearish candlesticks demonstrate the bears' determination to seize control, with confirmation occurring when the second bearish candle fills the gap. Many traders take short positions at this point to maximize profits from the pattern. Alternatively, some traders wait for a third bearish candle before entering a short position. Both approaches can be effective in generating profit. Confirmation of the pattern requires a breakout below the previous close. To manage risk, set a stop-loss order at the last high to protect against a bullish reversal triggering the stop loss.

#130 - Unique Three River Bottom

The Unique Three River Bottom is a bullish reversal pattern that resembles the Morning Star pattern and consists of three candles. It begins with a long red candlestick formed at the conclusion of a downtrend. On Day 2, the price opens higher and subsequently drops to establish a new low, creating a Hammer-like formation. Day 3 opens lower, but not below the low of the previous day, and closes higher, albeit below Day 2's close, forming a green candlestick. This pattern formation is uncommon but holds significance in signaling a potential trend reversal.

Figure 130: Unique Three River Bottom

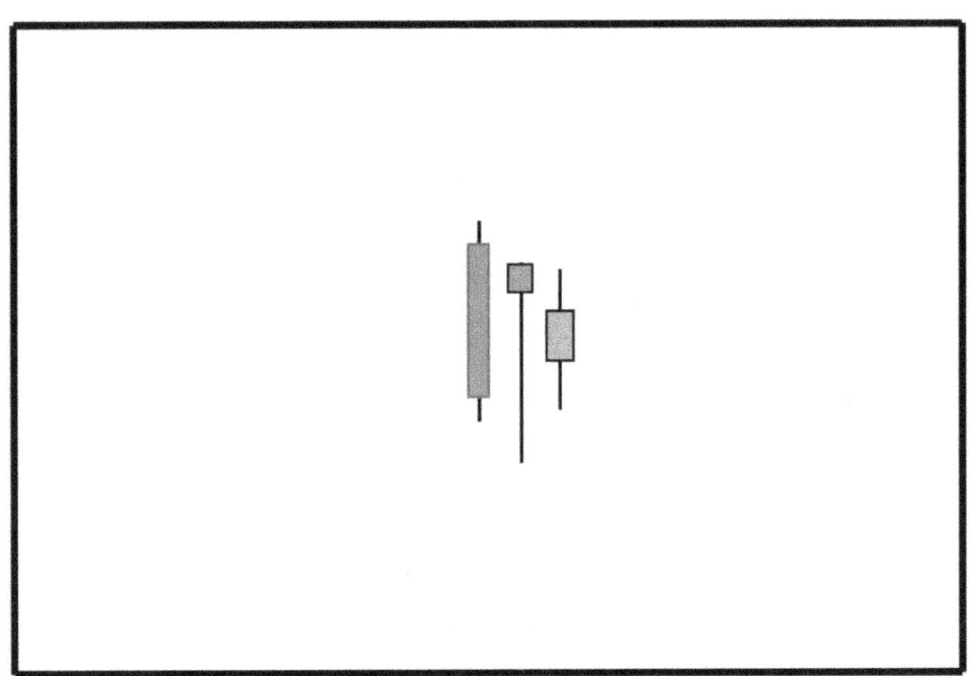

How to Trade Unique Three River Bottom

One notable characteristic of the Unique Three River Bottom pattern is its occurrence within a downtrend. The third candle, opening higher than the low of the second candle and displaying a bullish nature, suggests the potential for a bullish reversal. However, it is important to note that there have been instances where this pattern has resulted in a bearish reversal. Therefore, it is recommended to complement the analysis with other technical tools and carefully examine the preceding trend for confirmation. While the desire to enter a long position may arise at the close of the third candle, it is wiser to exercise patience and wait for the close of the fourth candle, as it provides the most reliable confirmation signal.

#131 - Upside Gap Three Method

The Upside Gap Three Method is a straightforward pattern that resembles the upside Tasuki gap. It occurs in a robust, trending market, typically during an uptrend. The pattern involves a gap up between two green candlesticks, with Day 3 opening within the real body of Day 2 and closing within the real body of Day 1's candlestick. This three-candle pattern is recognized as a bearish reversal signal.

Figure 131: Unique Three River Bottom

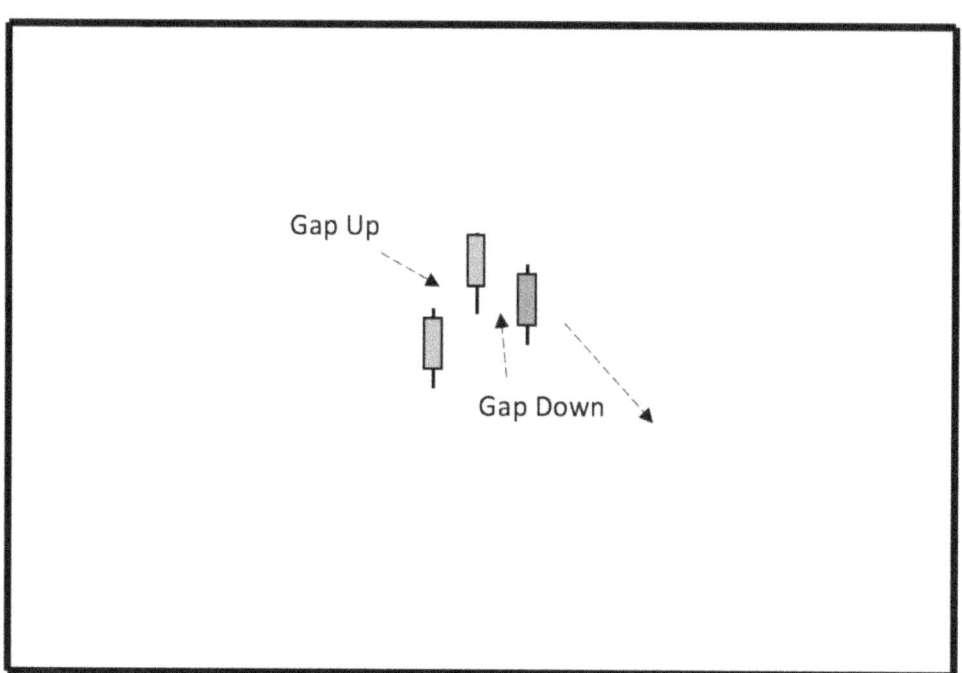

How to Trade Upside Gap Three Method

This is an uncommon pattern that requires the use of other technical analysis tools, like technical indicators and chart patterns, for confirmation as soon as it is identified. Because this pattern occurs within a current uptrend and resembles the Upside Tasuki Gap, traders are easily deceived into thinking it is a trend continuation pattern. However, in reality, it is the opposite. The key to trading this pattern is to observe if candle three closes the gap created between candles one and two. If it does, the likelihood of a reversal is reasonable, and you should   prepare   to   go   short.

#132 - Upside Gap Two Crows

This is a three-day pattern in which an upside gap is created between a long green candlestick and a small red candlestick on the first and second days. Day 3 does not bridge the gap between the first and second days and closes lower than Day 2. Day 3 also produces a real body that engulfs the candlestick from Day 2. This pattern is a bearish reversal signal that requires the previously described features as confirmation of its formation.

Figure 132: Upside Gap Two Crows

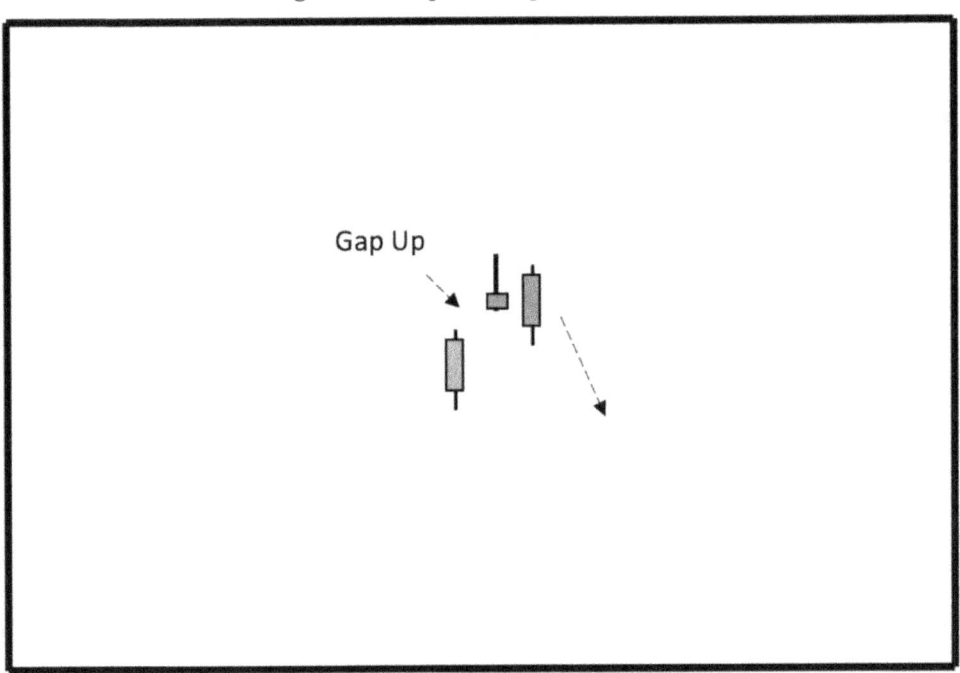

How to Trade Upside Gap Two Crows

As a bearish reversal pattern, the Upside Gap Two Crows must appear during an uptrend. It signifies that due to the strong opening from the last two days, the bears are gaining momentum and sentiments are changing. This presents an ideal opportunity for traders to position themselves for an upcoming reversal. You can establish support at the top of the candlestick before the gap and wait for the trend to break below the support line. However, if the upside gap is significant, your support should be placed below the low of the second candle. Gaps tend to retrace before continuing, so even if it was initially a bullish continuation gap, there is a likelihood that the gap will be filled in the near future, providing an opportunity for traders to benefit. By understanding this, traders can anticipate the trend of the price charts to some extent.

#133 - Upside Tasuki Gap

This pattern occurs when the market is in an uptrend, and it is a three-day signal. On Day 2, a green candlestick forms after a gap up from Day 1's green candlestick. On Day 3, the market opens and closes lower than Day 2. The Upside Tasuki Gap can be bullish if the gap is not filled, but it can also be bearish if the gap is filled. The candlesticks on Day 2 and Day 3 are of opposite colors and approximately the same size. This pattern is known to indicate the continuation of a bullish trend.

Figure 133: Upside Tasuki Gap

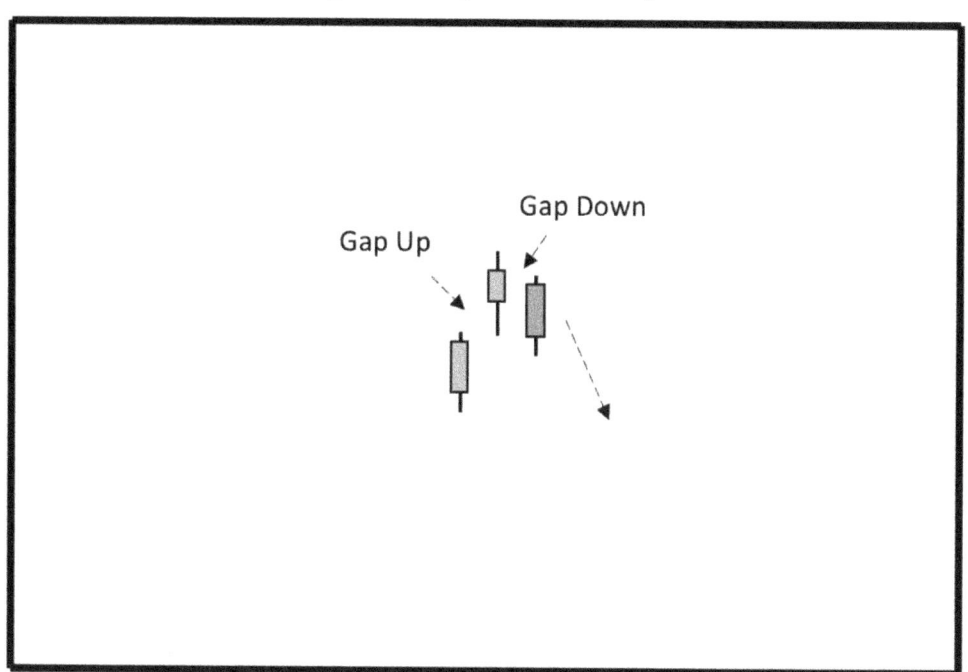

How to Trade Upside Tasuki Gap

A gap in price charts usually indicates a strong subsequent trend, and breakaway gaps are quite common in uptrends. Some of these gaps may even indicate a reversal, so understanding their characteristics is crucial. The size of the gap up can provide insight into the strength of the uptrend and the control exerted by the bulls in the market. Despite the bears' attempt to regain control, as evidenced by the single red candle, they fail to generate enough pressure to close the gap. This failure to reclaim the market confirms the continuation of the uptrend. To trade this pattern effectively, it is important to patiently observe the candles that follow the third red or black candle in the Upside Tasuki Gap. This confirmation is essential to prevent any misinterpretation of the pattern.

#134 – Extensive Series of Wicks at Top

This pattern occurs after a prolonged uptrend. Wicks extend to the upside as both bulls and bears engage in price battles. The longer the pattern persists, the higher the likelihood of the bulls giving way to the bears, as evidenced by the upward extension of the wicks. These signals include Long-Legged Doji, Shooting Stars, and Spinning Tops with predominantly upward wicks. Confirmation is provided by a bearish candle or a price gap down.

Figure 134: Extensive Series of Wicks at Top

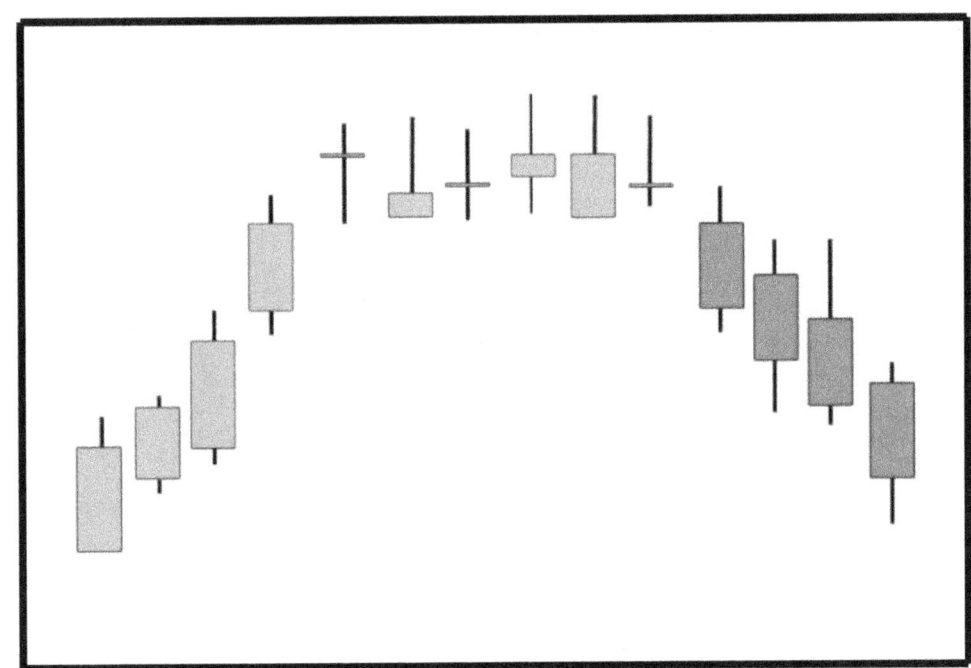

How to Trade Extensive Series of Wicks at Top

Generally, wicks are often seen as signals of potential reversals. Therefore, when a series of wicks appears at the end of a trend, it indicates a high likelihood of a strong reversal. When trading the Extensive Series of Wicks at the Top, it is important to consider the overall trend and not solely rely on the candlestick pattern. The longer the wick, the greater the chances of a reversal, similar to the concept of a long shadow. Since this pattern can be considered undefined, determining the right time to enter a trade can be challenging. However, once a trend consolidates with a cluster of wicks, particularly of the same color, it is advisable to wait for the subsequent candles before making any trading decisions.

Please feel free to stay connected by contacting me at kels1211@gmail.com or by following me on Twitter @KelsTrades. I would love to hear from you and engage in further discussions.

https://linktr.ee/BibleInspiredTruth